D0598568

MONSTERS

FOUNTAINHEAD PRESS V SERIES

Edited by
Brandy Ball Blake and L. Andrew Cooper

FOUNTAINHEAD
PRESS

Our green initiatives include:

Electronic Products
We deliver products in non-paper form whenever possible. This includes pdf downloadables, flash drives, & CDs.

Electronic Samples
We use Xample, a new electronic sampling system. Instructor samples are sent via a personalized web page that links to pdf downloads.

FSC Certified Printers
All of our printers are certified by the Forest Service Council which promotes environmentally and socially responsible management of the world's forests. This program allows consumer groups, individual consumers, and businesses to work together hand-in-hand to promote responsible use of the world's forests as a renewable and sustainable resource.

Recycled Paper
Most of our products are printed on a minimum of 30% post-consumer waste recycled paper.

Support of Green Causes
When we do print, we donate a portion of our revenue to green causes. Listed below are a few of the organizations that have received donations from Fountainhead Press. We welcome your feedback and suggestions for contributions, as we are always searching for worthy initiatives.
Rainforest 2 Reef
Environmental Working Group

Cover Image: Promotional photo of Boris Karloff from *The Bride of Frankenstein* as Frankenstein's monster. Universal Pictures (public domain)

Design by Susan Moore

Copyright © 2012 by Fountainhead Press

All rights reserved. No part of this book may be reproduced or utilized in any form or by any means, electronic or mechanical, including photocopying and recording, or by any informational storage and retrieval system without written permission from the publisher.

Books may be purchased for educational purposes.

For information, please call or write:

1-800-586-0330

Fountainhead Press
Southlake, TX 76092

Web Site: www.fountainheadpress.com
E-mail: customerservice@fountainheadpress.com

First Edition

ISBN: 978-1-59871-483-8

Printed in the United States of America

INTRODUCTION TO THE FOUNTAINHEAD PRESS V SERIES

By Brooke Rollins and Lee Bauknight
Series Editors

The *Fountainhead Press V Series* is a new collection of single-topic readers that take a unique look at some of today's most pressing issues. Designed to give writing students a more nuanced introduction to public discourse—on the environment, on food, and on digital life, to name a few of the topics—the books feature writing, research, and invention prompts that can be adapted to nearly any kind of college writing class. Each *V Series* textbook focuses on a single issue and includes multi-genre and multimodal readings and assignments that move the discourse beyond the most familiar patterns of debate—patterns usually fettered by entrenched positions and often obsessed with "winning."

The ultimate goal of the series is to help writing students—who tend to hover on the periphery of public discourse—think, explore, find their voices, and skillfully compose texts in a variety of media and genres. Not only do the books help students think about compelling issues and how they might address them, they also give students the practice they need to develop their research, rhetorical, and writing skills. Together, the readings, prompts, and longer assignments show students how to add their voices to the conversations about these issues in meaningful and productive ways.

With enough readings and composing tasks to sustain an entire quarter or semester, and inexpensive enough to be used in combination with other rhetorics and readers, the *Fountainhead Press V Series* provides instructors with the flexibility to build the writing courses they want and need to teach. An instructor interested in deeply exploring environmental issues, for example, could design a semester- or quarter-long course using *Green*, the first of the *V Series* texts. On the other hand, an instructor who wanted to teach discrete units on different issues could use two or more of the *V Series* books. In either case, the texts would give students ample opportunity—and a variety of ways—to engage with the issues at hand.

The *V Series* uses the term "composition" in its broadest sense. Of course, the textbooks provide students plenty of opportunities to write, but they also include assignments that take students beyond the page. Books in the series encourage students to explore other modes of communication by prompting them to design websites, for example; to produce videos, posters, and presentations; to conduct primary and secondary research; and to develop projects with community partners that might incorporate any number of these skills. Ultimately, we have designed the *Fountainhead Press V Series* to work for teachers and students. With their carefully chosen readings, built-in flexibility, and sound rhetorical grounding, the *V Series* books would be a dynamic and user-friendly addition to any writing class.

Books in the Series

978-1-59871-415-9

978-1-59871-431-9

978-1-59871-457-9

978-1-59871-472-9

978-1-59871-480-7

978-1-59871-553-8

978-1-59871-483-8

Future Titles

Tolerance, *Terror*, *Beauty*, *Sports*, *Music*, *Health*, and *Authenticity*

TABLE OF CONTENTS

INTRODUCTION: HAUNTING BOUNDARIES

BY BRANDY BALL BLAKE AND L. ANDREW COOPER

It's under the bed; it's in the closet. It's the thing in the basement, but it's also the thing in the mirror, hot breath on the back of your neck, cold eyes staring at you with loathing and hunger. The monster sometimes inspires heroes: a community's bravest members rise up and defend people's livelihoods against an indescribable threat. But in the dead of night, when no one can hear, even a hero might admit that a monster inspires one thing more than any other: fear.

Really? American culture of the last century has produced plenty of monsters that are more cuddly than blood-curdling. The title character in *Shrek* (2001) proves himself lovable, not despite being a monstrous ogre but in part because his monstrous appearance relegates him to the status of a misunderstood outcast. Even Count Dracula, originally one of the modern era's most dreaded creatures, becomes kid-friendly via *Sesame Street's* The Count ("I love to count: one, two, three!") and the sugary cereal Count Chocula ("Have a monster for breakfast today!"). While some vestiges of scariness survive—Shrek's overpowering size, the Count's neck-piercing fangs—these domesticated monstrosities nevertheless challenge the notion that the monster's sole purpose is to cause fear.

The monster's fearfulness is only the beginning of its significance. Monsters have appeared

1

across cultures and throughout history, and their meanings change with their contexts. The dragon, for example, was an ill omen in medieval England, but in imperial China, it heralded good luck. The diversity of monsters literally reflects the diversity of humanity, but what makes a monster monstrous is still the *difference* that sets it apart. Whether its appearance inspires fear or admiration, the monster always stands apart from the human, either at the enormous distance of the gigantic, serpentine dragon or the uncomfortable closeness of the human-looking vampire that only reveals its inhumanity when it is ready to feed on human blood. Defined both by humanity's cultural and historical contexts and by a difference that sets them apart, monsters are boundary-dwellers that help to define "us" by providing an identifiable "them." Their relationships with familiar contexts make them recognizable even as differences in their appearances, behaviors, and abilities allow us to claim that their faces in our mirrors are not our own. The closer we look, however, the more we might see that those faces are uncannily similar, and that similarity might be the most frightening thing of all.

MONSTROUS HISTORY

Monsters have always been symbolic creatures, generally representing darkness or evil, providing foils for the heroes of myth and legend. However, the etymology of the term *monster* points toward broader significance. The Latin word *monstrum*, which refers to both a monster and a portent, derives from *monere*, to warn. Most people today do not readily connect monsters with warnings, but in mythology and religion monsters often function in this manner. In Greek mythology, they warned of the power and anger of the gods. Lycaon attempted to serve Zeus the flesh of a child; in punishment, the god turned him into a wolf. Charybdis angered Zeus by flooding land on behalf of her father, Poseidon, and in response Zeus transformed her into a monstrous whirlpool. Monsters in religious literature, often defeated in combat by the good of heart, warn against the evils of sin. For example, giants appear often in medieval Christian literature, and their immense size, unnatural and outside of the human norm, acts as a warning against *moral* monstrosity. The size of giants often symbolizes pride, although their primitive nature, violent behavior, and aggressive sexuality could also emphasize wrath or lust. The Golem of Prague, one of several golems (artificial earthen creatures intended as guards) from Jewish tradition, expresses excessive wrath that becomes indiscriminately destructive and violent. Likewise, the wrath of Grendel, the giant man-eater from the medieval epic *Beowulf*, threatens social order with insatiable bloodlust. Monsters of folklore, on the other hand, may warn of the dangers of certain locations or activities. Knockers, who live in mines, make knocking noises before cave-ins or similar mining disasters, while parents use fear of the Grindylow, a long-armed monster known for killing children in marshes, to keep their children away from small bodies of water. The trend continues with modern monsters, though we do not always recognize the association. When Jason Voorhees and his mother (from the *Friday the 13th* films) kill camp counselors as punishment for teenage irresponsibility and excessive sexuality, they warn viewers not to make the same mistakes when they go to camp.

The etymology of *monster* challenges the assumption that monsters are necessarily evil because, as warnings, they can benefit humanity by teaching moral lessons. Similarly, scholars in the middle ages could not reconcile themselves to the singular categorization of monsters as evil creatures; many scholars, in search of definitive definition, questioned monsters' humanity and God's reasons for creating them. In fact, some medieval monsters were connected not to evil portents but to "miraculum," or miracles (Gilmore 55). Ronald Finucane explains the medieval notion of miracles: "Aquinas (d. 1274), the archetypal thirteenth-century theologian, defined miracle as whatever God did outside or beyond the order commonly determined or observed in nature" (51–52). Despite the seeming contradiction, monsters can be miracles if their appearances evoke the power of the divine.

The variety of monsters from myth, religion, folklore, and popular culture makes forming a singular definition of *monster* very difficult. Monsters take numerous forms. Some are full-fledged beasts, while others are hybrids, mixtures of animals and humans. These forms have so many different purposes, characteristics, and qualities that they barely have anything in common. For example, many of the beasts of the Bible (Leviathan and Behemoth) and from classical mythology (the Kraken, the Nemean Lion, and the Roc) are noted for their size, their immense power, and sometimes their indestructibility. However, some "monsters" seem physically frail and weak—certain fairies, for instance, or China's Dropa, which according to *Monstropedia.com* are ugly cloud-men whose giant heads contrast with their tiny, weak bodies. Many of the most well-known mythological monsters are hybrids—a bit from one animal, a bit from another. The Chimera (a lion with a snake for a tail and with a second head, a goat's) and the hydra (which is usually just a many-headed serpent but sometimes has a dog's body) directly oppose heroes, acting as obstacles that they must overcome on their adventures in order to rise in power and notoriety. Other monsters are mostly mischievous, such as Japan's Kappa, sometimes pictured as a monkey with a tortoise shell, scales, and webbed appendages, as well as a cavity of liquid on the top of its head. The Kappa's behavior ranges from harmful (drownings) to merely puckish (rude noises and vulgar behavior). However, not all hybrids are considered "bad." Griffins, which combine lions and eagles, are noble beasts that represent wisdom and strength, so respected that they often appear in heraldry—like unicorns, musimons (ram/ goat hybrids), and similar beasts. Good, bad, or somewhere in between, these monsters' animal characteristics emphasize their difference from humanity.

However, some of the most terrifying monsters are those with primarily human attributes. They emphasize similarity between the monstrous and the human, and thus they comment on the behaviors of humankind. The manticore, with the body of a lion, tail of a scorpion, and head of a man, was known for its brutally sharp teeth and voracious appetite; the minotaur, part bull and part man, for its violence; and harpies, with the bodies of vultures and the faces of women, for their cruelty. Over-sexual women, such as Medusa, the Lamia, and Error, were combined with snakes in order to emphasize the supposedly sinful nature of women and the temptations of their bodies (and thus Error, born from the Christian tradition, connects women with the serpent who

tempted Eve in the Garden). Each of these monsters, as part human, draws attention to humanity's propensity for wickedness and ruthlessness. On the other hand, even though many monstrous humanoids embody elements of pure destruction and evil, they almost always retain vestiges of humanity. In Shakespeare's *The Tempest*, the savage Caliban, despite his evil purposes, has a poetic nature that calls into question the relationship between man and monster, as does the behavior of Shakespeare's protagonist,

Prospero, who says of Caliban, "This thing of Darkness I acknowledge mine." In our studies of monstrosity, we are compelled to acknowledge our relationship with monsters and to question what separates us from them.

Over time, the humanoid monster has become the norm; most of the monster stories that hold our attention today (with a few famous exceptions such as Godzilla and some of Tolkien's fantastic creations) have a mostly human form: Frankenstein's creature; undead such as zombies, mummies, and vampires; devils and witches; and psychotic murderers. Even shapeshifters spend most of their time in a human form. Since monsters throughout history have embodied such a variety of shapes, why do modern monsters have such a direct tie to humanity? The proliferation of humanoid monsters and monstrous humans has forced us to recognize increasingly that monsters, however distorted, reflect on who we are.

The range of monsters across cultures and histories is too vast for any single book to cover thoroughly, so the editors of this volume have chosen to focus on monsters born in the "modern" era, primarily the nineteenth, twentieth, and twenty-first centuries, and in western cultures, primarily England, Ireland, and the United States. While the relative narrowness of this focus won't allow you to explore all of history's most famous monsters, it will encourage you to analyze some of today's most talked-about monsters in depth, from nineteenth-century superstars such as Frankenstein's Creature, Dr. Jekyll and Mr. Hyde, and Dracula, to more recent phenomena such as flesh-eating zombies and the *Twilight* series' kinder, gentler vampires.

MONSTROUS LITERATURE

The literary tradition that gave rise to the well-known wave of monsters that starts with Frankenstein's Creature is usually referred to as "Gothic" fiction, a type of fiction that focuses on the experiences of terror and horror and thus involves monstrosity in almost every text. Traditional histories of the Gothic trace it back to Horace Walpole's novel *The Castle of Otranto*, first published in 1764. The first edition claimed that the story was a translation of a recently rediscovered medieval romance, which links it to the centuries-old tradition of using inhuman and supernatural monsters not only as sources of fear but as portents of possibly miraculous origin. The monster in *Otranto* is a ghost so big that its helmet crushes to death the intended heir of a man who has wrongly usurped a noble's title and property. The reappearance of the ghost asserts a kind of divine justice that restores the proper aristocratic line. Thus the monster initially seemed to have all of the right medieval trappings of size and moral meaning, which is one of the reasons why critics felt scandalized when, in 1765, Walpole republished his novel, appended the subtitle "A Gothic Story," and admitted that he made the whole thing up. Suddenly what seemed to be a superstitious relic from more barbaric times in which people believed in monsters had to be read as a product of the era known as "the Age of Reason." This reappearance of monstrosity proved that humanity hadn't gotten quite as far from its monstrous fears as civilized people wanted to think.

Walpole's literary experiment proved hugely popular and became the first of many Gothic stories. Other eighteenth-century novelists, notably Clara Reeve and Ann Radcliffe, wrote tales that tamed the supernatural, minimalizing or ultimately consigning the apparent monstrosity of threats to characters' over-active imaginations. On the other hand, writers such as Matthew "Monk" Lewis, whose *The Monk* was even more scandalous than *Otranto*, gave eighteenth-century readers ghosts, demons, murderers, and other monstrosities that served up more sexual and moral perversion than many readers could stand. Meanwhile, William Godwin and Mary Wollstonecraft—the parents of Mary Shelley—used Gothic tales to make political points about the exploitation of society's disempowered groups, often framing powerful men as the world's real monsters. When Mary Shelley decided to have aristocratic Victor Frankenstein defy God by creating new life, she was building on the tradition that her parents helped to define, a tradition taken up by Robert Louis Stevenson in *The Strange Case of Dr. Jekyll and Mr. Hyde* and Bram Stoker in *Dracula* as well as by twentieth-century American writers in the vein of H.P. Lovecraft and Stephen King.

READING AND WRITING ABOUT MONSTERS

This volume offers selections that represent many of the achievements within the Gothic tradition, emphasizing particularly popular categories of monsters such as the undead and shapeshifters as well as magical, demonic, and psychotic forces. The examples in this book prompt you to think critically about monsters of many kinds, which provides the opportunity not only to learn about a phenomenon that stretches across multiple cultures and time periods but also helps you to participate in a conversation about the issues that surround monsters and the monstrous. Participating in this conversation will ultimately give you a better understanding of both cultural history and the world today. For example, because monsters deviate so drastically from the norms of society, they draw attention to the process of Othering, dividing people into two categories, the supposedly good "us" and the evil, other "them." From racism to xenophobia, from economic divisions to gender and sexual stereotyping, Othering enhances negative perceptions of difference; therefore, reading and writing about monsters could help you to explore how destructive Othering can be.

In addition, reading and writing about monsters could help you better understand monstrosity in everyday life. According to Bruno Bettelheim and Gerard Jones, overcoming monsters in literature, film, and the imagination can have a cathartic effect: people can face the darkness within themselves by embodying it in a monstrous form and finding ways to conquer it. Similarly, people can demonize the problems of the world today in order to help deal with them. The nightly news tells stories—of war and terrorism, of murder and assault, and of bullying and cruelty—that illustrate the violence, hatred, and anger of the world. Monsters provide a vocabulary to help define feelings on these issues, and critical thinkers can avoid the Othering of the past by learning to use that vocabulary to demonize acts rather than individuals: monsters can symbolize terrorism, not the terrorist, prejudice and not difference. The ambiguity of monsters acknowledges that these issues are more complicated than they may seem, and examining how the issues of the day connect to monstrosity can help to avoid repeating mistakes of the past.

To engage with the diversity of monstrosity in both historical and contemporary representations, this volume discusses examples from multiple media, providing selections from classic novels as well as overviews of films and references to video games and other media that you might choose to explore as well. While many of the examples come from fiction, the volume also includes nonfiction descriptions of real-life serial killer and a variety of essays about monsters and monstrosity. The combination of fiction and nonfiction will help you to articulate your ideas about monsters by providing both material for reflection and models for writing. Each selection appears alongside assignments that you might think through on your own or complete as part of a class. These assignments are multimodal—that is, they involve writing and other traditional forms of composition, but they also ask to you to make arguments in oral presentations, visual displays, and other forms. The modes and media you use for your communication about monsters might ultimately be as diverse as the monsters themselves.

MONSTROUS POLITICS: AN EXAMPLE

While many monsters exist across the boundaries of modes and media, few monsters have had the rich (un)lives of Frankenstein's Creature, so an example of a contemporary use of this monster demonstrates the strong connection between monstrosity and multimodal communication. As this book's selection from Mary Shelley's novel demonstrates, the Creature has always had strong political resonance. That resonance has continued through stage and film adaptations and through other media as well, including political cartoons.

Political cartoons use both humor and seriousness to comment on topical concerns and often use distortion and ambiguity to analyze and reveal the contradictions and problems that define political controversies. For example, Figure 1 presents the political cartoon "Health Care Monster" (2009), which highlights the issue of health care reform as pursued by the administration of Democratic President Barack Obama. The cartoon casts President Obama as Dr. Frankenstein and the Republicans (represented by their common symbol, the elephant) as his helper, Igor. Obama's gleeful shout of "It's Alive!" contrasts with Igor's "I'm not getting a pulse," emphasizing the opposition between political parties and their disagreement over the viability of reform. However, since Igor is assisting Frankenstein while disagreeing with him, the Republicans are shown to be complicit in the creation of the Democratically spearheaded reform effort, which is represented by the Creature itself, whose shirt proclaims his identity as "Some Kind of Health Care Reform."

Figure 1. "Health Care Monster:" A political cartoon uses Frankenstein's Creature to reflect on the monstrosity of political disagreements over health care in the United States.

The vagueness of the monster's identity, reflected in the uncertainty of "Some Kind" in the T-shirt, illustrates uncertainty about the form this *reform* will take. This uncertainty relates to ambiguity inherent to Frankenstein's Creature: as an assembly of corpses brought back to life, the Creature is the living dead, which calls its status as "alive" into question. Like the the health care reform effort, which seems to have produced *something*, the Creature is a huge presence that doesn't have a discernible pulse, or recognizable claim to vitality. All the political disagreements involved in the efforts to bring the reform to life, represented in the cartoon by Frankenstein/Obama and Igor/Republicans, have left the reform pulse-less on the floor of Congress. The reform itself, represented by the Creature, exists on the boundary between political parties as well as on the boundary between old and new political approaches to health care. Thus, like virtually all monsters, this version of Frankenstein's Creature is a boundary dweller, which makes him an apt tool for articulating some of the political challenges we face today.

Before reading any of the selections in this book, define the term "monster" in your own words. Your definition should be a brief paragraph that explains what a monster is—taking into account physical and behavioral characteristics—and why the monster is culturally significant.

In small groups, list monsters *not* mentioned in this introduction. Do the monsters on your list fit into particular categories? If so, what are those categories, and what commonalities make specific monsters fit specific categories? How might these commonalities add to or challenge the general claims the introduction makes about monsters?

Draw a cartoon that uses one or more monsters to express your views on a contemporary political issue. After you finish the drawing, write a reflective paragraph that answers these questions:

- Did you use a familiar monster (such as Frankenstein's Creature) or invent a new monster? What difference does (un)familiarity make in your cartoon?

- Does your representation of the monster(s) create "Othering"— does it frame any ideas or people, perhaps those opposed to your own position, as a bad "them" in relation to a good "us"? If so, what or who is framed as the Other, and what problems might this Othering pose? If not, who or what does your monster represent, and how does it avoid Othering them?

- Finally, how might your use of monstrosity in your cartoon serve as a warning about society approaching the issue you've chosen in a dangerous or misguided way?

Jeffrey Jerome Cohen is an expert on medievalism and monstrosity, having published numerous books on monsters and the theories surrounding them, including Hybridity, Identity and Monstrosity in Medieval Britain: Of Difficult Middles *(2006);* Of Giants: Sex, Monsters, and the Middle Ages *(1999); and* Monster Theory: Reading Culture *(1996).*

In this chapter from Monster Theory, *Cohen "offer[s] seven theses toward understanding cultures through the monsters they bear." These theses show that definitions of "monster," as well as the term's connotations, have fluctuated throughout history and depend on the cultures and taboos of different periods. They also depend on representations of the Other, a term used to describe individuals or groups who do not conform to the ideologies of the dominant culture. Before you read this essay, consider your own definition of "monster," determining what qualities you perceive as monstrous. Once you've finished Cohen's essay, consider how your definition relates to, or might change in response to, Cohen's claims.*

MONSTER CULTURE (SEVEN THESES)

BY JEFFREY JEROME COHEN

What I will propose here by way of a first foray, as entrance into this book of monstrous content, is a sketch of a new *modus legendi,* a method of reading cultures from the monsters they engender. In doing so, I will partially violate two of the sacred dicta of recent cultural studies: the compulsion to historical specificity and the insistence that all knowledge (and hence all cartographies of that knowledge) is local. Of the first I will say only that in cultural studies today history (disguised perhaps as "culture") tends to be fetishized as a *telos,* as a final determinant of meaning; post de Man, post Foucault, post Hayden White, one must bear in mind that history is just another text in a procession of texts, and not a guarantor of any singular signification. A movement away from the *longue durée* and toward microeconomics (of capital or of gender) is associated most often with Foucauldian criticism; yet recent critics have found that where Foucault went wrong was mainly in his details, in his minute specifics. Nonetheless, his methodology—his archaeology of ideas, his histories of unthought—remains with good reason the chosen route of inquiry for most cultural critics today, whether they work in postmodern cyberculture or in the Middle Ages.

And so I would like to make some grand gestures. We live in an age that has rightly given up on Unified Theory, an age when we realize that history (like "individuality," "subjectivity," "gender," and "culture") is composed of a multitude of fragments, rather than of smooth epistemological wholes. Some fragments will be collected here and bound temporarily together to form a loosely integrated net—or, better, an unassimilated hybrid, a monstrous body. Rather than argue a "theory of teratology," I offer by way of introduction to the essays that follow a set of breakable postulates in search of specific cultural moments. I offer seven theses toward understanding cultures through the monsters they bear.

THESIS I: THE MONSTER'S BODY IS A CULTURAL BODY

Vampires, burial, death: inter the corpse where the road forks, so that when it springs from the grave, it will not know which path to follow. Drive a stake through its heart: it will be stuck to the ground at the fork, it will haunt that place that leads to many other places, that point of indecision. Behead the corpse, so that, acephalic, it will not know itself as subject, only as pure body.

The monster is born only at this metaphoric crossroads, as an embodiment of a certain cultural moment—of a time, a feeling, and a place.[1] The monster's body quite literally incorporates fear, desire, anxiety, and fantasy (ataractic or incendiary), giving them life and an uncanny independence. The monstrous body is pure culture. A construct and a projection, the monster exists only to be read: the *monstrum* is etymologically "that which reveals," "that which warns," a glyph that seeks a hierophant. Like a letter on the page, the monster signifies something other than itself: it is always a displacement, always inhabits the gap between the time of upheaval that created it and the moment into which it is received, to be born again. These epistemological spaces between the monster's bones are Derrida's familiar chasm of *différance*: a genetic uncertainty principle, the essence of the monster's vitality, the reason it always rises from the dissection table as its secrets are about to be revealed and vanishes into the night.

THESIS II: THE MONSTER ALWAYS ESCAPES

We see the damage that the monster wreaks, the material remains (the footprints of the yeti across Tibetan snow, the bones of the giant stranded on a rocky cliff), but the monster itself turns immaterial and vanishes, to reappear someplace else (for who is the yeti if not the medieval wild man? Who is the wild man if not the biblical and classical giant?). No matter how many times King Arthur killed the ogre of Mount Saint Michael, the monster reappeared in another heroic chronicle, bequeathing the Middle Ages an abundance of *morte d'Arthurs*. Regardless of how many times Sigourney Weaver's beleaguered Ripley utterly destroys the ambiguous Alien that stalks her, its monstrous progeny return, ready to stalk again in another bigger-than-ever sequel. No monster tastes of death but once. The anxiety that condenses like green vapor into the form of the vampire can be dispersed temporarily, but the revenant by definition returns. And so the monster's body is both corporal and incorporeal; its threat is its propensity to shift.

Each time the grave opens and the unquiet slumberer strides forth ("come from the dead, / Come back to tell you all"), the message proclaimed is transformed by the air that gives its speaker new life. Monsters must be examined within the intricate matrix of relations (social, cultural, and literary-historical) that generate them. In speaking of the new kind of vampire invented by Bram Stoker, we might explore the foreign count's transgressive but compelling sexuality, as subtly alluring to Jonathan Harker as Henry Irving, Stoker's mentor, was to Stoker.[2] Or we might analyze Murnau's self-loathing appropriation of the same demon in *Nosferatu*, where in the face of nascent fascism the undercurrent of desire surfaces in plague and bodily corruption. Anne Rice has given the myth a modern rewriting in which homosexuality and vampirism have been conjoined, apotheosized; that she has created a pop culture phenomenon in the process is not insignificant, especially at a time when gender as a construct has been scrutinized at almost every social register. In Francis Coppola's recent blockbuster, *Bram Stoker's Dracula*, the homosexual subtext present at least since the appearance of Sheridan Le Fanu's lesbian lamia (*Carmilla*, 1872) has, like the red corpuscles that serve as the film's leitmotif, risen to the surface, primarily as an AIDS awareness that transforms the disease of vampirism into a sadistic (and very medieval) form of redemption through the torments of the body in pain. No coincidence, then, that Coppola was putting together a documentary on AIDS at the same time he was working on *Dracula*.

In each of these vampire stories, the undead returns in slightly different clothing, each time to be read against contemporary social movements or a specific, determining event: *la decadence* and its new possibilities, homophobia and its hateful imperatives, the acceptance of new subjectivities unfixed by binary gender, a fin de siècle social activism paternalistic in its embrace. Discourse extracting a transcultural, transtemporal phenomenon labeled "the vampire" is of rather limited utility; even if vampire figures are found almost worldwide, from ancient Egypt to modern Hollywood, each reappearance and its analysis is still bound in a double act of construction and reconstitution.[3] "Monster theory" must therefore concern itself with strings of cultural moments, connected by a logic that always threatens to shift; invigorated by change and escape, by the impossibility of achieving what Susan Stewart calls the desired "fall or death, the stopping" of its gigantic subject,[4] monstrous interpretation is as much process as epiphany, a work that must content itself with fragments (footprints, bones, talismans, teeth, shadows, obscured glimpses—signifiers of monstrous passing that stand in for the monstrous body itself).

THESIS III: THE MONSTER IS THE HARBINGER OF CATEGORY CRISIS

The monster always escapes because it refuses easy categorization. Of the nightmarish creature that Ridley Scott brought to life in *Mien*, Harvey Greenberg writes:

> It is a Linnean nightmare, defying every natural law of evolution; by turns bivalve, crustacean, reptilian, and humanoid. It seems capable of lying dormant within its egg indefinitely. It sheds its skin like a snake, its carapace like an arthropod. It deposits its young into other species like a wasp. . . It responds according to Lamarckian *and* Darwinian principles.[5]

This refusal to participate in the classificatory "order of things" is true of monsters generally: they are disturbing hybrids whose externally incoherent bodies resist attempts to include them in any systematic structuration. And so the monster is dangerous, a form suspended between forms that threatens to smash distinctions.

Because of its ontological liminality, the monster notoriously appears at times of crisis as a kind of third term that problematizes the clash of extremes—as "that which questions binary thinking and introduces a crisis."[6] This power to evade and to undermine has coursed through the monster's blood from classical times, when despite all the attempts of Aristotle (and later Pliny, Augustine, and Isidore) to incorporate the monstrous races[7] into a coherent epistemological system, the monster always escaped to return to its habitations at the margins of the world (a purely conceptual locus rather than a geographic one).[8] Classical "wonder books" radically undermine the Aristotelian taxonomic system, for by refusing an easy compartmentalization of their monstrous contents, they demand a radical rethinking of boundary and normality. The too-precise laws of nature as set forth by science are gleefully violated in the freakish compilation of the monster's body. A mixed category, the monster resists any classification built on hierarchy or a merely binary opposition, demanding instead a "system" allowing polyphony, mixed response (difference in sameness, repulsion in attraction), and resistance to integration—allowing what Hogle has called with a wonderful pun "a deeper play of differences, a nonbinary polymorphism at the 'base' of human nature."[9]

The horizon where the monsters dwell might well be imagined as the visible edge of the hermeneutic circle itself: the monstrous offers an escape from its hermetic path, an invitation to explore new spirals, new and interconnected methods of perceiving the world.[10] In the face of the monster, scientific inquiry and its ordered rationality crumble. The monstrous is a genus too large to be encapsulated in any conceptual system; the monster's very existence is a rebuke to boundary and enclosure; like the giants of *Mandevilles Travels*, it threatens to devour "all raw & quyk" any thinker who insists otherwise. The monster is in this way the living embodiment of the phenomenon Derrida has famously labeled the "supplement" *(ce dangereux supplément)*[11]: it breaks apart bifurcating, "either/or" syllogistic logic with a kind of reasoning closer to "and/or," introducing what Barbara Johnson has called "a revolution in the very logic of meaning."[12]

Full of rebuke to traditional methods of organizing knowledge and human experience, the geography of the monster is an imperiling expanse, and therefore always a contested cultural space.

THESIS IV: THE MONSTER DWELLS AT THE GATES OF DIFFERENCE

The monster is difference made flesh, come to dwell among us. In its function as dialectical Other or third-term supplement, the monster is an incorporation of the Outside, the Beyond—of all those loci that are rhetorically placed as distant and distinct but originate Within. Any kind of alterity can be inscribed across (constructed through) the monstrous body, but for the most part monstrous difference tends to be cultural, political, racial, economic, sexual. ✳

The exaggeration of cultural difference into monstrous aberration is familiar enough. The most famous distortion occurs in the Bible, where the aboriginal inhabitants of Canaan are envisioned as menacing giants to justify the Hebrew colonization of the Promised Land (Numbers 13). Representing an anterior culture as monstrous justifies its displacement or extermination by rendering the act heroic. In medieval France the *chansons de geste* celebrated the crusades by transforming Muslims into demonic caricatures whose menacing lack of humanity was readable from their bestial attributes; by culturally glossing "Saracens" as "monstra," propagandists rendered rhetorically admissible the annexation of the East by the West. This representational project was part of a whole dictionary of strategic glosses in which "monstra" slipped into significations of the feminine and the hypermasculine. ✳

A recent newspaper article on Yugoslavia reminds us how persistent these divisive mythologies can be, and how they can endure divorced from any grounding in historical reality:

> A Bosnian Serb militiaman, hitchhiking to Sarajevo, tells a reporter in all earnestness that the Muslims are feeding Serbian children to the animals in the zoo. The story is nonsense. There aren't any animals left alive in the Sarajevo zoo. But the militiaman is convinced and can recall all the wrongs that Muslims may or may not have perpetrated during their 500 years of rule.[13]

In the United States, Native Americans were presented as unredeemable savages so that the powerful political machine of Manifest Destiny could push westward with disregard. Scattered throughout Europe by the Diaspora and steadfastly refusing assimilation into Christian society, Jews have been perennial favorites for xenophobic misrepresentation, for here was an alien culture living, working, and even at times prospering within vast communities dedicated to becoming homogeneous and monolithic. The Middle Ages accused the Jews of crimes ranging from the bringing of the plague to bleeding Christian children to make their Passover meal. Nazi Germany simply brought these ancient traditions of hate to their conclusion, inventing a Final Solution that differed from earlier persecutions only in its technological efficiency.

Political or ideological difference is as much a catalyst to monstrous representation on a micro level as cultural alterity in the macrocosm. A political figure suddenly out of favor is transformed like an unwilling participant in a science experiment by the appointed historians of the replacement regime: "monstrous history" is rife with sudden, Ovidian metamorphoses, from Vlad Tepes to Ronald Reagan. The most illustrious of these propaganda-bred demons is the English king Richard III, whom Thomas More famously described as "little of stature, ill fetured of limmes, croke backed, his left shoulder much higher then his right, hard fauoured of visage. . . . hee came into the worlde with feete forward, . . . also not vntothed."[14] From birth, More declares, Richard was a monster, "his deformed body a readable text"[15] on which was inscribed his deviant morality (indistinguishable from an incorrect political orientation).

The almost obsessive descanting on Richard from Polydor Vergil in the Renaissance to the Friends of Richard III Incorporated in our own era demonstrates the process of "monster theory" at its most active: culture gives birth to a monster before our eyes, painting over the normally proportioned Richard who once lived, raising his shoulder to deform simultaneously person, cultural response, and the possibility of objectivity.[16] History itself becomes a monster: defeaturing, self-deconstructive, always in danger of exposing the sutures that bind its disparate elements into a single, unnatural body. At the same time Richard moves between Monster and Man, the disturbing suggestion arises that this incoherent body, denaturalized and always in peril of disaggregation, may well be our own.

The difficult project of constructing and maintaining gender identities elicits an array of anxious responses throughout culture, producing another impetus to teratogenesis. The woman who oversteps the boundaries of her gender role risks becoming a Scylla, Weird Sister, Lilith ("die erste Eva," "la mère obscuré"),[17] Bertha Mason, or Gorgon.[18] "Deviant" sexual identity is similarly susceptible to monsterization. The great medieval encyclopedist Vincent of Beauvais describes the visit of a hermaphroditic cynocephalus to the French court in his *Speculum naturale* (31.126).[19] Its male reproductive organ is said to be disproportionately large, but the monster could use either sex at its own discretion. Bruno Roy writes of this fantastic hybrid: "What warning did he come to deliver to the king? He came to bear witness to sexual norms.... He embodied the punishment earned by those who violate sexual taboos."[20] This strange creature, a composite of the supposedly discrete categories "male" and "female," arrives before King Louis to validate heterosexuality over homosexuality, with its supposed inversions and transformations ("Equa fin equus," one Latin writer declared; "The horse becomes a mare").[21] The strange dog-headed monster is a living excoriation of gender ambiguity and sexual abnormality, as Vincent's cultural moment defines them heteronormalization incarnate.

From the classical period into the twentieth century, race has been almost as powerful a catalyst to the creation of monsters as culture, gender, and sexuality. Africa early became the West's significant other, the sign of its ontological difference simply being skin color. According to the Greek myth of Phaeton, the denizens of mysterious and uncertain Ethiopia were black because they had been scorched by the too-close passing of the sun. The Roman naturalist Pliny assumed nonwhite skin to be symptomatic of a complete difference in temperament and attributed Africa's darkness to climate; the intense heat, he said, had burned the Africans' skin and malformed their bodies (*Natural History*, 2.80). These differences were quickly moralized through a pervasive rhetoric of deviance. Paulinus of Nola, a wealthy landowner turned early church homilist, explained that the Ethiopians had been scorched by sin and vice rather than by the suni and the anonymous commentator to Theodulus's influential *Edoga* (tenth century) succinctly glossed the meaning of the word *Ethyopium*: "Ethiopians, that is, sinners. Indeed, sinners can rightly be compared to Ethiopians, who are black men presenting a terrifying appearance to those beholding them."[22] Dark skin was associated with the fires of hell, and so signified in Christian mythology demonic provenance. The perverse and exaggerated sexual appetite of monsters generally was quickly affixed to the Ethiopian; this linking was only strengthened by a xenophobic backlash as dark-skinned people were forcibly imported into Europe early in the Renaissance. Narratives of miscegenation arose and circulated to sanction official policies of exclusion; Queen Elizabeth is famous for her anxiety over "blackamoores" and their supposed threat to the "increase of people of our own nation."[23]

Through all of these monsters the boundaries between personal and national bodies blur. To complicate this category confusion further, one kind of alterity is often written as another, so that national difference (for example) is transformed into sexual difference. Giraldus Cambrensis demonstrates just this slippage of the foreign in his *Topography of Ireland*; when he writes of the Irish (ostensibly simply to provide information about them to a curious English court, but actually as a first step toward invading and colonizing the island), he observes:

> It is indeed a most filthy race, a race sunk in vice, a race more ignorant than all other nations of the first principles of faith— These people who have customs so different from others, and so opposite to them, on making signs either with the hands or the head, beckon when they mean that you should go away, and nod backwards as often as they wish to be rid of you. Likewise, in this nation, the men pass their water sitting, die women standing—The women, also, as well as the men, ride astride, with their legs stuck out on each side of the horse.[24]

One kind of inversion becomes another as Giraldus deciphers the alphabet of Irish culture—and reads it backwards, against the norm of English masculinity. Giraldus creates a vision of monstrous gender (aberrant, demonstrative): the violation of the cultural codes that valence gendered behaviors creates a rupture that must be cemented with (in this case) the binding, corrective mortar of English normalcy. A bloody war of subjugation followed immediately after the promulgation of this text, remained potent throughout the High Middle Ages, and in a way continues to this day.

Through a similar discursive process the East becomes feminized (Said) and the soul of Africa grows dark (Gates).[25] One kind of difference becomes another as the normative categories of gender, sexuality, national identity, and ethnicity slide together like the imbricated circles of a Venn diagram, abjecting from the center that which becomes the monster. This violent foreclosure erects a self-validating, Hegelian master/slave dialectic that naturalizes the subjugation of one cultural body by another by writing the body excluded from personhood and agency as in every way different, monstrous. A polysemy is granted so that a greater threat can be encoded; multiplicity of meanings, paradoxically, iterates the same restricting, agitprop representations that narrowed signification performs. Yet a danger resides in this multiplication: as difference, like a Hydra, sprouts two heads where one has been lopped away, the possibilities of escape, resistance, disruption arise with more force.

René Girard has written at great length about the real violence these debasing representations enact, connecting monsterizing depiction with the phenomenon of the scapegoat. Monsters are never created *ex nihilo*, but through a process of fragmentation and recombination in which elements are extracted "from various forms" (including—indeed, especially—marginalized social groups) and then assembled as the monster, "which can then claim an independent identity."[26] The political-cultural monster, the embodiment of radical difference, paradoxically threatens to *erase* difference in the world of its creators, to demonstrate

> the potential for the system to differ from its own difference, in other words not to be different at all, to cease to exist as a system . . . Difference that exists outside the system is terrifying because it reveals the truth of the system, its relativity, its fragility, and its mortality . . . Despite what is said around us persecutors are never obsessed with difference but rather by its unutterable contrary, the lack of difference.[27]

By revealing that difference is arbitrary and potentially free-floating, mutable rather than essential, the monster threatens to destroy not just individual members of a society, but the very cultural apparatus through; which individuality is constituted and allowed. Because it is a body across which difference has been repeatedly written, the monster (like Frankenstein's creature, that combination of odd somatic pieces stitched together from a community of cadavers) seeks out its author to demand its raison d'etre—and to bear witness to the fact that it could have been constructed Otherwise. Godzilla trampled Tokyo; Girard frees him here to fragment the delicate matrix of relational systems that unite every private body to the public world.

THESIS V: THE MONSTER POLICES THE BORDERS OF THE POSSIBLE

The monster resists capture in the epistemological nets of the erudite, but it is something more than a Bakhtinian ally of the popular. From its position at the limits of knowing, the monster stands as a warning against exploration of its uncertain demesnes. The giants of Patagonia, the dragons of the Orient, and the dinosaurs of Jurassic Park together declare that curiosity is more often punished than rewarded, that one is better off safely contained within one's own domestic sphere than abroad, away from the watchful eyes of the state. The monster prevents mobility (intellectual, geographic, or sexual), delimiting the social spaces through which private bodies may move. To step outside this official geography is to risk attack by some monstrous border patrol or (worse) to become monstrous oneself.

Lycaon, the first werewolf in Western literature, undergoes his lupine metamorphosis as the culmination of a fable of hospitality.[28] Ovid relates how the primeval giants attempted to plunge the world into anarchy by wrenching Olympus from the gods, only to be shattered by divine thunderbolts. From their scattered blood arose a race of men who continued their fathers' malignant ways.[29] Among this wicked progeny was Lycaon, king of Arcadia, When Jupiter arrived as a guest at his house, Lycaon tried to kill the ruler of the gods as he slept, and the next day served him pieces of a servant's body as a meal. The enraged Jupiter punished this violation of the host-guest relationship by transforming Lycaon into a monstrous semblance of that lawless, godless state to which his actions would drag humanity back:

> The king himself flies in terror and, gaining the fields, howls aloud, attempting in vain to speak. His mouth of itself gathers foam, and with his accustomed greed for blood he turns against the sheep, delighting still in slaughter. His garments change to shaggy hair, his arms to legs. He turns into a wolf, and yet retains some traces of his former shape.[30]

The horribly fascinating loss of Lycaon's humanity merely reifies his previous moral state; the king's body is rendered all transparence, instantly and insistently readable. The power of the narrative prohibition peaks in the lingering description of the monstrously composite Lycaon, at that median where he is both man and beast, dual natures in a helpless tumult of assertion. The fable concludes when Lycaon can no longer speak, only signify.

Whereas monsters born of political expedience and self-justifying nationalism function as living invitations to action, usually military (invasions, usurpations, colonizations), the monster of prohibition polices the borders of the possible, interdicting through its grotesque body some behaviors and actions, envaluing others. It is possible, for example, that medieval merchants intentionally disseminated maps depicting sea serpents like Leviathan at the edges of their trade routes in order to discourage further exploration and to establish monopolies.[31] Every monster is in this way a double narrative, two living stories: one that describes how the monster came to be and another, its testimony, detailing what cultural use the monster serves. The monster of prohibition exists to demarcate the bonds that hold together that system of relations we call culture, to call horrid attention to the borders that cannot—*must* not— be crossed.

Primarily these borders are in place to control the traffic in women, or more generally to establish strictly homosocial bonds, the ties between men that keep a patriarchal society functional. A kind of herdsman, this monster delimits the social space through which cultural bodies may move, and in classical times (for example) validated a tight, hierarchical system of naturalized leadership and control where every man had a functional place.[32] The prototype in Western culture for this kind of "geographic" monster is Homer's Polyphemos. The quintessential xenophobic rendition of the foreign (the *barbaric*—that which is unintelligible within a given cultural-linguistic system),[33] the Cyclopes are represented as savages who have not "a law to bless them" and who lack the *techne* to produce (Greek-style) civilization. Their archaism is conveyed through their lack of hierarchy and of a politics of precedent. This dissociation from community leads to a rugged individualism that in Homeric terms can only be horrifying. Because they live without a system of tradition and custom, the Cyclopes are a danger to the arriving Greeks, men whose identities are contingent upon a compartmentalized function within a deindividualizing system of subordination and control. Polyphemos's victims are devoured, engulfed, made to vanish from the public gaze: cannibalism as incorporation into the wrong cultural body.

The monster is a powerful ally of what Foucault calls "the society of the panopticon," in which "polymorphous conducts [are] actually extracted from people's bodies and from their pleasures ... [to be] drawn out, revealed, isolated, intensified, incorporated, by multifarious power devices."[34] Susan Stewart has observed that "the monster's sexuality takes on a separate life"[35]; Foucault helps us to see why. The monster embodies those sexual practices that must not be committed, or that may be committed only through the body of the monster. *She* and *Them!:* the monster enforces the cultural codes that regulate sexual desire.

Anyone familiar with the low-budget science fiction movie craze of the 1950s will recognize in the preceding sentence two superb films of the genre, one about a radioactive virago from outer space who kills every man she touches, the other a social parable in which giant ants (really, Communists) burrow beneath Los Angeles (that is, Hollywood) and threaten world peace (that is, American conservatism). I connect these two seemingly unrelated titles here to call attention to the anxieties that monsterized their subjects in the first place, and to enact syntactically an even deeper fear: that the two will join in some unholy miscegenation. We have seen that the monster arises at the gap where difference is perceived as dividing a recording voice from its captured subject; the criterion of this division is arbitrary, and can range from anatomy or skin color to religious belief, custom, and political ideology. The monster's destructiveness is really a deconstructiveness: it threatens to reveal that difference originates in process, rather than in fact (and that "fact" is subject to constant reconstruction and change). Given that the recorders of the history of the West have been mainly European and male, women (*She*) and nonwhites (*Them!*) have found themselves repeatedly transformed into monsters, whether to validate specific alignments of masculinity and whiteness, or simply to be pushed from its realm of thought.[36] Feminine and cultural others are monstrous enough by themselves in patriarchal society, but when they threaten to mingle, the entire economy of desire comes under attack.

As a vehicle of prohibition, the monster most often arises to enforce the laws of exogamy, both the incest taboo (which establishes a traffic in women by mandating that they marry outside their families) and the decrees against interracial sexual mingling (which limit the parameters of that traffic by policing the boundaries of culture, usually in the service of some notion of group "purity").[37] Incest narratives are common to every tradition and have been extensively documented, mainly owing to Levi-Strauss's elevation of the taboo to the founding base of patriarchal society. Miscegenation, that intersection of misogyny (gender anxiety) and racism (no matter how naive), has received considerably less critical attention. I will say a few words about it here.

The Bible has long been the primary source for divine decrees against interracial mixing. One of these pronouncements is a straightforward command from God that comes through the mouth of the prophet Joshua (Joshua 23:12ff); another is a cryptic episode in Genesis much elaborated during the medieval period, alluding to "sons of God" who impregnate the "daughters of men" with a race of wicked giants (Genesis 6:4). The monsters are here, as elsewhere, expedient representations of other cultures, generalized and demonized to enforce a strict notion of group sameness. The fears of contamination, impurity, and loss of identity that produce stories like the Genesis episode are strong, and they reappear incessantly. Shakespeare's Caliban, for example, is the product of such an illicit mingling, the "freckled whelp" of the Algerian witch Sycorax and the devil. Charlotte Brontë reversed the usual paradigm in *Jane Eyre* (white Rochester and lunatic Jamaican Bertha Mason), but horror movies as seemingly innocent as *King Kong* demonstrate miscegenation anxiety in its brutal essence. Even a film as recent as 1979's immensely successful *Alien* may have a cognizance of the fear in its underworkings: the grotesque creature that stalks the heroine (dressed in the final scene only in her underwear) drips a glistening slime of K-Y Jelly from its teeth; the jaw tendons are constructed of shredded condoms; and the man inside the rubber suit is Bolaji Badejo, a Masai tribesman standing seven feet tall who happened to be studying in England at the time the film was cast.[38]

The narratives of the West perform the strangest dance around that fire in which miscegenation and its practitioners have been condemned to burn. Among the flames we see the old women of Salem hanging, accused of sexual relations with the black devil; we suspect they died because they crossed a different border, one that prohibits women from managing property and living solitary, unmanaged lives. The flames devour the Jews of thirteenth-century England, who stole children from proper families and baked seder matzo with their blood; as a menace to the survival of English race and culture, they were expelled from the country and their property confiscated. A competing narrative again implicates monstrous economics—the Jews were the money lenders, the state and its commerce were heavily indebted to them—but this second story is submerged in a horrifying fable of cultural purity and threat to Christian continuance. As the American frontier expanded beneath the banner of Manifest Destiny in the nineteenth century, tales circulated about how "Indians" routinely kidnapped white women to furnish wives for themselves; the West was a place of danger waiting to be tamed into farms, its menacing native inhabitants fit only to be dispossessed. It matters little that the protagonist of Richard Wright's *Native Son* did not rape and butcher his employer's daughter; that narrative is supplied by the police, by an angry white society, indeed by Western history itself. In the novel, as in life, the threat occurs when a nonwhite leaves the reserve abandoned to him; Wright envisions what happens when the horizon of narrative expectation is firmly set, and his conclusion (born out in seventeenth-century Salem, medieval England, and nineteenth-century America) is that the actual circumstances of history tend to vanish when a narrative of miscegenation can be supplied.

The monster is transgressive, too sexual, perversely erotic, a lawbreaker; and so the monster and all that it embodies must be exiled or destroyed. The repressed, however, like Freud himself, always seems to return.

THESIS VI: FEAR OF THE MONSTER IS REALLY A KIND OF DESIRE

The monster is continually linked to forbidden practices, in order to normalize and to enforce. The monster also attracts. The same creatures who terrify and interdict can evoke potent escapist fantasies; the linking of monstrosity with the forbidden makes the monster all the more appealing as a temporary egress from constraint. This simultaneous repulsion and attraction at the core of the monster's composition accounts greatly for its continued cultural popularity, for the fact that the monster seldom can be contained in a simple, binary dialectic (thesis, antithesis... no synthesis). We distrust and loathe the monster at the same time we envy its freedom, and perhaps its sublime despair.

Through the body of the monster fantasies of aggression, domination, and inversion are allowed safe expression in a clearly delimited and permanently liminal space. Escapist delight gives way to horror only when the monster threatens to overstep these boundaries, to destroy or deconstruct the thin walls of category and culture. When contained by geographic, generic, or epistemic marginalization, the monster can function as an alter ego, as an alluring projection of (an Other) self. The monster awakens one to the pleasures of the body, to the simple and fleeting joys of being frightened, or frightening—to the experience of mortality and corporality. We watch the monstrous spectacle of the horror film because we know that the cinema is a temporary place, that the jolting sensuousness of the celluloid images will be followed by reentry into the world of comfort and light.[39] Likewise, the story on the page before us may horrify (whether it appears in the *New York Times* news section or Stephen King's latest novel matters little), so long as we are safe in the knowledge of its nearing end (the number of pages in our right hand is dwindling) and our liberation from it. Aurally received narratives work no differently; no matter how unsettling the description of the giant, no matter how many unbaptized children and hapless knights he devours, King Arthur will ultimately destroy him. The audience knows how the genre works.

Times of carnival temporally marginalize the monstrous, but at the same time allow it a safe realm of expression and play: on Halloween everyone is a demon for a night. The same impulse to ataractic fantasy is behind much lavishly bizarre manuscript marginalia, from abstract scribblings at the edges of an ordered page to preposterous animals and vaguely humanoid creatures of strange anatomy that crowd a biblical text. Gargoyles and ornately sculpted grotesques, lurking at the crossbeams or upon the roof of the cathedral, likewise record the liberating fantasies of a bored or repressed hand suddenly freed to populate the margins. Maps and travel accounts inherited from antiquity invented whole geographies of the mind and peopled them with exotic and fantastic creatures; Ultima Thule, Ethiopia, and the Antipodes were the medieval equivalents of outer space and virtual reality, imaginary (wholly verbal) geographies accessible from anywhere, never meant to be discovered but always waiting to be explored. Jacques Le Goff has written that the Indian Ocean (a "mental horizon" imagined, in the Middle Ages, to be completely enclosed by land) was a cultural space

> where taboos were eliminated or exchanged for others. The weirdness of this world produced an impression of liberation and freedom. The strict morality imposed by the Church was contrasted with the discomfiting attractiveness of a world of bizarre tastes, which practiced coprophagy and cannibalism; of bodily innocence, where man, freed of the modesty of clothing, rediscovered nudism and sexual freedom; and where, once rid of restrictive monogamy and family barriers, he could give himself over to polygamy, incest, and eroticism.[40]

The habitations of the monsters (Africa, Scandinavia, America, Venus, the Delta Quadrant—whatever land is sufficiently distant to be exoticized) are more than dark regions of uncertain danger: they are also realms of happy fantasy, horizons of liberation. Their monsters serve as secondary bodies through which the possibilities of other genders, other sexual practices, and other social customs can be explored. Hermaphrodites, Amazons, and lascivious cannibals beckon from the edges of the world, the most distant planets of the galaxy.

The co-optation of the monster into a symbol of the desirable is often accomplished through the neutralization of potentially threatening aspects with a liberal dose of comedy: the thundering giant becomes the bumbling giant.[41] Monsters may still function, however, as the vehicles of causative fantasies even without their valences reversed. What Bakhtin calls "official culture" can transfer all that is viewed as undesirable in itself into the body of the monster, performing a wish-fulfillment drama of its own; the scapegoated monster is perhaps ritually destroyed in the course of some official narrative, purging the community by eliminating its sins. The monster's eradication functions as an exorcism and, when retold and promulgated, as a catechism. The monastically manufactured *Queste del Saint Graal* serves as an ecclesiastically sanctioned antidote to the looser morality of the secular romances; when Sir Bors comes across a castle where "ladies of high descent and rank" tempt him to sexual indulgence, these ladies are, of course, demons in lascivious disguise. When Bors refuses to sleep with one of these transcorporal devils (described as "so lovely and so fair that it seemed all earthly beauty was embodied in her"), his steadfast assertion of control banishes them all shrieking back to hell.[42] The episode valorizes the celibacy so central to the authors' belief system (and so difficult to enforce) while inculcating a lesson in morality for the work's intended secular audience, the knights and courtly women fond of romances.

Seldom, however, are monsters as uncomplicated in their use and manufacture as the demons that haunt Sir Bors. Allegory may flatten a monster rather thin, as when the vivacious demon of the Anglo-Saxon hagio-graphic poem *Juliana* becomes the one-sided complainer of Cynewulf's *Elene*. More often, however, the monster retains a haunting complexity. The dense symbolism that makes a thick description of the monsters in Spenser, Milton, and even *Beowulf* so challenging reminds us how permeable the monstrous body can be, how difficult to dissect.

This corporal fluidity, this simultaneity of anxiety and desire, ensures that the monster will always dangerously entice. A certain intrigue is allowed even Vincent of Beauvais's well-endowed cynocephalus, for he occupies a textual space of allure before his necessary dismissal, during which he is granted an undeniable charm. The monstrous lurks somewhere in that ambiguous, primal space between fear and attraction, close to the heart of what Kristeva calls "abjection":

> There looms, within abjection, one of those violent, dark revolts of being, directed against a threat that seems to emanate from an exorbitant outside or inside, ejected beyond the scope of the possible, the tolerable, the thinkable. It lies there, quite close, but it cannot be assimilated. It beseeches, worries, fascinates desire, which, nonetheless, does not let itself be seduced. Apprehensive, desire turns aside; sickened, it rejects . . . But simultaneously, just the same, that impetus, that spasm, that leap is drawn toward an elsewhere as tempting as it is condemned. Unflaggingly, like an inescapable boomerang, a vortex of summons and repulsion places the one haunted by it literally beside himself.[43]

And the self that one stands so suddenly and so nervously beside is the monster.

The monster is the abjected fragment that enables the formation of all kinds of identities—personal, national, cultural, economic, sexual, psychological, universal, particular (even if that "particular" identity is an embrace of the power/status/knowledge of abjection itself); as such it reveals their partiality, their contiguity. A product of a multitude of morphogeneses (ranging from somatic to ethnic) that align themselves to imbue meaning to the Us and Them behind every cultural mode of seeing, the monster of abjection resides in that marginal geography of the Exterior, beyond the limits of the Thinkable, a place that is doubly dangerous: simultaneously "exorbitant" and "quite dose." Judith Butler calls this conceptual locus "a domain of unlivability and unintelligibility that bounds the domain of intelligible effects," but points out that even when discursively closed off, it offers a base for critique, a margin from which to reread dominant paradigms.[44] Like Grendel thundering from the mere or Dracula creeping from the grave, like Kristeva's "boomerang, a vortex of summons" or the uncanny Freudian-Lacanian return of the repressed, the monster is always coming back, always at the verge of irruption.

Perhaps it is time to ask the question that always arises when the monster is discussed seriously (the inevitability of the question a symptom of the deep anxiety about what is and what should be thinkable, an anxiety that the process of monster theory is destined to raise): Do monsters really exist?

Surely they must, for if they did not, how could we?

THESIS VII: THE MONSTER STANDS AT THE THRESHOLD ... OF BECOMING

"This thing of darkness I acknowledge mine."

Monsters are our children. They can be pushed to the farthest margins of geography and discourse, hidden away at the edges of the world and in the forbidden recesses of our mind, but they always return. And when they come back, they bring not just a fuller knowledge of our place in history and the history of knowing our place, but they bear self-knowledge, *human* knowledge—and a discourse all the more sacred as it arises from the Outside. These monsters ask us how we perceive the world, and how we have misrepresented what we have attempted to place. They ask us to reevaluate our cultural assumptions about race, gender, sexuality, our perception of difference, our tolerance toward its expression. They ask us why we have created them.

MONSTER CULTURE (SEVEN THESES)

Notes

1. Literally, here, *Zeitgeist*. Time Ghost, the bodiless spirit that uncannily incorporates a "place" that is a series of places, die crossroads that is a point in a *movement* toward an uncertain elsewhere. Bury the Zeitgeist by the crossroads: it is confused as it awakens, it is not going anywhere, it intersects everyplace; all roads lead back to the monster.

2. I realize that this is an interpretive biographical maneuver Barthes would surely have called "the living death of the author."

3. Thus the superiority of Joan Copjec's "Vampires, Breast-feeding, and Anxiety," *October* 58 (Fall 1991): 25-43, to Paul Barber's *Vampires, Burial, and Death: Folklore and Reality* (New Haven, Conn.: Yale University Press, 1988).

4. "The giant is represented through movement, through being in time. Even in the ascription of the still landscape to the giant, it is the activities of the giant, his or her legendary actions, that have resulted in the observable trace. In contrast to the still and perfect universe of the miniature, the gigantic represents the order and disorder of historical forces." Susan Stewart, *On Longing: Narratives of the Miniature, the Gigantic, the Souvenir, the Collection* (Baltimore: Johns Hopkins University Press, 1984), 86.

5. Harvey R. Greenberg, "Reimaging the Gargoyle: Psychoanalytic Notes *on Alien,*" in *Close Encounters: Film, Feminism, and Science Fiction*, ed. Constance Penley, Elisabeth Lyon, Lynn Spigel, and Janet Bergstrom (Minneapolis: University of Minnesota Press, 1991), 90–91.

6. Marjorie Garber, *Vested Interests: Cross-Dressing and Cultural Anxiety* (New York: Routledge, 1992), 11. Garber writes at some length about "category crisis," which she defines as "a failure of definitional distinction, a borderline that becomes permeable, that permits of border crossings from one (apparently distinct) category to another: black/white, Jew/Christian, noble/bourgeois, master/servant, master/slave . . . That which crosses the border, like the transvestite will always function as a mechanism of overdetermination—a mechanism of displacement from one blurred boundary to another. An analogy here might be the so-called 'tagged' gene that shows up in a genetic chain, indicating the presence of some otherwise hidden condition. It is not the gene itself, but its presence, that marks the trouble spot, indicating the likelihood of a crisis somewhere, elsewhere" (pp. 16–17). Note, however, that whereas Garber insists that the transvestite must be read *with* rather than *through*, the monster can be read only *through*—for the monster, pure culture, is nothing of itself.

7. These are the ancient monsters recorded first by the Greek writers Ktesias and Megasthenes, and include such wild imaginings as the Pygmies, the Sciapods (men with one large foot with which they can hop about at tremendous speed or that they can lift over their reclining bodies as a sort of beach umbrella), Blemmyae ("men whose heads / Do grow beneath their shoulders," in Othello's words), and Cynocephali, ferocious dog-headed men who are anthropophagous to boot. John Block Friedman has called these creatures the Plinian races, after the classical encyclopedist who bestowed them to the Middle Ages and early modern period. *The Monstrous Races in Medieval Art and Thought* (Cambridge: Harvard University Press, 1981).

8. The discussion of the implication of the monstrous in the manufacture of heuristics is partially based upon my essay "The Limits of Knowing: Monsters and the Regulation of Medieval Popular Culture," *Medieval Folklore* 3 (Fall 1994): 1–37.

9. Jerrold E. Hogle, "The Struggle for a Dichotomy: Abjection in Jekyll and His Interpreters," in *Dr. Jekyll and Mr. Hyde after One Hundred Years,* ed. William Veeder and Gordon Hirsch (Chicago: University of Chicago Press, 1988), 161.

10. "The hermeneutic circle does not permit access or escape to an uninterrupted reality; but we do not [have to] keep going around in the same path." Barbara Herrnstein Smith, "Belief and Resistance: A Symmetrical Account," *Critical Inquiry* 18 (Autumn 1991): 137–38.

11. Jacques Derrida, *Of Grammatology,* trans. Gayatri Chakravorty Spivak (Baltimore: Johns Hopkins University Press, 1974).

12. Barbara Johnson, "Introduction," in Jacques Derrida, *Dissemination,* trans. Barbara Johnson (Chicago: University of Chicago Press, 1981), xiii.

13. H. D. S. Greenway, "Adversaries Create Devils of Each Other," *Boston Globe,* December 15, 1992, 1.

14. Thomas More, *The Yale Edition of the Complete Works of Thomas More,* vol. 2, *The History of King Richard III,* ed. Richard S. Sylvester (New Haven, Conn.: Yale University Press, 1963), 7.

15. Marjorie Garber, *Shakespeare's Ghost Writers: Literature as Uncanny Causality* (New York: Routledge, Chapman & Hall, 1988), 30. My discussion of Richard is indebted to Marjorie Garber's provocative work.

16. "A portrait now in the Society of Antiquaries of London, painted about 1505, shows a Richard with straight shoulders. But a second portrait, possibly of earlier date, in the Royal Collection, seems to emblematize the whole controversy [over Richard's supposed monstrosity], for in it, X-ray examination reveals an original straight shoulder line, which was subsequently painted over to present the raised right shoulder silhouette so often copied by later portraitists," Ibid., 35.

17. I am hinting here at the possibility of a feminist recuperation of the gendered monster by citing the titles of two famous books about Lilith (a favorite figure in feminist writing): Jacques Bril's *Lilith, ou, La Mere obscure* (Paris: Payot, 1981), and Siegmund Hurwitz's *Lilith, die erste Eva: Eine Studie uber dunkle Aspekte des Weiblichen* (Zurich: Daimon Verlag, 1980).

18. "The monster-woman, threatening to replace her angelic sister, embodies intransigent female autonomy and thus represents both the author's power to allay 'his' anxieties by calling their source bad names (witch, bitch, fiend, monster) and simultaneously, the mysterious power of the character who refuses to stay in her textually ordained 'place' and thus generates a story that 'gets away' from its author." Sandra M. Gilbert and Susan Gubar, *The Madwoman in the Attic: The Woman Writer and the Nineteenth Century Literary Imagination* (New Haven, Conn.: Yale University Press, 1984), 28. The "dangerous" role of feminine will in the engendering of monsters is also explored by Marie-Hélène Huet in *Monstrous Imagination* (Cambridge: Harvard University Press, 1993).

19. A cynocephalus is a dog-headed man, like the recently decanonized Saint Christopher. Bad enough to be a cynocephalus without being hermaphroditic to boot: the monster accrues one kind of difference on top of another, like a magnet that draws differences into an aggregate, multivalent identity around an unstable core.

20. Bruno Roy, "En marge du monde connu: Les races de monstres," in Aspects *de la marginalia au Moyen Age*, ed. Guy-H Allard. (Quebec: Les Éditions de bAurore, 1975), 77. This translation is mine.

21. See, for example, Monica E. McAlpine, "The Pardoner's Homosexuality and How It Matters," *PMLA 95* (1980): 8–22.

22. Cited by Friedman, *The Monstrous Races*, 64.

23. Elizabeth deported "blackamoores" in 1596 and again in 1601. See Karen Newman, "'And Wash the Ethiop White': Femininity and the Monstrous in Othello," in *Shakespeare Reproduced: The Text in History and Ideology*, ed. Jean E. Howard and Marion F. O'Connor (New York: Methuen, 1987), 148.

24. See Giraldus Cambrensis, *Topographia Hibemae (The History and Topography of Ireland)*, trans. John J. O'Meara (Atlantic Highlands, N.J.: Humanities Press, 1982), 24.

25. See Edward Said, *Orientalism* (New York: Pantheon, 1978); Henry Louis Gates Jr., *The Signifying Monkey: A Theory of Afro-American Literature* (New York: Oxford University Press, 1988).

26. René Girard, *The Scapegoat*, trans. Yvonne Freccero (Baltimore: Johns Hopkins University Press, 1986), 33.

27. Ibid., 21–22.

28. Extended travel was dependent in both the ancient and medieval world on the promulgation of an ideal of hospitality that sanctified the responsibility of host to guest. A violation of that code is responsible for the destruction of the biblical Sodom and Gomorrah, for the devolution from man to giant in *Sir Gawain and the Carl of Carlisle*, and for the first punitive transformation in Ovid's *Metamorphoses*. This popular type of narrative may be conveniently labeled the fable of hospitality; such stories envalue the practice whose breach they illustrate through a drama repudiating the dangerous behavior. The valorization is accomplished in one of two ways: the host is a monster already and learns a lesson at the hands of his guest, or the host becomes a monster in the course of the narrative and audience members realize how they should conduct themselves. In either case, the cloak of monstrousness calls attention to those behaviors and attitudes the text is concerned with interdicting.

29. Ovid, *Metamorphoses* (Loeb Classical Library no. 42), ed. G. P. Goold (Cambridge: Harvard University Press, 1916, rpr. 1984), I.156–62.

30. Ibid., I. 231–39.

31. I am indebted to Keeryung Hong of Harvard University for sharing her research on medieval map production for this hypothesis.

32. A useful (albeit politically charged) term for such a collective is *Männerbunde*, "all-male groups with aggression as one major function." See Joseph Harris, "Love and Death in the *Männerbund*: An Essay with Special Reference to the *Bjarkamál and The Battle of Maldon*," in *Heroic Poetry in the Anglo-Saxon Period*, ed. Helen Damico and John Leyerle (Kalamazoo: Medieval Institute/Western Michigan State University, 1993), 78. See also the Interscripta discussion of "Medieval Masculinities," moderated and edited by Jeffrey Jerome Cohen, accessible via WWW: http://www.georgetown.edu/labyrinth/e-center/interscripts/mm.html (the piece is also forthcoming in a nonhypertext version in *Arthuriana*, as "The Armour of an Alienating Identity").

33. The Greek word *barbaros*, from which we derive the modern English word *barbaric*, means "making the sound *bar bar*"—that is, not speaking Greek, and therefore speaking nonsense.

34. Michel Foucault, *The History of Sexuality*, vol. 1, *An introduction*, trans. Robert Hurley (New York: Vintage, 1990), 47–48.

35. Stewart, *On Longing*. See especially "The Imaginary Body," 104–31.

36. The situation was obviously far more complex than these statements can begin to show; "European," for example, usually includes only males of the Western Latin tradition. Sexual orientation further complicates the picture, as we shall see. Donna Haraway, following Trinh Minh-ha, calls the humans beneath the monstrous skin "inappropriate/d others": "To be 'inappropriate/d' does not mean 'not to be in relation with'—i.e., to be in a special reservation, with the status of the authentic, the untouched, in the allochronic and allotropic condition of innocence. Rather to be an 'inappropriate/d other' means to be in critical deconstructive relationality, in a diffracting rather than reflecting (ratio) nality—as the means of making potent connection that exceeds domination." "The Promises of Monsters," in *Simians, Cyborgs, and Women: The Reinvention of Nature* (New York: Routledge, 1991), 299.

37. This discussion owes an obvious debt to Mary Douglas, *Purity and Danger: An Analysis of the Concepts of Pollution and Taboo* (New York: Routledge & Kegan Paul, 1966).

38. John Eastman, *Retakes: Behind the Scenes of 500 Classic Movies*, 9–10.

39. Paul Coates interestingly observes that "the horror film becomes the essential form of cinema, monstrous content manifesting itself in the monstrous form of the gigantic screen." *The Gorgon's Gaze* (Cambridge: Cambridge University Press, 1991), 77. Carol Clover locates some of the pleasure of the monster film in its cross-gender game of identification; see *Men, Women, and Chain Saws: Gender in the Modern Horror Film* (Princeton, N. J.: Princeton University Press, 1992). Why not go further, and call the pleasure cross-somatic?

40. Jacques Le Goff, "The Medieval West and the Indian Ocean," in *Time, Work and Culture in the Middle Ages*, trans. Arthur Goldhammer (Chicago: University of Chicago Press, 1980), 197. The postmodern equivalent of such spaces is Gibsoniair cyberspace, with its MOOs and MUSHes and other arenas of unlimited possibility.

41. For Mikhail Bakhtin, famously, this is the transformative power of laughter: "Laughter liberates not only from external censorship but first of all from the great internal censor;

it liberates from the fear that developed in man during thousands of years: fear of the sacred, fear of the prohibitions, of the past, of power." *Rabelais and His World,* trans. Hélène Iswolsky (Indianapolis: Indiana University Press, 1984), 94. Bakhtin traces the moment of escape to the point at which laughter became a part of the "higher levels of literature," when Rabelais wrote *Gargantua et Pantagruel.*

42. *The Quest for the Holy Grail,* trans. Pauline Matarasso (London: Penguin Books, 1969), 194.

43. Julia Kristeva, *The Powers of Honor: An Essay on Abjection,* trans. Leon S. Roudiez (New York: Columbia University Press, 1982), 1.

44. Judith Butler, *Bodies That Matter: On the Discursive Limits of "Sex"* (New York: Routledge, 1993). 22. Both Butler and I have in mind here Foucault's notion of an emancipation of thought "from what it silently thinks" that will allow "it to think differently." Michael Foucault, *The Use of Pleasure,* trans. Robert Hurley (New York: Vintage, 1985), 9. Michael Uebel amplifies and applies this practice to the monster in his essay in this volume.

Explore

Consider Cohen's assertion that monsters can represent "cultural, political, racial, economic, [and/or] sexual" difference. In what ways have you seen this process occurring in your everyday life? For example, in what ways do modern media present people as Others? When have you seen monstrous attributes projected onto individual people or groups? Find two examples in which the media uses monstrous attributes to vilify a particular individual or a group, and analyze how language and imagery contribute to the negative characterization.

Collaborate

In a small group, choose a monster with which everyone is already familiar. Discuss why people might consider it to be "monstrous." Then, use the internet or other resources to learn about the monster's original cultural significance. In what time period did it originate? Why was it considered "monstrous" at the time? Finally, discuss how this monster resonates with your culture today. How do people "read" this monster today? How might today's understandings of this monster differ from its original cultural meanings? As you read this book, continue to consider how the monsters within it represent the cultures from which they come.

Compose

Cohen emphasizes that monsters "are disturbing hybrids whose externally incoherent bodies resist attempts to include them in any systematic structuration." Create an essay or a poster that analyzes how a monster "refuses easy categorization," illustrating and explaining the significance of the different hybrid parts and how they conflict with typical definitions and categories. Also explain how this monster "offers … an invitation to explore new spirals, new and interconnected methods of perceiving the world." In other words, how does the monster's lack of categorization open up new possibilities for interpreting its significance?

Frankenstein (1818) was written in the summer of 1816 in response to Lord Byron's suggestion that he, John Polidori, Percy Shelley, and Mary Shelley each write a supernatural tale. Mary Shelley, daughter of authors Mary Wollstonecraft and William Godwin and wife of poet Percy Shelley, completed the task but published the novel anonymously. Frankenstein was originally controversial, the topic considered by some to be immoral, improper, or impious, but it has become a classic of Gothic fiction, ultimately making Mary Shelley more widely recognized than her other famous family members.

This selection, from the 1818 edition, describes Victor Frankenstein's obsessive frenzy of creation and the disgust and horror he experiences once he gives his monster life. In a revised version of the tale published in 1831, Shelley mitigates Victor Frankenstein's responsibility as the creator of a monster, making him more a victim of fate than a mad scientist, but in the original work, Frankenstein's ego overcomes his morals. He creates his monster with no regard for the consequences. As you read, consider how much of the creature's "monstrosity" comes from his appearance and how much originates from Victor Frankenstein's reaction to him.

----

excerpts from

FRANKENSTEIN

BY MARY SHELLEY

[. . .] When I found so astonishing a power placed within my hands, I hesitated a long time concerning the manner in which I should employ it. Although I possessed the capacity of bestowing animation, yet to prepare a frame for the reception of it, with all its intricacies of fibres, muscles, and veins, still remained a work of inconceivable difficulty and labour. I doubted at first whether I should attempt the creation of a being like myself, or one of simpler organization; but my imagination was too much exalted by my first success to permit me to doubt of my ability to give life to an animal as complex and wonderful as man. The materials at present within my command hardly appeared adequate to so arduous an undertaking, but I doubted not that I should ultimately succeed. I prepared myself for a multitude of reverses; my operations might be incessantly baffled, and at last my work be imperfect: yet, when I considered the improvement which every day takes place in science and mechanics, I was encouraged to hope my present attempts would at least lay the foundations of future success. Nor could I consider the magnitude and complexity of my plan as any argument of its impracticability. It was with these feelings that I began the creation of a human being. As the minuteness of the parts formed a great hindrance to my speed, I resolved, contrary to my first intention, to make the being of a gigantic stature; that is to say, about eight feet in height, and proportionably large. After having formed this determination, and having spent some months in successfully collecting and arranging my materials, I began.

No one can conceive the variety of feelings which bore me onwards, like a hurricane, in the first enthusiasm of success. Life and death appeared to me ideal bounds,[1] which I should first break through, and pour a torrent of light into our dark world. A new species would bless me as its creator and source; many happy and excellent natures would owe their being to me. No father could claim the gratitude of his child so completely as I should deserve theirs. Pursuing these reflections, I thought that if I could bestow animation upon lifeless matter, I might in process of time (although I now found it impossible) renew life where death had apparently devoted the body to corruption.

These thoughts supported my spirits, while I pursued my undertaking with unremitting ardour. My cheek had grown pale with study, and my person had become emaciated with confinement. Sometimes, on the very

Figure 2. The first illustration of Frankenstein, an engraving by Theodor von Holst, was created for the frontispiece of the book's 1831 edition. Compare the appearance of the creature with Shelley's description, noting its muscular form; its long, black hair; the awkward proportion of body, limbs, and head.

1 Imaginary boundaries.

brink of certainty, I failed; yet still I clung to the hope which the next day or the next hour might realize. One secret which I alone possessed was the hope to which I had dedicated myself, and the moon gazed on my midnight labours, while, with unrelaxed and breathless eagerness, I pursued nature to her hiding places. Who shall conceive the horrors of my secret toil, as I dabbled among the unhallowed damps of the grave, or tortured the living animal to animate the lifeless clay? My limbs now tremble, and my eyes swim with the remembrance; but then a resistless, and almost frantic impulse, urged me forward; I seemed to have lost all soul or sensation but for this one pursuit. It was indeed but a passing trance, that only made me feel with renewed acuteness so soon as, the unnatural stimulus ceasing to operate, I had returned to my old habits. I collected bones from charnel houses; and disturbed, with profane fingers, the tremendous secrets of the human frame. In a solitary chamber, or rather cell, at the top of the house, and separated from all the other apartments by a gallery and staircase, I kept my workshop of filthy creation; my eyeballs were starting from their sockets in attending to the details of my employment. The dissecting room and the slaughter-house furnished many of my materials; and often did my human nature turn with loathing from my occupation, whilst, still urged on by an eagerness which perpetually increased, I brought my work near to a conclusion.

The summer months passed while I was thus engaged, heart and soul, in one pursuit. It was a most beautiful season; never did the fields bestow a more plentiful harvest or the vines yield a more luxuriant vintage: but my eyes were insensible to the charms of nature. And the same feelings which made me neglect the scenes around me caused me also to forget those friends who were so many miles absent, and whom I had not seen for so long a time. I knew my silence disquieted them; and I well remembered the words of my father: "I know that while you are pleased with yourself, you will think of us with affection, and we shall hear regularly from you. You must pardon me, if I regard any interruption in your correspondence as a proof that your other duties are equally neglected."

I knew well therefore what would be my father's feelings; but I could not tear my thoughts from my employment, loathsome in itself, but which had taken an irresistible hold of my imagination. I wished, as it were, to procrastinate all that related to my feelings of affection until the great object, which swallowed up every habit of my nature, should be completed.

Figure 3. This famous physical presentation of the creature, played by Boris Karloff, originated in the 1931 film *Frankenstein*. Pay particular attention to the bolts on his neck and the square skull, both of which appear in virtually all cartoon images of the creature. Since Shelley never mentions these features, why might the film add them? What is their purpose?

I then thought that my father would be unjust if he ascribed my neglect to vice, or faultiness on my part; but I am now convinced that he was justified in conceiving that I should not be altogether free from blame. A human being in perfection ought always to preserve a calm and peaceful mind, and never to allow passion or a transitory desire to disturb his tranquillity. I do not think that the pursuit of knowledge is an exception to this rule. If the study to which you apply yourself has a tendency to weaken your affections, and to destroy your taste for those simple pleasures in which no alloy can possibly mix, then that study is certainly unlawful, that is to say, not befitting the human mind. If this rule were always observed; if no man allowed any pursuit whatsoever to interfere with the tranquillity of his domestic affections, Greece had not been enslaved; Cæsar would have spared his country; America would have been discovered more gradually; and the empires of Mexico and Peru had not been destroyed.

But I forget that I am moralizing in the most interesting part of my tale; and your looks remind me to proceed.

My father made no reproach in his letters; and only took notice of my silence by inquiring into my occupations more particularly than before. Winter, spring, and summer passed away during my labours; but I did not watch the blossom or the expanding leaves—sights which before always yielded me supreme delight—so deeply was I engrossed in my occupation. The leaves of that year had withered before my work drew near to a close; and now every day shewed me more plainly how well I had succeeded. But my enthusiasm was checked by my anxiety, and I appeared rather like one doomed by slavery to toil in the mines, or any other unwholesome trade, than an artist occupied by his favourite employment. Every night I was oppressed by a slow fever, and I became nervous to a most painful degree; a disease that I regretted the more because I had hitherto enjoyed the most excellent health, and had always boasted of the firmness of my nerves. But I believed that exercise and amusement would soon drive away such symptoms; and I promised myself both of these, when my creation should be complete.

CHAPTER IV

It was on a dreary night of November, that I beheld the accomplishment of my toils. With an anxiety that almost amounted to agony, I collected the instruments of life around me, that I might infuse a spark of being into the lifeless thing that lay at my feet. It was already one in the morning; the rain pattered dismally against the panes, and my candle was nearly burnt out, when, by the glimmer of the half-extinguished light, I saw the dull yellow eye of the creature open; it breathed hard, and a convulsive motion agitated its limbs.

How can I describe my emotions at this catastrophe, or how delineate the wretch whom with such infinite pains and care I had endeavoured to form? His limbs were in proportion, and I had selected his features as beautiful. Beautiful!—Great God! His yellow skin scarcely covered the work of muscles and arteries beneath; his hair was of a lustrous black, and flowing; his teeth of a pearly whiteness; but these luxuriances only formed a more horrid contrast with his watery eyes, that seemed almost of the same colour as the dun-white sockets in which they were set, his shrivelled complexion and straight black lips.

The different accidents of life are not so changeable as the feelings of human nature. I had worked

Figure 4. Robert DeNiro plays Frankenstein's creature in the 1994 adaptation Mary Shelley's *Frankenstein*. This version of the creature focuses on his assembly by drawing attention to the stitches all over his body.

hard for nearly two years, for the sole purpose of infusing life into an inanimate body. For this I had deprived myself of rest and health. I had desired it with an ardour that far exceeded moderation; but now that I had finished, the beauty of the dream vanished, and breathless horror and disgust filled my heart. Unable to endure the aspect of the being I had created, I rushed out of the room and continued a long time traversing my bed-chamber, unable to compose my mind to sleep. At length lassitude succeeded to the tumult I had before endured, and I threw myself on the bed in my clothes, endeavouring to seek a few moments of forgetfulness. But it was in vain: I slept indeed, but I was disturbed by the wildest dreams. I thought I saw Elizabeth, in the bloom of health, walking in the streets of Ingolstadt. Delighted and surprised, I embraced her; but as I imprinted the first kiss on her lips, they became livid with the hue of death; her features appeared to change, and I thought that I held the corpse of my dead mother in my arms; a shroud enveloped her form, and I saw the grave-worms crawling in the folds of the flannel. I started from my sleep with horror; a cold dew covered my forehead, my teeth chattered, and every limb became convulsed; when, by the dim and yellow light of the moon, as it forced its way through the window-shutters, I beheld the wretch— the miserable monster whom I had created. He held up the curtain of the bed; and his eyes, if eyes they may be called, were fixed on me. His jaws opened, and he muttered some inarticulate sounds, while a grin wrinkled his cheeks. He might have spoken, but I did not hear; one hand was stretched out, seemingly to detain me, but I escaped, and rushed downstairs. I took refuge in the courtyard belonging to the house which I inhabited; where I remained during the rest of the night, walking up and down in the greatest agitation, listening attentively, catching and fearing each sound as if it were to announce the approach of the demoniacal corpse to which I had so miserably given life.

Oh! No mortal could support the horror of that countenance. A mummy again endued with animation could not be so hideous as that wretch. I had gazed on him while unfinished; he was ugly then; but when those muscles and joints were rendered capable of motion, it became a thing such as even Dante[2] could not have conceived.

I passed the night wretchedly. Sometimes my pulse beat so quickly and hardly, that I felt the palpitation of every artery; at others, I nearly sank to the ground through languor and extreme weakness. Mingled with this horror, I felt the

---

2   Dante Alighieri (1265–1321), Italian Poet; *The Inferno*, the first book of his *Divine Comedy*, is a guided tour of hell.

bitterness of disappointment: dreams that had been my food and pleasant rest for so long a space were now become a hell to me; and the change was so rapid, the overthrow so complete! [. . .]

Modern audiences confuse the creature and its creator, often referring to the monster itself as Frankenstein. What does this confusion say about the two characters? Brainstorm a list of attributes possessed by each of the characters. What do they have in common? How are they different? Then discuss which traits from either list could be considered monstrous and which emphasize humanity.

Mary Shelley's descriptive details of Frankenstein's creature are vague enough that representations of the monster (from illustrations to movies) vary widely. Pick two of the images included in this selection to compare and contrast. In a short paper, analyze how the different visual interpretations of the creature change your perception of him. What do these differences say about the nature of the creature itself? About Victor Frankenstein's enthusiasm for his creation?

Both *Frankenstein* and this book's selection from *The Strange Case of Dr. Jekyll and Mr. Hyde* are written from the point of view of the monsters' creators. What does Frankenstein's behavior as he is creating the monster tell us about him and his state of mind? How does this behavior compare to that of Dr. Jekyll? Once Frankenstein gives life to his monster, how do his emotional responses change? Why? How do these changes connect to those of Dr. Jekyll after Jekyll loses control of his transformations?

MONSTERS

Anne K. Mellor is an expert in British literature, specializing in the Romantic and Victorian periods and in feminist criticism and theory. Her published works include Mary Shelley: Her Life, Her Fiction, Her Monsters *(1988) and* Romanticism and Gender *(1993); in addition, she has acted as editor for* Romanticism and Feminism *(1988),* British Literature 1780-1830 *(1996), and* The Other Mary Shelley *(1993). Her essay "Frankenstein: A Feminist Critique of Science" was originally published in* One Culture: Essays in Science and Literature *(1987).*

This essay details relationships between Mary Shelley's work and the scientific theories and innovations of her time, connecting the genesis of the creature to "bad" scientific practices and suggesting that this connection causes, at least in part, the creature's monstrosity. In addition, the essay elucidates nineteenth-century patriarchal society's fears of female sexuality, particularly those of Britain's scientific community. These fears are revealed as Frankenstein attempts "to usurp the function of the female in the reproductive cycle." As you read this essay, consider how modern scientific advances are often demonized in literature, television, and movies.

FRANKENSTEIN:
A FEMINIST CRITIQUE OF SCIENCE

By Anne K. Mellor

In *One Culture: Essays in Science and Literature*, ed. George Levine and Alan Rauch (Madison: Univ. of Wisconsin Press, 1987), pp. 287–312

[*This essay was subsequently reprinted as Chap. 5 of* Mary Shelley: Her Life, Her Fictions, Her Monsters *(1988): up to subsection II in this version, with one exception linked as an addendum, differences between the texts are essentially stylistic. Where the texts eventually diverge at subsection II, then, the simplest solution has seemed to be that of representing the 1988 text as a separate, linked entity. Up to that point, for convenient reference to this second version, its page demarcations are given in double curled brackets* {{--}}.]

{287} {{89}} From a feminist perspective, the most significant dimension of the relationship between literature and science is the degree to which both enterprises are grounded on the use of metaphor and image. The explanatory models of science, like the plots of literary works, depend on linguistic structures which are shaped by metaphor and metonymy. The feminist reader is perhaps most sensitized to those symbolic structures which employ gender as a major variable or value. When Francis Bacon announced, "I am come in very truth leading to you Nature with all her children to bind her to your service and make her your slave,"[1] he identified the pursuit of modern science with a form of sexual politics: the aggressive, virile male scientist legitimately captures and enslaves a passive, fertile female nature. Mary Shelley was one of the first to comprehend and illustrate the dangers inherent in the use of sexist metaphors in the seventeenth-century scientific revolution.

Mary Shelley grounded her fiction of the scientist who creates a monster he can't control upon an extensive understanding of the most recent scientific developments of her day. More important, she used this knowledge both to analyze and to criticize the more dangerous implications of both the scientific method and its practical results. Implicitly, she contrasted what she considered "good" science—the detailed and reverent description of the workings of nature—to "bad" science, the hubristic manipulation of the forces of nature to serve man's private ends. In *Frankenstein, or the Modern Prometheus*, she illustrated the potential evils of scientific hubris and at the same time challenged any conception of science and the scientific method that rested on a gendered definition of nature as female. Fully to appreciate the {{90}} significance of Mary Shelley's feminist critique of modern science, {288} we must look first at the particular scientific research upon which her novel is based.

I

The works of three of the most famous scientists of the late eighteenth and early nineteenth century—Humphry Davy, Erasmus Darwin, and Luigi Galvani—together with the teachings of two of their ardent disciples, Adam Walker and Percy Shelley, were crucial to Mary Shelley's understanding of science and the scientific enterprise. While no scientist herself (her description of Victor Frankenstein's laboratory is both vague and naive; apparently Victor does all his experiments in a small attic room by the light of a single candle), Mary Shelley nonetheless had a sound grasp of the concepts and implications of some of the most important scientific work of her day. In her novel, she distinguishes between those scientific researches which attempt to describe accurately the functionings of the physical universe and those which attempt to control or change that universe through human intervention. Implicitly, she celebrates the former, which she associates most closely with the work of Erasmus Darwin, while she calls attention to the dangers inherent in the latter, found in the work of Davy, Galvani, and Walker. [...]

[...] In relation to *Frankenstein*, Erasmus Darwin's most significant evolutionary concept was that of the hierarchy of reproduction. Darwin insisted that sexual reproduction is at a higher evolutionary level than hermaphroditic or solitary paternal propagation.

This concept of the superiority of sexual reproduction over paternal propagation was so important to Erasmus Darwin that it forced him radically to revise his concept of reproduction in his third, "corrected" edition of *Zoonomia*. In 1794, Darwin had argued, following Aristotle, that male plants produce the seed or embryon, while female plants provide only nourishment to this seed, and by analogy, had contended "that the mother does not contribute to the formation of the living ens in normal generation, but is necessary only for supplying its nutriment and oxigenation" (*Zoonomia*, 1794, I: 487). He then attributed all monstrous births to the female, saying that deformities result from either excessive or insufficient nourishment in the egg or uterus (p. 497). But by 1801, Darwin's observations of both animal and vegetable mules had convinced him that both male and female seeds contribute to the innate characteristics of the species (see *Zoonomia*, 1801, 2: 296–97. Interestingly, while Darwin no longer attributed monstrous births to uterine deficiencies or excesses, he continued to hold the male imagination at the moment of conception responsible for determining both the sex of the child and its outstanding traits. [...]

II

[...] Reading *Frankenstein* against the background of Darwin's work, we can see that Mary Shelley directly pitted Victor Frankenstein, that modern Prometheus, against those gradual evolutionary processes of nature described by Darwin. Victor Frankenstein wants to originate a new life form quickly, by chemical means. In his Faustian thirst for knowledge and power, he dreams:

> Life and death appeared to me ideal bounds, which I should first break through, and pour a torrent of light into our dark world. A new species would bless me as its creator and source; many happy and excellent natures would owe their being to me. (F, p. 49)

Significantly, in his attempt to create a new species, Victor Frankenstein substitutes solitary paternal propagation for sexual reproduction. He thus reverses the evolutionary ladder described by Darwin. And he engages in a notion of science that Mary Shelley deplores, the idea that science should manipulate and control rather than describe and understand nature.

{299} Moreover, his imagination at the moment of conception is fevered and unhealthy; as he tells Walton,

Every night I was oppressed by a slow fever, and I became nervous to a most painful degree; . . . my voice became broken, my trembling hands almost refused to accomplish their task; I became as timid as a love-sick girl, and alternate tremor and passionate ardour took the place of wholesome sensation and regulated ambition. (*F*, p. 51)

Under such mental circumstances, according to Darwin, the resultant creation could only be a monster. Frankenstein has further increased the monstrousness of his creation by making a form that is both larger and more simple than a normal human being. As he acknowledges to Walton, "As the minuteness of the parts formed a great hindrance to my speed, I resolved, contrary to my first intention, to make the being of a gigantic stature; that is to say, about eight feet in height, and proportionably large" (*F*, p. 49). {{101}} Darwin had observed that nature moves "from simpler things to more compound" (*Phytologia*, p. 118); in defying nature's law, Victor Frankenstein has created not a more perfect species but a degenerative one.

In his attempt to override natural evolutionary development and to create a new species *sui generis*, Victor Frankenstein enacts a parody of the orthodox creationist theory. While he denies the unique power of God to create organic life, he confirms the capacity of a single creator to originate a new species. Thus he simultaneously upholds the creationist theory and parodies it by creating only a monster. In both ways, he blasphemes against the natural order of things. He moves down rather than up the evolutionary ladder; he reverses human progress and perverts the law of the survival of the fittest. And he denies the natural mode of human reproduction through sexual procreation. […]

[…] Mary Shelley's novel implicitly invokes Darwin's theory of gradual evolutionary progress to suggest both the error and the evil of Victor

Frankenstein's bad science. The genuine improvement of the species can result only from the fusing of both male and female sexuality. In trying to have a baby without a woman, Frankenstein denies to his child the maternal love and nurturance it requires, the very nourishment that Darwin explicitly equated with the female sex. Frankenstein's failure to embrace his smiling creature with maternal love, his horrified rejection of his own creation, spells out the narrative consequences of solitary paternal propagation. But even if Frankenstein had been able to provide his child with a mother's care, he could not have prevented its social ostracism and misery.

Moreover, in trying to create a human being as God created Adam, out of earth and water, all at once, Victor Frankenstein robs nature of something more than fertilizer. "On a dreary night in November, . . . with an anxiety that almost amounted to agony," Victor Frankenstein infused "a spark of being into the lifeless thing that lay" at his feet (*F*, p. 52). At that moment Victor Frankenstein became the modern Prometheus, stealing fire from the gods to give to mankind and thus overthrowing the established, sacred order of both earth and heaven. At that moment he transgressed against nature.

To understand the full implications of Frankenstein's transgression, {301} we must recognize that his stolen "spark of life" is not merely fire; it is also that recently discovered caloric fluid called electricity. Victor's interest in legitimate science is first aroused by the sight of lightning destroying an old oak tree; it is then that he learns of the existence of electricity and replicates Benjamin Franklin's experiment with kite and key and draws down "that fluid from the clouds" (*F*, p. 35). In the late eighteenth century, there was widespread interest in Franklin's and Father Beccaria's discoveries of atmospheric electricity, in static electricity, and in artificial or mechanical electricity generated through such machines as the Leyden jar. Many scientists explored the possibility, derived from Newton's concept of the ether as an elastic medium capable of transmitting the pulsations of light, heat, gravitation, magnetism, and electricity, that the atmosphere was filled with a thin fluid that was positively and negatively charged and that could be identified as a single animating principle appearing under multiple guises (as light, heat, magnetism, etc.). [...]

[...] {303} Fully to appreciate the science that lies behind Victor Frankenstein's endeavors, however, we must remember that in the 1831 Preface to *Frankenstein*, Mary Shelley specifically associated electricity with galvanism. [...]

In 1791 the Bolognese physiologist Luigi Galvani published his *De Viribus Electricitatis in Motui Musculari* (or *Commentary on the Effects of Electricity on Muscular Motion*),[2] in which he came to the conclusion that animal tissue contained a heretofore neglected innate vital force, which he called "animal electricity" but which was subsequently widely known as "galvanism"; this force activated both nerves and muscles when spanned by an arc of metal wires {{105}} connected to a pile of copper and zinc plates. Galvani believed that his new vital force was a form of electricity different from both the "natural" form of electricity produced by lightning or by the torpedo and electric eel and the "artificial" form produced by friction (i.e., static electricity). Galvani argued that the brain is the most important source of the production of this "electric fluid" and that the nerves acted as conductors of this fluid to other nerves and muscles, the tissues of which act much like the outer and inner surfaces of the widely used Leyden jar. Thus the flow of animal electric fluid provided a stimulus which produced contractions of convulsions in the irritable muscle fibers.

Galvani's theories made the British headlines in December 1802 when, in the presence of their Royal Highnesses the Prince of Wales and the dukes of York, Clarence, and Cumberland, Galvani's nephew, disciple, and ardent defender, Professor Luigi Aldini of Bologna University, applied a voltaic pile connected by metallic wires to the ear and nostrils of a recently killed ox head. At that moment, "the eyes were seen to open, the ears to shake, the tongue to be agitated, and the {304} nostrils to swell, in the same manner as those of the living animal, when irritated and desirous of combating another of the same species."[3] But Professor Aldini's most notorious demonstration of galvanic electricity took place on 17 January 1803—On that day he applied galvanic electricity to the corpse of the murderer Thomas Forster. The body of the recently hanged criminal was collected from Newgate, where it had lain in the prison yard at a temperature of 30 degrees Fahrenheit for one hour, by the president of the College of Surgeons, Mr. Keate, and brought immediately to Mr. Wilson's anatomical theater where the following experiments were performed. When wires attached to a pile composed of 120 plates of zinc and 120 plates of copper were connected to the ear and mouth of the dead criminal, Aldini later reported, "the jaw began to quiver, the adjoining muscles were horribly contorted, and the left eye actually opened" (p. 193)— When the wires were applied to the dissected thumb muscles, they "induced a forcible effort to clench the hand;" when applied to the ear and rectum, they "excited in the muscles contractions much stronger . . . The action even of those muscles furthest distant from the points of contact with the arc was so much increased as almost to give an appearance of re-animation." And when volatile alkali was smeared on the nostrils and mouth before the galvanic stimulus was applied, "the convulsions appeared to be much increased . . . and extended from the muscles of the head, face, and neck, as far as the deltoid. The effect in this case surpassed our most sanguine expectations," Aldini exults, and remarkably concludes that "vitality might, perhaps, have been {{106}} restored, if many circumstances had not rendered it impossible" (pp. 194–95). Here is the scientific prototype of Victor Frankenstein, restoring life to dead bodies. [...]

II

[...] Mary Shelley based Victor Frankenstein's attempt to create a new species from dead organic matter through the use of chemistry and electricity on the most advanced scientific research of the early nineteenth century. But *Frankenstein* reflects much more than merely an intelligent use of the latest scientific knowledge. Perhaps because she was a woman, Mary Shelley understood that much of the scientific research of her day incorporated an attempt to dominate the female.

Francis Bacon heralded the seventeenth-century scientific revolution as a calculated attempt to control and exploit female Nature: "I am come in very truth leading to you Nature with all her children to bind her to your service and make her your slave." Bacon's metaphor of a passive, possessable female nature radically transformed the traditional image of female nature as Dame Kind, the "all creating" and bounteous mother earth who single-handedly bore and nourished her children. As Brian Easlea concludes, many seventeenth-century natural philosophers and their successors viewed the scientific quest as a virile masculine penetration into a passive and by herself uncreative female nature, a penetration that would, in Bacon's words, not merely exert a "gentle guidance over nature's course" but rather "conquer and subdue her" and even "shake her to her foundations."[5]

A product of the scientific revolution of the seventeenth century, Frankenstein had been taught to see nature the way Bacon did, as female but inert. He sees nature "objectively," as something separate from himself, a passive and even dead "object of my affection"[5] that can and should be penetrated, analyzed, and controlled. He thus accords nature no living soul or "personhood" that requires recognition or respect.

Mary Shelley perceived a potentially dangerous metaphor inherent in the scientific thought of her day. {307} Nature is female, Dame Kind, Mother Earth. As "all creating nature," she can be seen as the abundantly providing, ever nurturing mother, the blessed source of life itself. But this sacramental view of female nature has been foresworn by Waldman, Frankenstein, and many of the leading scientists of Mary Shelley's day. As Professor Waldman proclaims, scientists "penetrate into the recesses of nature, and shew how *she* works in *her* hiding places" (*F*, p. 42, my emphasis). Nature has become the passive female whose sole function is to satisfy male desires. The scientist who analyzes, manipulates, and attempts to control nature unconsciously engages in a form of oppressive sexual politics. Construing nature as the female other, he attempts to make nature serve his own ends, to gratify his own desires for power, wealth, reputation.

Frankenstein's scientific project is clearly an attempt to gain power. He is inspired by Waldman's description of scientists who "have acquired new and almost unlimited powers; they can command the thunders of the heaven, mimic the earthquake, and even mock the invisible world with its own shadows" (*F*, p. 42). He has sought the power of a father over his children, of God over his creation. "A new species would bless me as its creator and source; many happy and excellent natures would owe their being to me. No father could claim the gratitude of his child so completely as I should deserve theirs," he exults (*F*, p. 49). More subtly yet more pervasively, Frankenstein has sought power over the female. He has "pursued nature to her hiding {308} places" (*F*, p. 49) in an attempt not only to penetrate nature and show how her hidden womb works but actually to steal or appropriate that womb. In effect, Frankenstein has tried to usurp the function of the female in the reproductive cycle and thus eliminate the necessity, at least for the purposes of the biological survival of mankind, of female sexuality.

But Mary Shelley portrays Frankenstein's desire to penetrate and usurp the female as monstrous, unattainable, and finally self-destructive. For nature is not the passive, inert, or "dead" matter that Frankenstein imagines;[34] she resists and revenges his attempts. During his research, nature denies to Victor Frankenstein both mental and physical health: "my enthusiasm was checked by my anxiety, and I appeared rather like one doomed by slavery to toil in the mines, or any other unwholesome trade, than an artist occupied by his favourite employment. Every night I was oppressed by a slow fever, and I became nervous to a most painful degree" (*F*, p. 51). Victor continues to be tormented by anxiety attacks, bouts of delirium, periods of distraction and madness. As soon as he determines to blaspheme against nature a second time, by creating a female human being, nature torments him with a return of his mental illness: "Every thought that was devoted to it was an extreme anguish, and every word that I spoke in allusion to it caused my lips to quiver and my heart to palpitate" (*F*, p. 156); "my spirits became unequal -- I grew restless and nervous" (*F*, p. 162). In the end, Frankenstein's obsession with destroying his creature exposes him to such mental and physical distress that he dies before his twenty-fifth birthday.

The novel thus calls into question the gendered metaphor on which much Western scientific theory and practice are founded. The attempt of science to penetrate, possess, and control Mother Nature entails both a violation of the sacred rights of nature and a false belief in the "objectivity" or "rationality" of scientific research. When it construes nature as a passive and possessable female, Western science encodes a sexist metaphor that has profoundly troubling implications, not only for women but for human survival. As Frankenstein's monster tells him, "Remember that I have power; . . . I can make you so wretched that the light of day will be hateful to you" (*F*, p. 165). Like Victor Frankenstein, modern scientists have too often treated nature as the "other," to be exploited rather than understood and served through detailed, loving, and noninterventionist description. In their search for the truth about the workings of the physical universe, they have ignored the possibility that their manipulations of nature might harm her. Too often, they have failed to take responsibility for the predictable consequences of their research, failed to care for their own technological progeny. As Mary Shelley first perceived, a scientific method founded on the gendered construction of nature as the female other, as the passive object of desire, hence possessable and exploitable, can produce monsters, even monsters of biological, chemical, and nuclear warfare capable of destroying civilization as we know it.

Notes

1. Quoted in Benjamin Farrington, "Temporis Partus Masculus: An Untranslated Writing of Francis Bacon," *Centaurus* 1 (1951), p. 197.

2. Luigi Galvani, *De Viribus Electricitatis in Motui Musculari. Commentarius* (Bologna, 1791); *Commentary on the Effects of Electricity on Muscular Motion*, trans. M. G. Foley, with notes and introduction by I. Bernard Cohen (Norwalk, Conn.: Burndy Library, 1953).

3. John Aldini, *An Account of the Late Improvements in Galvanism, with a series of Curious and Interesting Experiments performed before the Commissioners of the French National Institute and repeated lately ill the Anatomical Theatres of London; to which is added, An Appendix, containing the author's Experiments on the Body of a Malefactor executed at New Gate* (London: Cuthell and Martin, 1803), p. 54. (This book is an English translation of the original French text, *Essai théorique et expérimentale sur le galvanisme* published in Paris in 1802 and translated into German by F. H. Martens and published at Leipzig in 1804.)

4. Brian Easlea, *Science and Sexual Oppression, Patriarchy's Confrontation with Woman and Nature* (London: Weidenfeld and Nicolson, 1981), pp. 83–86.

5. This phrase was deleted by Percy Shelley from Mary Shelley's manuscript of *Frankenstein* (now in the Bodleian Library, Abinger Dep. c. 477/1). Her original version of the passage at F, 50, lines 31-33 reads thus: "I wished, as it were, to procrastinate my feelings of affection, until the great object of my affection was compleated."

According to Mellor, Shelley disapproves of "'bad' science, the hubristic manipulation of the forces of nature to serve man's private ends" including "scientific researches … which attempt to control or change that universe through human intervention." How could this sort of science be considered "monstrous"? With a partner, brainstorm a list of scientific advances that try to *control* or *change* nature. In front of the class, make an argument for why these advances are or are not monstrous. Be aware that your argument could be controversial.

Research Erasmus Darwin or Luigi Galvani, and answer the following questions: How was he received in his own time? What were common opinions of him and his theories? In what way might his theories have been considered "monstrous"? How might Mary Shelley's feelings about him reflect or differ from the common opinions of her time?

FRANKENSTEIN: A FEMINIST CRITIQUE OF SCIENCE

Mellor claims that Shelley takes a feminist stance, condemning Frankenstein not only for his "bad science" but also for his usurpation of female roles and for his attack against Nature, which she claims is the embodiment of femininity. In a small group, discuss your definitions of feminism. How do definitions differ within your group? How do your group's definitions differ from Mellor's? What assumptions come across in your discussion? Find a definition online of a feminist literary approach, and compare it with your ideas about feminism. Then look back at the selection from *Frankenstein* in this book, and discuss how Mellor's position fits the various definitions of feminism you have examined. Be prepared to discuss your discoveries in class.

How might a monster be used as a metaphor for science or scientific advances, and how could such a metaphor be considered social commentary about science? According to Mellor's essay, Frankenstein's creature comments on the science of Shelley's day. In *The Strange Case of Dr. Jekyll and Mr. Hyde*, how might Hyde accomplish a similar goal? In contemporary texts, zombies often provide similar metaphors for science. Choose either *Dr. Jekyll and Mr. Hyde* or a modern zombie story, and write a research paper with a thesis about how the monster provides a metaphor for scientific advances. Your essay should compare Jekyll/Hyde or zombies with Frankenstein and his creature—how is the monster you've chosen similar to this pair?

MONSTERS

GEORGE ROMERO'S ZOMBIE FILMS: A PLAGUE OF MEANING

By L. Andrew Cooper and Brandy Ball Blake

Director George Romero's *Night of the Living Dead* (1968) changed the horror genre, and arguably all of cinema, forever. Remarkably successful for an independent film, *Night*'s brutal black-and-white images of cannibalistic walking corpses revolted imaginations around the world. Ever since, critics have alternately condemned and celebrated the film for its innovative depictions of violence and potentially subversive political resonance. Romero has said that he didn't intend all of the political messages that the film's enthusiasts have associated with it, but he certainly capitalized on the controversy. Ten years after *Night*, he released the sequel *Dawn of the Dead* (1978), with bigger production values, more elaborate violence, and more pointed social satire. The film that completed the original trilogy, *Day of the Dead* (1985), received a lukewarm reception from critics and fans. The director's disappointment with *Day* as an ending for the series led him to expand the trilogy into a quadrilogy that includes *Land of the Dead* (2005) as its final film. After *Land*, Romero rebooted the series with *Diary of the Dead* (2007) and *Survival of the Dead* (2009), which include the slow-moving, cannibalistic, mindless zombies popularized in the original films but don't conform to the earlier films' timeline. Despite his focus on the undead, Romero isn't a zombies-only filmmaker—his movie *The Crazies* (1973) earned a remake in 2010, and his adaptations of Stephen King stories in *Creepshow* (1982) and of a King novel in *The Dark Half* (1993) reached wide audiences—but his films of the living dead are the contributions for which he will be remembered.

The premise of *Night of the Living Dead* is simple: it combines traditional ideas about the voodoo zombie (explored in films such as *White Zombie*, 1932, and *I Walked with a Zombie*, 1943) with newer ideas about a monster plague (hinted at in Bram Stoker's novel *Dracula*, 1897, but not really explored until Richard Matheson's novel *I am Legend*, 1954). The result is a story about a small group of people trapped in a rural farmhouse who fight for their lives against a swarm of undead. This relatively uncomplicated scenario might not have been recognized as an ingenious commentary on its political milieu had it not been released in 1968, a year that saw the assassinations of Martin Luther King, Jr. and Robert F. Kennedy as well as serious developments in both the Civil Rights Movement and the antiwar movement that would eventually convince the United States to withdraw from Vietnam. In this context, the horde of mindless attackers suddenly seemed like metaphors for every possible social ill. They were simultaneously antiwar protesters and the Vietnamese people. They were paradoxically agitators for racial equality and the reactionary white mobs that fought to maintain the status quo. They offered a grim reflection on the braindead generations being raised on the relatively new phenomenon of television and other mass media, on which the film reflects extensively, and they gave new form to the menace of Communism, which people saw as threatening to assimilate America and thereby annihilate individual freedoms and identities. Referred to as ghouls rather than zombies, the first film's monstrous masses had the potential to signify any Other whose threat came from the possibility of overwhelming numbers.

Dawn of the Dead traded *Night*'s setting, a rural farmhouse, for a suburban shopping mall, shifting the metaphoric potential of the zombies onto American consumerism and capitalism. Called simply *Zombi* for its European release, *Dawn* popularized the term for which Romero's monsters are now known. Like the original, the sequel makes some subtle and some not-so-subtle moves that tear down a simplistic "us versus them" understanding of the humans versus zombies struggle. Humans often seem just as bad, and sometimes worse, than the zombies, so if the zombies are mindless consumers of the shopping mall's materialistic excesses, then so are we. *Day of the Dead* changed the setting once more, making the survivors an uneasy combination of scientists and soldiers in an underground military bunker besieged by the undead, and thus *Day*'s critical lens of zombie-ness falls squarely on the United States' military-industrial complex.

Since *Day*, all three films in the original trilogy have been remade, with Zack Snyder's *Dawn of the Dead* (2004) rising above the other remakes due to its big budget and graphic infusion of action-genre energy. Romero-inspired zombies have also infiltrated virtually every aspect of culture, from the parody film *Shaun of the Dead* (2004), to the series of graphic-novels-turned-TV-hit *The Walking Dead* (2010), to rewrites of classic novels such as *Pride and Prejudice and Zombies* (2009), to the live action role-playing game *Humans vs. Zombies* that has been popularized on many college campuses. As far as the media are concerned, Romero's zombies have indeed spread like a plague.

Figure 5. Romero's zombies in *Night of the Living Dead* are slow-moving corpses who reach hungrily for their prey. Dressed in everything from nightgowns to formalwear, the zombies look like white, middle-class Americans.

Figure 6. This image of a TV from *Dawn of the Dead* continues a theme introduced in *Night*. In both films, TV newscasts offer images and descriptions of horror—just as TV news brought the atrocities of the Vietnam War into millions of Americans' living rooms.

Figure 7. High-contrast black-and-white cinematography obscures much of the gore in *Night,* but the camera still provides a nauseating look at the ghouls' appetites. If they are human, they are cannibals, but newscasts within the film insist the ghouls only look human. Their diets are one of the features that might disqualify them from the category of human, making them pure monster.

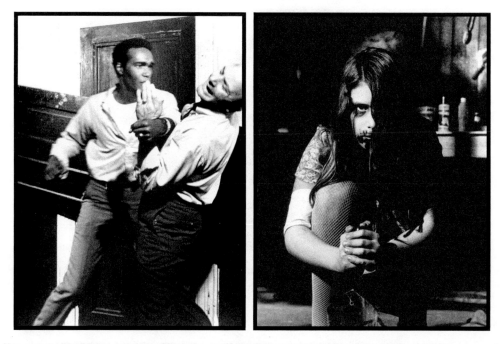

Figure 8. Violence within *Night's* rural farmhouse resonates strongly with many of the political and social tensions of America in 1968. For much of the film, Ben (Duane Jones) and Harry (Karl Hardman) struggle with one another over who will lead the group of people in the farmhouse. When the tension between them finally erupts in violence (left), the image of a black man (Ben) beating up a white man (Harry) reflects the anxieties of the white majority during the Civil Rights Movement. Throughout the film, another sort of violence is also preparing to erupt as the daughter of Harry and his wife Helen succumbs to a ghoul's infectious bite. When the girl finally dies and becomes a ghoul, she picks up a spade and murders her mother. This violence reflects another anxiety of the period, as the anti-war movement led to protests in which the young rose up against their elders.

Figure 9. *Dawn of the Dead's* setting in a suburban shopping mall makes the zombies look like mindless shoppers, shuffling through a maze of products. Instead of consuming products, however, the zombies would consume people, and thus one form of consumerism blends into another.

Figure 10. The inhumanity of the humans becomes even more graphic in *Day of the Dead* as scientists in an underground military bunker perform horrific experiments on zombies. The military takes its experiments to the point of chaining a zombie and watching it (re)learn rudimentary tool use and language skills. As the zombie becomes more human, the humans become less sympathetic, and the line between human and monster almost seems to vanish.

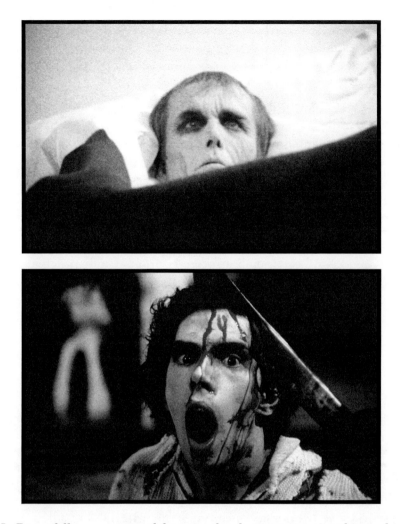

Figure 11. *Dawn* follows a group of four people who try to survive the zombie menace by hiding in a shopping mall. One of the four (top) eventually succumbs to a zombie bite, and his slow transformation charts the passing from human to monster. The humans have a difficult time shooting their transformed friend, but otherwise, they kill zombies gleefully, hacking them to pieces as if killing zombies were a sport (bottom). The humans' predatory behavior might actually make them worse than the zombies, whose killing at least lacks playfulness and glee.

Romero's influence has spread across media, inspiring novels, comics, TV shows, and, of course, other films. Find three representations of zombies that arguably demonstrate Romero's influence. What details of these representations are similar to the details discussed here? What details seem to depart from Romero's vision? What is significant about these similarities and differences? Create a short slideshow (such as a PowerPoint®) that discusses the representations you've found. Either use your software's option to record audio and advance slides automatically, or present the slideshow to your class in person.

Romero's zombies are fairly easy to handle individually. They are slow, weak, and soft, so an informed human can dispatch an individual with a relatively effortless blow to the head. When they're in groups, however, the zombies are lethal—you might be able to hit one on the head, but while you're attempting the hit, the others are liable to get you. In a group, discuss the type(s) of collaboration modeled by zombies. Identify a task that would be hard (perhaps impossible) for an individual zombie but easier (or at least possible) for a group. Act out the completion of this task twice, first behaving like zombies and then behaving like humans. What do your performances reveal about zombie and human forms of collaboration?

Write an extended definition of "human," specifying the criteria that allow something/someone to qualify as human. Then write an extended definition of "zombie," specifying the criteria that allow something/someone to qualify as a zombie. In both definitions, refer to what you know about Romero's zombie films, either from the descriptions here or from outside viewing, as examples. Finally, write a short reflective essay about your definitions.

- What difficulties arose as you composed the definitions?

- What, according to your definitions, distinguishes human from zombie?

- In what ways do the definitions inevitably overlap?

- What do your definitions reveal about the capacity of the zombie, as a monster, to reflect on both the strengths and the weaknesses of humanity?

Author, screenwriter, and actor Max Brooks has written numerous fictional accounts of zombies, including The Zombie Survival Guide *(2003) and* The Zombie Survival Guide: Recorded Attacks *(2009), as well as the introduction to the graphic mini-series* Raise the Dead *(2007). His best-known work,* World War Z *(2006), presents "An Oral History of the Zombie War," composed of first-person accounts of a world-wide zombie plague. The novel's narrator interviews key figures in and survivors of the war in order to provide "the human factor" of the devastating conflict.*

As the narrator explains, "the human factor" is "the only true difference between us and the enemy we now refer to as 'the living dead'". The story, therefore, focuses on the emotional impact of the zombie plague, including fear, heroism, anger, resentment, and other responses that illustrate the human condition. The selections included here, which describe the first outbreak of the plague in China and, from much later in the conflict, the plan that allows many world governments to retake their countries from the zombie threat, provide initial reactions to the outbreak as well as the desperate measures that world governments have to adopt in order to thwart the plague. As you read, consider the "human" reactions to the zombie plague and whether any of these reactions could be defined as "monstrous."

excerpts from

WORLD WAR Z

BY MAX BROOKS

GREATER CHONGQING, THE UNITED FEDERATION OF CHINA

[At its prewar height, this region boasted a population of over thirty-five million people. Now, there are barely fifty thousand. Reconstruction funds have been slow to arrive in this part of the country, the government choosing to concentrate on the more densely populated coast. There is no central power grid, no running water besides the Yangtze River. But the streets are clear of rubble and the local "security council" has prevented any postwar outbreaks. The chairman of that council is Kwang Jing-shu, a medical doctor who, despite his advanced age and wartime injuries, still manages to make house calls to all his patients.]

The first outbreak I saw was in a remote village that officially had no name. The residents called it "New Dachang," but this was more out of nostalgia than anything else. Their former home, "Old Dachang," had stood since the period of the Three Kingdoms, with farms and houses and even trees said to be centuries old. When the Three Gorges Dam was completed, and reservoir waters began to rise, much of Dachang had been disassembled, brick by brick, then rebuilt on higher ground. This New Dachang, however, was not a town anymore, but a "national historic museum." It must have been a heartbreaking irony for those poor peasants, to see their town saved but then only being able to visit it as a tourist. Maybe that is why some of them chose to name their newly constructed hamlet "New Dachang" to preserve some connection to their heritage, even if it was only in name. I personally didn't know that this other New Dachang existed, so you can image how confused I was when the call came in.

The hospital was quiet; it had been a slow night, even for the increasing number of drunk-driving accidents. Motorcycles were becoming very popular. We used to say that your Harley-Davidson killed more young Chinese than all the GIs in the Korean War. That's why I was so grateful for a quiet shift. I was tired, my back and feet ached. I was on my way out to smoke a cigarette and watch the dawn when I heard my name being paged. The receptionist that night was new and couldn't quite understand the dialect. There had been an accident, or an illness. It was an emergency, that part was obvious, and could we please send help at once.

What could I say? The younger doctors, the kids who think medicine is just a way to pad their bank accounts, they certainly weren't going to go help some "nongmin" just for the sake of helping. I guess I'm still an old revolutionary at heart. "Our duty is to hold ourselves responsible to the people."[1] Those words still mean something to me...and I tried to remember that as my Deer[2] bounced and banged over dirt roads the government had promised but never quite gotten around to paving.

I had a devil of a time finding the place. Officially, it didn't exist and therefore wasn't on any map. I became lost several times and had to ask directions from locals who kept thinking I meant the museum town. I was in an impatient mood by the time I reached the small collection of hilltop homes. I remember

---

1 From "Quotations from Chairman Maozedong," originally from "The Situation and Our Policy After the Victory in the War of Resistance Against Japan," August 13, 1945.
2 A prewar automobile manufactured in the People's Republic.

thinking. *This had better be damned serious.* Once I saw their faces, I regretted my wish.

There were seven of them, all on cots, all barely conscious. The villagers had moved them into their new communal meeting hall. The walls and floor were bare cement. The air was cold and damp. *Of course they're sick,* I thought. I asked the villagers who had been taking care of these people. They said no one, it wasn't "safe." I noticed that the door had been locked from the outside. The villagers were clearly terrified. They cringed and whispered; some kept their distance and prayed. Their behavior made me angry, not at them, you understand, not as individuals, but what they represented about our country. After centuries of foreign oppression, exploitation, and humiliation, we were finally reclaiming our rightful place as humanity's middle kingdom. We were the world's richest and most dynamic superpower, masters of everything from outer space to cyber space. It was the dawn of what the world was finally acknowledging as "The Chinese Century" and yet so many of us still lived like these ignorant peasants, as stagnant and superstitious as the earliest Yangshao savages.

I was still lost in my grand, cultural criticism when I knelt to examine the first patient. She was running a high fever, forty degrees centigrade, and she was shivering violently. Barely coherent, she whimpered slightly when I tried to move her limbs. There was a wound in her right forearm, a bite mark. As I examined it more closely, I realized that it wasn't from an animal. The bit radius and teeth marks had to have come from a small, or possibly young, human being. Although I hypothesized this to be the source of the infection, the actual injury was surprisingly clean. I asked the villagers, again, who had been taking care of these people. Again, they told me no one. I knew this could not be true. The human mouth is packed with bacteria, even more so than the most unhygienic dog. If no one had cleaned this woman's wound, why wasn't it throbbing with infection?

I examined the six other patients. All showed similar symptoms, all had similar wounds on various parts of their bodies. I asked one man, the most lucid of the group, who or what had inflicted these injuries. He told me it had happened when they had tried to subdue "him."

"Who?" I asked.

I found "Patient Zero" behind the locked door of an abandoned house across town. He was twelve years old. His wrists and feet were bound with plastic packing twine. Although he'd rubbed off the skin around his bonds, there was no blood. There was also no blood on his other wounds, not on the gouges on his legs or arms, or from the large dry gap where his right big toe had been. He was writhing like an animal; a gag muffled his growls.

At first the villagers tried to hold me back. They warned me not to touch him, that he was "cursed." I shrugged them off and reached for my mask and gloves. The boy's skin was as cold and gray as the cement on which he lay. I could find neither his heartbeat nor his pulse. His eyes were wild, wide and sunken back in their sockets. They remained locked on me like a predatory beast. Throughout the examination he was inexplicably hostile, reaching for me with his bound hands and snapping at me through his gag.

His movements were so violent I had to call for two of the largest villagers to help me hold him down. Initially they wouldn't budge, cowering in the doorway like baby rabbits. I explained that there was no risk of infection if they used gloves and masks. When they shook their heads, I made it an order, even though I had no lawful authority to do so.

That was all it took. The two oxen knelt beside me. One held the boy's feet while the other grasped his hands. I tried to take a blood sample and instead extracted only brown, viscous matter. As I was withdrawing the needle, the boy began another bout of violent struggling.

One of my "orderlies," the one responsible for his arms, gave up trying to hold them and thought it might be safer if he just braced them against the floor with his knees. But the boy jerked again and I heard his left arm snap. Jagged ends of both radius and ulna bones stabbed through his gray flesh. Although the boy didn't cry out, didn't even seem to notice, it was enough for both assistants to leap back and run from the room.

I instinctively retreated several paces myself. I am embarrassed to admit this; I have been a doctor for most of my adult life. I was trained and...you could even say "raised" by the People's Liberation Army. I've treated more than my share of combat injuries, faced my own death on more than one occasion, and now I was scared, truly scared, of this frail child.

The boy began to twist in my direction, his arm ripped completely free. Flesh and muscle tore from one another until there was nothing except the stump. His now free right arm, still tied to the severed left hand, dragged his body across the floor.

I hurried outside, locking the door behind me. I tried to compose myself, control my fear and shame. My voice still cracked as I asked the villagers how the boy had been infected. No one answered. I began to hear banging on the door, the boy's fist pounding weakly against the think wood. It was all I could do not to jump at the sound. I prayed they would not notice the color draining from my face. I shouted, as much from fear as frustration, that I *had* to know what happened to this child.

A young woman came forward, maybe his mother. You could tell that she has been crying for days; her eyes were dry and deeply red. She admitted that it had happened when the boy and his father were "moon fishing," a term that describes diving for treasure among the sunken ruins of the Three Gorges Reservoir. With more than eleven hundred abandoned villages, towns, and even cities, there was always the hope of recovering something valuable. It was a very common practice in those days, and also very illegal. She explained that they weren't looting, that it was their own village, Old Dachang, and they were just trying to recover some heirlooms from the remaining houses that hadn't been moved. She repeated the point, and I had to interrupt her with promises not to inform the police. She finally explained that the boy came up crying with a bite mark on his foot. He didn't know what had happened, the water had been too dark and muddy. His father was never seen again.

I reached for my cell phone and dialed the number of Doctor Gu Wen Kuei, an old comrade from my army days who now worked at the Institute of Infectious Diseases at Chongqing University.[3] We exchanged pleasantries, discussing our health, our grandchildren; it was only proper. I then told him about the outbreak and listened as he made some joke about the hygiene habits of hillbillies. I tried to chuckle along but continued that I thought the incident might be significant. Almost reluctantly he asked me what the symptoms were. I told him everything; the bites, the fever, the boy, the arm...his face suddenly stiffened. His smile died.

---

3 The Institute of Infectious and Parasitic Diseases of the First Affiliated Hospital, Chongqing Medical University.

He asked me to show him the infected. I went back into the meeting hall and waved the phone's camera over each of the patients. He asked me to move the camera closer to some of the wounds themselves. I did so and when I brought the screen back to my face, I saw that his video image had been cut.

"Stay where you are," he said, just a distant, removed voice now. "Take the names of all who have had contact with the infected. Restrain those already infected. If any have passed into coma, vacate the room and secure the exit." His voice was flat, robotic, as if he had rehearsed this speech or was reading from something. He asked me, "Are you armed?" "Why would I be?" I asked. He told me he would get back to me, all business again. He said he had to make a few calls and that I should expect "support" within several hours.

They were there in less than one, fifty men in large army Z-8A helicopters; all were wearing hazardous materials suits. They said they were from the Ministry of Health. I don't know who they thought they were kidding. With their bullying swagger, their intimidating arrogance, even these backwater bumpkins could recognize the Guoanbu.[4]

Their first priority was the meeting hall. The patients were carried out on stretchers, their limbs shackled, their mouths gagged. Next, they went for the boy. He came out in a body bag. His mother was wailing as she and the rest of the village were rounded up for "examinations." Their names were taken, their blood drawn. One by one they were stripped and photographed. The last one to be exposed was a withered old woman. She had a thin, crooked body, a face with a thousand lines and tiny feet that had to have been bound when she was a girl. She was shaking her bony fist at the "doctors." "This is your punishment!" she shouted. "This is revenge for Fengdu!"

She was referring to the City of Ghosts, whose temples and shrines were dedicated to the underworld. Like Old Dachang, it had been an unlucky obstacle to China's next Great Leap Forward. It had been evacuated, then demolished, then almost entirely drowned. I've never been a superstitious person and I've never allowed myself to be hooked on the opiate of the people. I'm a doctor, a scientist. I believe only in what I can see and touch. I've never seen Fengdu as anything but a cheap, kitschy tourist trap. Of course this ancient crone's words had no effect on me, but her tone, her anger...she had witnessed enough calamity in her years upon the earth: the warlords, the

---

4 Guokia Anquan Bu: The prewar Ministry of State Security.

Japanese, the insane nightmare of the Cultural Revolution...she knew that another storm was coming, even if she didn't have the education to understand it.

My colleague Dr. Kuei had understood all too well. He's even risked his neck to warn me, to give me enough time to call and maybe alert a few others before the "Ministry of Health" arrived. It was something he had said...a phrase he hadn't used in a very long time, not since those "minor" border clashes with the Soviet Union. That was back in 1969. We had been in an earthen bunker on our side of the Ussuri, less than a kilometer downriver from Chen Bao. The Russians were preparing to retake the island, their massive artillery hammering our forces.

Gu and I had been trying to remove shrapnel from the belly of this soldier not much younger than us. The boy's lower intestines had been torn open, his blood and excrement were all over our gowns. Every seven seconds a round would land close by and we would have to bend over his body to shield the wound from falling earth, and every time we would be close enough to hear him whimper softly for his mother. There were other voices, too, rising from the pitch darkness just beyond the entrance to our bunker, desperate, angry voices that weren't supposed to be on our side of the river. We had two infantrymen stationed at the bunker's entrance. One of them shouted "Spetsnaz!" and started firing into the dark. We could hear other shots now as well, ours or theirs, we couldn't tell.

Another round hit and we bent over the dying boy. Gu's face was only a few centimeters from mine. There was sweat pouring down his forehead. Even in the dim light of one paraffin lantern, I could see that he was shaking and pale. He looked at the patient, then at the doorway, then at me, and suddenly he said, "Don't worry, everything's going to be all right." Now, this is a man who has never said a positive thing in his life. Gu was a worrier, a neurotic curmudgeon. If he had a headache, it was a brain tumor; if it looked like rain, this year's harvest was ruined. This was his way of controlling the situation, his lifelong strategy for always coming out ahead. Now, when reality looked more dire than any of his fatalistic predictions, he had no choice but to turn tail and charge in the opposite direction. "Don't worry, everything's going to be all right." For the first time everything turned out as he predicted. The Russians never crossed the river and we even managed to save our patient.

For years afterward I would tease him about what it took to pry out a little ray of sunshine, and he would always respond that it would take a hell of a lot worse to get him to do it again. Now we were old men, and something worse was about to happen. It was right after he asked me if I was armed. "No," I said, "why should I be?" There was a brief silence, I'm sure other ears were listening. "Don't worry," he said, "everything's going to be all right." That was when I realized that this was not an isolated outbreak. I ended the call and quickly placed another to my daughter in Guangzhou.

Her husband worked for China Telecom and spent at least one week of every month abroad. I told her it would be a good idea to accompany him the next time he left and that she should take my granddaughter and stay for as long as they could. I didn't have time to explain; my signal was jammed just as the first helicopter appeared. The last thing I managed to say to her was "Don't worry, everything's going to be all right."

[Kwang Jingshu was arrested by the MSS and incarcerated without formal charges. By the time he escaped, the outbreak had spread beyond China's borders.]

TURNING THE TIDE

Robben Island, Cape Town Province, United States of Southern Africa

> [Xolelwa Azania greets me at his writing desk, inviting me to switch places with him so I can enjoy the cool ocean breeze from his window. He apologizes for the "mess" and insists on clearing the notes off his desk before we continue. Mister Azania is halfway through his third volume of *Rainbow Fist: South Africa at War*. This volume happens to be about the subject we are discussing, the turning point against the living dead, the moment when his country pulled itself back from the brink.]

Dispassionate, a rather mundane word to describe one of history's most controversial figures. Some revere him as a savior, some revile him as a monster, but if you ever met Paul Redeker, ever discussed his views of the world and the problems, or more importantly, the solutions to the problems that plague the world, probably the one word that would always cling to your impression of the man is *dispassionate*.

Paul always believed, well, perhaps not always, but at least in his adult life, that humanity's one fundamental flaw was emotion. He used to say that the heart should only exist to pump blood to the brain, that anything else was a waste of time and energy. His papers from university, all dealing with alternate "solutions" to historical, societal quandaries, were what first brought him to the attention of the apartheid government. Many psychobiographers have tried to label him a racist, but, in his own words, "racism is a regrettable by-product of irrational emotion." Others have argued that, in order for a racist to hate one group, he must at least love another. Redeker believed both love and hate to be irrelevant. To him, they were "impediments of the human condition," and, in his words again, "imagine what could be accomplished if the human race would only shed its humanity." Evil? Most would call it that, while others, particularly that small cadre in the center of Pretoria's power, believed it to be "an invaluable source of liberated intellect."

It was the early 1980s, a critical time for the apartheid government. The country was resting on a bed of nails. You had the ANC, you had the Inkatha Freedom Party, you even had extremist, right-wing elements of the Afrikaner population that would have liked nothing better than open revolt in order to bring about a complete racial showdown. On her border, South Africa faced nothing but hostile nations, and, in the case of Angola, a Soviet-backed, Cuban-spearheaded civil war. Add to this mixture a growing isolation from the Western democracies (which included a critical arms embargo) and it was no surprise that a last-ditch fight for survival was never far from Pretoria's mind.

This is why they enlisted the aid of Mister Redeker to revise the government's ultrasecret "Plan Orange." "Orange" had been in existence since the apartheid government first came to power in 1948. It was the doomsday scenario for the country's white minority, the plan to deal with an all-out uprising of its indigenous African population. Over the years it had been updated with the changing strategic outlook of the region. Every decade that situation grew more and more grim. With multiplying independence of her neighbor states, and multiplying voices for freedom from the majority of her own people, those in Pretoria realized that a full-blown confrontation might not just mean the end for the Afrikaner government, but the Afrikaners themselves.

This is where Redeker stepped in. His revised Plan Orange, appropriately completed in 1984, was the ultimate survival strategy for the Afrikaner people. No variable was ignored. Population figures, terrain, resources, logistics . . .

Redeker not only updated the plan to include both Cuba's chemical weapons and his own country's nuclear option, but also, and this is what made "Orange Eighty-Four" so historic, the determination of which Afrikaners would be saved and which had to be sacrificed.

SACRIFICED?

Redeker believed that to try to protect everyone would stretch the government's resources to the breaking point, thus dooming the entire population. He compared it to survivors from a sinking ship capsizing a lifeboat that simply did not have room for them all. Redeker had even gone so far as to calculate who should be "brought aboard." He included income, IQ, fertility, an entire checklist of "desirable qualities," including the subject's location to a potential crisis zone. "The first casualty of the conflict must be our own sentimentality" was the closing statement tor his proposal, "for its survival will mean our destruction."

Orange Eighty-Four was a brilliant plan. It was clear, logical, efficient, and it made Paul Redeker one of the most hated men in South Africa. His first enemies were some of the more radical, fundamentalist Afrikaners, the racial ideologues and the ultrareligious. Later, after the fall of apartheid, his name began circulating among the general population. Of course he was invited to appear before the "Truth and Reconciliation" hearings, and, of course, he refused. "I won't pretend to have a heart simply to save my skin," he stated publicly, adding, "No matter what I do, I'm sure they will come for me anyway."

And they did, although it probably was not in the manner Redeker could have expected. It was during our Great Panic, which began several weeks before yours. Redeker was holed up in the Drakensberg cabin he had bought with the accumulated profits of a business consultant. He liked business, you know. "One goal, no soul," he used to say. He wasn't surprised when the door blew off its hinges and agents of the National Intelligence Agency rushed in. They confirmed his name, his identity, his past actions. They asked him point-blank if he had been the author of Orange Eighty-Four. He answered without emotion, naturally. He suspected, and accepted, this intrusion as a last-minute revenge killing; the world was going to hell anyway, why not take a few "apartheid devils" down first. What he could have never predicted was the sudden lowering of their firearms, and the removal of the gas masks of the NIA agents. They were of all colors: black, Asian, colored, and even a white man, a tall Afrikaner who stepped forward, and without giving his name or rank, asked abruptly . . . "You've got a plan for this, man, don't you?"

Redeker had, indeed, been working on his own solution to the undead epidemic. What else could he do in this isolated hideaway? It had been an intellectual exercise; he never believed anyone would be left to read it. It had no name, as explained later "because names only exist to distinguish one from others," and, until that moment, there had been no other plan like his. Once again, Redeker had taken everything into account, not only the strategic situation of the country, but also the physiology, behavior, and "combat doctrine" of the living dead. While you can research the details of the "Redeker Plan" in any public library around the world, here are some of the fundamental keys:

First of all, there was no way to save everyone. The outbreak was too far gone. The armed forces had already been too badly weakened to effectively isolate the threat, and, spread so thinly throughout the country, they could only grow weaker with each passing day. Our forces had to be consolidated, withdrawn to a special "safe zone," which, hopefully, would be aided by some natural obstacle such as mountains, rivers, or even an offshore island. Once concentrated within this zone, the armed forces could eradicate the infestation within its borders, then use what resources were available to defend it against further onslaughts of the living dead. That was the first part of the plan and it made as much sense as any conventional military retreat.

The second part of the plan dealt with the evacuation of civilians, and this could not have been envisioned by anyone else but Redeker. In his mind, only a small fraction of the civilian population could be evacuated to the safe zone. These people would be saved not only to provide a labor pool for the eventual wartime economic restoration, but also to preserve the legitimacy and stability of the government, to prove to those already within the zone that their leaders were "looking out for them."

There was another reason for this partial evacuation, an eminently logical and insidiously dark reason that, many believe, will forever ensure Redeker the tallest pedestal in the pantheon of hell. Those who were left behind were to be herded into special isolated zones. They were to be "human bait," distracting the undead from following the retreating army to their safe zone. Redeker argued that these isolated, uninfected refugees must be kept alive, well defended and even resupplied, if possible, so as to keep the undead hordes firmly rooted to the spot. You see the genius, the sickness? Keeping people as prisoners because "every zombie besieging those survivors will be one less zombie throwing itself against our defenses." That was the moment when the Afrikaner agent looked up at Redeker, crossed himself, and said, "God help you, man." Another one said, "God help us all." That was the black one who appeared to be in charge of the operation. "Now let's get him out of here."

Within minutes they were on a helicopter for Kimberley, the very underground base where Redeker had first written Orange Eighty-Four. He was ushered into a meeting of the president's surviving cabinet, where his report was read aloud to the room. You should have heard the uproar, with no voice louder than the defense minister's. He was a Zulu, a ferocious man who'd rather be fighting in the streets than cowering in a bunker.

The vice president was more concerned about public relations. He didn't want to imagine what his backside would be worth if news of this plan ever leaked to the population.

The president looked almost personally insulted by Redeker. He physically grabbed the lapels of the safety and security minister and demanded why in hell he brought him this demented apartheid war criminal.

The minister stammered that he didn't understand why the president was so upset, especially when it was he who gave the order to find Redeker.

The president threw his hands in the air and shouted that he never gave such an order, and then, from somewhere in the room, a faint voice said, "I did."

He had been sitting against the back wall; now he stood, hunched over by age, and supported by canes, but with a spirit as strong and vital as it had ever been. The elder statesman, the father of our new democracy, the man whose birth name had been Rolihlahla, which some have translated simply into "Troublemaker." As he stood, all others sat, all others except Paul Redeker. The old man locked eyes on him, smiled with that warm squint so famous the world over, and said, "Molo, mhlobo wam." "Greetings, person of my region." He walked slowly over to Paul, turned to the governing body of South Africa, then lifted the pages from the Afrikaner's hand and said in a suddenly loud and youthful voice, "This plan will save our people." Then, gesturing to Paul, he said, "This *man* will save our people." And then came that moment, the one that historians will probably debate until the subject fades from memory. He embraced the white Afrikaner. To anyone else this was simply his signature bear hug, but to Paul Redeker . . . I know that the majority of psychobiographers continue to paint this man without a soul. That is the generally accepted notion. Paul Redeker: no feelings, no compassion, no heart. However, one of our most revered authors, Biko's old friend and biographer, postulates that Redeker was actually a deeply sensitive man, too sensitive, in fact, for life in apartheid South Africa. He insists that Redeker's lifelong jihad against emotion was the only way to protect his sanity from the hatred and brutality he witnessed on a daily basis. Not much is known about Redeker's childhood, whether he even had parents, or was raised by the state, whether he had friends or was ever loved in any way. Those who knew him from work were hard-pressed to remember witnessing any social interaction or even any physical act of warmth. The embrace by our nation's father, this genuine emotion piercing his impenetrable shell . . .

[Azania smiles sheepishly.]

Perhaps this is all too sentimental. For all we know he was a heartless monster, and the old man's embrace had absolutely no impact. But I can tell you that that was the last day anyone ever saw Paul Redeker. Even now, no one knows what really happened to him. That is when I stepped in, in those chaotic weeks when the Redeker Plan was implemented throughout the country. It took some convincing to say the least, but once I'd convinced them that I'd worked for many years with Paul Redeker, and, more importantly, I understood his way of thinking better than anyone left alive in South Africa, how could they refuse? I worked on the retreat, then afterward, during the consolidation months, and right up until the end of the war. At least they were appreciative of my services, why else would they grant me such luxurious accommodations? **[Smiles.]** Paul Redeker, an angel and a devil. Some hate him, some worship him. Me, I just pity him. If he still exists, somewhere out there, I sincerely hope he's found his peace.

[After a parting embrace from my guest, I am driven back to my ferry for the mainland. Security is tight as I sign out my entrance badge. The tall Afrikaner guard photographs me again. "Can't be too careful, man," he says, handing me the pen. "Lot of people out there want to send him to hell." I sign next to my name, under the heading of Robben Island Psychiatric Institution. NAME OF PATIENT YOU ARE VISITING: PAUL REDEKER.]

Consider how these two stories comment on the societies they present. Choose one of the following two research options, and then write an essay that responds to the related questions:

1. Research some of the differences between modern agrarian and industrial China. Why is Kwang Jingshu so angry at the "ignorant peasants"? Why might a virulent outbreak occur in a place like New Dachang, and why would it spread so easily from there? How does the government react to the outbreak? How do the answers to these questions reflect the differences between these conflicting Chinese cultures?

2. Research the history of South Africa, particularly the concept of apartheid. How does understanding this concept change your feelings toward Paul Redeker? What is the connection between apartheid and the Redeker Plan? How could the use of an apartheid-era plan during a zombie apocalypse be considered social commentary?

Unlike in many zombie stories, the focus in "New Dachang" on emotion outweighs its action and gore. In a small group, discuss the different emotions presented throughout the story and how those emotions come across. Compare and contrast the two selections from *World War Z*. Compile a list of specific ways that the stories create emotional impact, paying particular attention to choices in diction and characterization. How do the stories differ in purpose, in emotional impact, and in how the zombie situation is handled? What aspects of the war do these stories portray? What different emotions come across throughout each story, and what causes those emotions? How do various characters respond to the zombie threat, and what do their responses indicate about the variety of emotions that an outbreak such as this could cause? How does this chapter's use of emotion affect our perception of the approaching zombie plague? Discuss how the variety of responses contributes to a larger picture and a greater understanding of the Zombie War. Examine how the presentation of these stories, particularly their focus on "the human factor," provides social commentary that is similar to or different from the social commentary in other zombie narratives with which your group is familiar.

Brooks relies on first-person perspective in his writing. What is effective about first-person writing's presentation of zombies? What is its emotional impact? How does this impact compare to first-person perspective in film (a type of perspective attributed to film when the camera adopts a character's point of view or when a character describes personal experiences in a voiceover)? After watching one of the Romero zombie movies, create a mock interview of one of the characters, incorporating questions and first-person narrative responses. Then, in a short response paper, explain how writing down the interview responses changes the story. How does the emotion change? The social commentary? Alternatively, work with a partner and create an interview about a monster attack, carefully crafting both the questions and the responses in order to best show "the human factor" of the attack. Define the medium and audience for this interview (for example, is it for television or a newspaper? for CNN, a tabloid, or a talk show?).

Monsters

Among late Victorian authors, Robert Louis Stevenson was one of the most diverse, a writer of poetry, children's verse, adventure stories, travel narratives, and horror. He penned a number of short stories in the horror genre, including "The Body-Snatcher" (1884), "Markheim" (1885) and "Thrawn Janet" (1887), but his best-known tale of terror remains The Strange Case of Dr. Jekyll and Mr. Hyde (1886), which follows the physical and psychological decline of a man struggling with his divided moral nature.

While literally the story of a shapeshifter, Jekyll and Hyde does not incorporate the sort of animal transformation that is most common in this tradition. Instead, the monster of this story is a man who changes into an alternate humanoid form in which he commits atrocious acts, including trampling a small girl and murdering an aged member of Parliament, Sir Danvers Carew. While Hyde has some animalistic features, descriptions of him focus more on the disquietude with which people react to his appearance. The story narrates these reactions from multiple perspectives: it begins in third person, focusing on Mr. Utterson's attempts to understand the relationship between Jekyll and Hyde, but it ends with a chapter written from Jekyll's perspective. As a result, the story shows the monster from both an external and an internal perspective. Consider how reading the story from the monster's perspective might shape your understanding of his monstrosity. Pay attention to Jekyll's language, particularly the excuses he makes and the way in which he switches between the pronouns "I" and "he."

excerpts from

THE STRANGE CASE OF DR. JEKYLL AND MR. HYDE

By Robert Louis Stevenson

[. . .] The lawyer stood awhile when Mr. Hyde had left him, the picture of disquietude. Then he began slowly to mount the street, pausing every step or two and putting his hand to his brow like a man in mental perplexity. The problem he was thus debating as he walked, was one of a class that is rarely solved. Mr. Hyde was pale and dwarfish, he gave an impression of deformity without any nameable malformation, he had a displeasing smile, he had borne himself to the lawyer with a sort of murderous mixture of timidity and boldness, and he spoke with a husky, whispering and somewhat broken voice; all these were points against him, but not all of these together could explain the hitherto unknown disgust, loathing and fear with which Mr. Utterson regarded him. "There must be something else," said the perplexed gentleman. "There *is* something more, if I could find a name for it. God bless me, the man seems hardly human! Something troglodytic, shall we say? or can it be the old story of Dr. Fell? or is it the mere radiance of a foul soul that thus transpires through, and transfigures, its clay continent? The last, I think; for, O my poor old Harry Jekyll, if ever I read Satan's signature upon a face, it is on that of your new friend." [. . .]

HENRY JEKYLL'S FULL STATEMENT OF THE CASE.

[. . .] I was born in the year 18— to a large fortune, endowed besides with excellent parts[1], inclined by nature to industry, fond of the respect of the wise and good among my fellow-men, and thus, as might have been supposed, with every guarantee of an honourable and distinguished future. And indeed the worst of my faults was a certain impatient gaiety of disposition[2], such as has made the happiness of many, but such as I found it hard to reconcile with my imperious desire to carry my head high, and wear a more than commonly grave countenance before the public. Hence it came about that I concealed my pleasures; and that when I reached years of reflection, and began to look round me and take stock of my progress and position in the world, I stood already committed to a profound duplicity of life. Many a man would have even blazoned such irregularities as I was guilty of; but from the high views that I had set before me, I regarded and hid them with an almost morbid sense of shame. It was thus rather the exacting nature of my aspirations than any particular degradation in my faults, that made me what I was and, with even a deeper trench than in the majority of men, severed in me those provinces of good and ill which divide and compound man's dual nature. In this case, I was driven to reflect deeply and inveterately on that hard law of life[3], which lies at the root of religion and is one of the most plentiful springs

---

1 Abilities.

2 Victorian usages of "gay" do not shed much light on this vague phrase. "Gay had not yet taken on what would later become its central slang association with homosexuality, but according to the OED, it could have either the straightforward meaning of "light-hearted, exuberantly cheerful, merry," or the sardonic sense of "addicted to social pleasures and dissipations" (with a slang application to a woman of "living by prostitution"). Even supposing a relatively innocent meaning, however, Jekyll's categorization of his "impatient gaiety of disposition" as a "fault" needs to be understood in the light of the Evangelical cast of Victorian Christianity, with its call for renunciation of soul-endangering levity in favor of self-disciplined moral earnestness.

3 Presumably the "law" which ordains that desires of the soul will often be pitted against desires of the body.

of distress. Though so profound a double-dealer, I was in no sense a hypocrite[4]; both sides of me were in dead earnest; I was no more myself when I laid aside restraint and plunged in shame, than when I laboured, in the eye of day, at the furtherance of knowledge or the relief of sorrow and suffering. And it chanced that the direction of my scientific studies, which led wholly toward the mystic and the transcendental, reacted and shed a strong light on this consciousness of the perennial war among my members[5]. With every day, and from both sides of my intelligence, the moral and the intellectual, I thus drew steadily nearer to that truth, by whose partial discovery I have been doomed to such a dreadful shipwreck: that man is not truly one, but truly two. I say two, because the state of my own knowledge does not pass beyond that point. Others will follow, others will outstrip me on the same lines; and I hazard the guess that man will be ultimately known for a mere polity of multifarious, incongruous, and independent denizens. I, for my part, from the nature of my life, advanced infallibly in one direction and in one direction only. It was on the moral side, and in my own person, that I learned to recognise the thorough and primitive duality of man; I saw that, of the two natures that contended in the field of my consciousness, even if I could rightly be said to be either, it was only because I was radically both; and from an early date, even before the course of my scientific discoveries had begun to suggest the most naked possibility of such a miracle, I had learned to dwell with pleasure, as a beloved daydream, on the thought of the separation of these elements. If each, I told myself, could but be housed in separate identities, life would be relieved of all that was unbearable; the unjust delivered from the aspirations might go his way, and remorse of his more upright twin; and the just could walk steadfastly and securely on his upward path, doing the good things in which he found his pleasure, and no longer exposed to disgrace and penitence by the hands of this extraneous evil[6]. It was the curse of mankind that these

---

4 Jekyll may be straining the bounds of common word usage in claiming that someone who genuinely *desires* virtue is not a hypocrite, even if he pretends to a higher *level* of virtue than he really possesses.

5 Conflicts among parts of the self, especially between body and spirit. The phrase echoes James 4:1, "From whence come war and fightings among you? come they not hence, even of your lusts that war in your members?" and, less directly, Romans 7:22–23, "For I delight in the law of God after the inward man: But I see another law in my members, warring against the law of my mind, and bringing me into captivity to the law of sin which is in my members."

6 I.e., This alien evil. Various influences have been suggested for Stevenson's interest in the mental condition which divorces the sinful from the virtuous self. Among them are the biblical text of Romans (e.g. 7:20 "Now if I do that I would not, it is no more that I do it, but the sin

incongruous faggots[7] were thus bound together—that in the agonised womb of consciousness, these polar twins should be continuously struggling. How, then, were they dissociated[8]?

I was so far in my reflections when, as I have said, a side light began to shine upon the subject from the laboratory table. I began to perceive more deeply than it has ever yet been stated, the trembling immateriality, the mist-like transience of this seemingly so solid body in which we walk attired. Certain agents I found to have the power to shake and to pluck back that fleshly vestment, even as a wind might toss the curtains of a pavilion[9]. For two good reasons, I will not enter deeply into this scientific branch of my confession. First, because I have been made to learn that the doom and burthen of our life is bound for ever on man's shoulders, and when the attempt is made to cast it off, it but returns upon us with more unfamiliar and more awful pressure. Second, because, as my narrative will make, alas! too evident, my discoveries were incomplete. Enough, then, that I not only recognised my natural body for the mere aura and effulgence of certain of the powers that made up my spirit, but managed to compound a drug by which these powers should be dethroned from their supremacy, and a second form and countenance substituted, none the less natural to me because they were the expression, and bore the stamp, of lower elements in my soul.

I hesitated long before I put this theory to the test of practice. I knew well that I risked death; for any drug that so potently controlled and shook the very fortress of identity, might by the least scruple of an overdose or at the least inopportunity in the moment of exhibition, utterly blot out that immaterial tabernacle[10] which I looked to it to change. But the temptation of a discovery so singular and profound, at last overcame the suggestions of

---

that dwelleth in me"); the Edinburgh legend of Deacon Brodie (1741–88, master craftsman by day and burglar by night); and James Hogg's novel *The Private Memoirs and Confessions of a Justified Sinner* (1824), in which a young Scotch Calvanist puffed up by a conviction of being among the Elect falls under the spell of a double whom he fails to recognize as the devil.

7 A faggot is a collection of twigs or sticks bundled together for use as fuel; or, figuratively, a collection of things not forming any genuine unity.

8 I.e., How, then, were they to be be dissociated?

9 A large, often stately, tent.

10 Scruple: a very small unit of weight or measurement (20 grams or 1/24th ounce); tabernacle i.e., the body (a usage found in 2 Corinthians 5: 1–4 and 2 Peter 1: 13–14, where the body, as a perishable abode for the soul, is likened to the "tabernacle," or tent sanctuary, used for religious worship during the Israelite wandering in the wilderness).

alarm. I had long since prepared my tincture; I purchased at once, from a firm of wholesale chemists, a large quantity of a particular salt which I knew, from my experiments, to be the last ingredient required; and late one accursed night, I compounded the elements, watched them boil and smoke together in the glass, and when the ebullition had subsided, with a strong glow of courage, drank off the potion.

The most racking pangs succeeded: a grinding in the bones, deadly nausea, and a horror of the spirit that cannot be exceeded at the hour of birth or death. Then these agonies began swiftly to subside, and I came to myself as if out of a great sickness. There was something strange in my sensations, something indescribably new and, from its very novelty, incredibly sweet. I felt younger, lighter, happier in body; within I was conscious of a heady recklessness, a current of disordered sensual images running like a mill race in my fancy, a solution[11] of the bonds of obligation, an unknown but not an innocent freedom of the soul. I knew myself, at the first breath of this new life, to be more wicked, tenfold more wicked, sold a slave to my original evil; and the thought, in that moment, braced and delighted me like wine. I stretched out my hands, exulting in the freshness of these sensations; and in the act, I was suddenly aware that I had lost in stature.

There was no mirror, at that date, in my room; that which stands beside me as I write, was brought there later on and for the very purpose of these transformations. The night, however, was far gone into the morning—the morning, black as it was, was nearly ripe for the conception of the day—the inmates of my house were locked in the most rigorous hours of slumber; and I determined, flushed as I was with hope and triumph, to venture in my new shape as far as to my bedroom. I crossed the yard, wherein the constellations looked down upon me, I could have thought, with wonder, the first creature of that sort that their unsleeping vigilance had yet disclosed to them; I stole through the corridors, a stranger in my own house; and coming to my room, I saw for the first time the appearance of Edward Hyde.

I must here speak by theory alone, saying not that which I know, but that which I suppose to be most probable. The evil side of my nature, to which I had now transferred the stamping efficacy[12], was less robust and less developed than the good which I had just deposed. Again, in the course of my life, which

---

11 Mill race: the current of water that drives a mill-wheel; solution: dissolving.
12 I.e., the shape-giving power.

had been, after all, nine tenths a life of effort, virtue, and control, it had been much less exercised and much less exhausted. And hence, as I think, it came about that Edward Hyde was so much smaller, slighter, and younger than Henry Jekyll. Even as good shone upon the countenance of the one, evil was written broadly and plainly on the face of the other. Evil besides (which I must still believe to be the lethal side of man) had left on that body an imprint of deformity and decay. And yet when I looked upon that ugly idol[13] in the glass, I was conscious of no repugnance, rather of a leap of welcome. This, too, was myself. It seemed natural and human. In my eyes it bore a livelier image of the spirit, it seemed more express[14] and single, than the imperfect and divided countenance I had been hitherto accustomed to call mine. And in so far I was doubtless right. I have observed that when I wore the semblance of Edward Hyde, none could come near to me at first without a visible misgiving of the flesh. This, as I take it, was because all human beings, as we meet them, are commingled out of good and evil: and Edward Hyde, alone in the ranks of mankind, was pure evil.

I lingered but a moment at the mirror: the second and conclusive experiment had yet to be attempted; it yet remained to be seen if I had lost my identity beyond redemption and must flee before daylight from a house that was no longer mine; and hurrying back to my cabinet, I once more prepared and drank the cup, once more suffered the pangs of dissolution, and came to myself once more with the character, the stature, and the face of Henry Jekyll.

That night I had come to the fatal cross roads. Had I approached my discovery in a more noble spirit, had I risked the experiment while under the empire of generous or pious aspirations, all must have been otherwise, and from these agonies of death and birth, I had come forth an angel instead of a fiend. The drug had no discriminating action; it was neither diabolical nor divine; it but shook the doors of the prisonhouse of my disposition; and like the captives of Philippi, that which stood within ran forth[15]. At that time my

---

13 Carries the specialized meaning of "a visible but unsubstantial appearance, an image caused by reflexion as in a mirror" (OED, which quotes this usage by Stevenson), but also suggests the more familiar meaning of an image or representation of a deity, especially as an object of false worship.

14 Truly depicted; exactly resembling.

15 As recounted in Acts 16:26, when God visited an earthquake upon the prision in Philippi where the apostle Paul and his companion Silas were being held captive, "immediately all the doors were opened and everyone's bands were loosed." Paul and Silas, however, rather than fleeing, honorably turned themselves over to their captors.

virtue slumbered; my evil, kept awake by ambition, was alert and swift to seize the occasion; and the thing that was projected was Edward Hyde. Hence, although I had now two characters as well as two appearances, one was wholly evil, and the other was still the old Henry Jekyll, that incongruous compound of whose reformation and improvement I had already learned to despair. The movement was thus wholly toward the worse.

Even at that time, I had not yet conquered my aversion to the dryness of a life of study. I would still be merrily disposed at times; and as my pleasures were (to say the least) undignified, and I was not only well known and highly considered, but growing toward the elderly man, this incoherency of my life was daily growing more unwelcome. It was on this side that my new power tempted me until I fell in slavery. I had but to drink the cup, to doff at once the body of the noted professor, and to assume, like a thick cloak, that of Edward Hyde. I smiled at the notion; it seemed to me at the time to be humorous; and I made my preparations with the most studious care. I took and furnished that house in Soho, to which Hyde was tracked by the police; and engaged as housekeeper a creature whom I well knew to be silent and unscrupulous. On the other side, I announced to my servants that a Mr. Hyde (whom I described) was to have full liberty and power about my house in the square; and to parry mishaps, I even called and made myself a familiar object, in my second character. I next drew up that will to which you so much objected; so that if anything befell me in the person of Dr. Jekyll, I could enter on that of Edward Hyde without pecuniary loss. And thus fortified, as I supposed, on every side, I began to profit by the strange immunities of my position.

Men have before hired bravos[16] to transact their crimes, while their own person and reputation sat under shelter. I was the first that ever did so for his pleasures. I was the first that could thus plod in the public eye with a load of genial respectability, and in a moment, like a schoolboy, strip off these lendings[17] and spring headlong into the sea of liberty. But for me, in my impenetrable mantle, the safety was complete. Think of it—I did not even exist! Let me but escape into my laboratory door, give me but a second or two to mix and swallow the draught that I had always standing ready; and whatever he had done, Edward Hyde would pass away like the stain of breath upon a mirror; and there in his

---

16 Paid desperados or assassins.

17 Something lent, here referring to clothes in an echo of King Lear's line, "Off, off, you lendings!" as he tears off his garments on the heath in a sudden access of fellow-feeling for the naked madman he encounters there (*King Lear* 3.4.114).

stead, quietly at home, trimming the midnight lamp in his study, a man who could afford to laugh at suspicion, would be Henry Jekyll.

The pleasures which I made haste to seek in my disguise were, as I have said, undignified; I would scarce use a harder term. But in the hands of Edward Hyde, they soon began to turn toward the monstrous. When I would come back from these excursions, I was often plunged into a kind of wonder at my vicarious depravity. This familiar that I called out of my own soul, and sent forth alone to do his good pleasure[18], was a being inherently malign and villainous; his every act and thought centered on self; drinking pleasure with bestial avidity from any degree of torture to another; relentless like a man of stone. Henry Jekyll stood at times aghast before the acts of Edward Hyde; but the situation was apart from ordinary laws, and insidiously relaxed the grasp of conscience. It was Hyde, after all, and Hyde alone, that was guilty. Jekyll was no worse; he woke again to his good qualities seemingly unimpaired; he would even make haste, where it was possible, to undo the evil done by Hyde. And thus his conscience slumbered.

Into the details of the infamy at which I thus connived (for even now I can scarce grant that I committed it)[19] I have no design of entering; I mean but to point out the warnings and the successive steps with which my chastisement approached. I met with one accident which, as it brought on no consequence, I shall no more than mention. An act of cruelty to a child aroused against me the anger of a passer by, whom I recognised the other day in the person of your kinsman; the doctor and the child's family joined him; there were moments when I feared for my life; and at last, in order to pacify their too just resentment, Edward Hyde had to bring them to the door, and pay them in a cheque drawn in the name of Henry Jekyll. But this danger was easily eliminated from the future, by opening an account at another bank in the name of Edward Hyde himself; and when, by sloping my own hand backward, I had supplied my double with a signature, I thought I sat beyond the reach of fate.

18 Familiar: a spirit or demon supposed to be in association with or under the power of a particular person; his good pleasure: i.e., pleasure that is satisfying or suitable to him (the phrase occurs frequently in the Bible in reference to God's "good pleasure," e.g., Psalms 51:18, Luke 12:32, Philippians 2:13).

19 This parenthesis makes more sense in light of what the OED defines as the ordinary meaning at the time of "connive":"to shut one's eye to an action that one ought to oppose, but which one covertly sympathizes with; to wink at, be secretly privy or accessory."

Some two months before the murder of Sir Danvers, I had been out for one of my adventures, had returned at a late hour, and woke the next day in bed with somewhat odd sensations. It was in vain I looked about me; in vain I saw the decent furniture and tall proportions of my room in the square; in vain that I recognised the pattern of the bed curtains and the design of the mahogany frame; something still kept insisting that I was not where I was, that I had not wakened where I seemed to be, but in the little room in Soho where I was accustomed to sleep in the body of Edward Hyde. I smiled to myself, and, in my psychological way began lazily to inquire into the elements of this illusion, occasionally, even as I did so, dropping back into a comfortable morning doze. I was still so engaged when, in one of my more wakeful moments, my eyes fell upon my hand. Now the hand of Henry Jekyll (as you have often remarked) was professional in shape and size: it was large, firm, white, and comely. But the hand which I now saw, clearly enough, in the yellow light of a mid-London morning, lying half shut on the bed-clothes, was lean, corded, knuckly, of a dusky pallor and thickly shaded with a swart[20] growth of hair. It was the hand of Edward Hyde.

I must have stared upon it for near half a minute, sunk as I was in the mere stupidity of wonder, before terror woke up in my breast as sudden and startling as the crash of cymbals; and bounding from my bed, I rushed to the mirror. At the sight that met my eyes, my blood was changed into something exquisitely thin and icy. Yes, I had gone to bed Henry Jekyll, I had awakened Edward Hyde. How was this to be explained? I asked myself; and then, with another bound of terror—how was it to be remedied? It was well on in the morning; the servants were up; all my drugs were in the cabinet—a long journey, down two pairs of stairs, through the back passage, across the open court and through the anatomical theatre, from where I was then standing horror-struck. It might indeed be possible to cover my face; but of what use was that, when I was unable to conceal the alteration in my stature? And then with an overpowering sweetness of relief, it came back upon my mind that the servants were already used to the coming and going of my second self. I had soon dressed, as well as I was able, in clothes of my own size: had soon passed through the house, where Bradshaw stared and drew back at seeing Mr. Hyde at such an hour and in such a strange array; and ten minutes later, Dr. Jekyll had returned to his own shape and was sitting down, with a darkened brow, to make a feint of breakfasting.

---

20 Swarthy, dark.

Small indeed was my appetite. This inexplicable incident, this reversal of my previous experience, seemed, like the Babylonian finger on the wall, to be spelling out the letters of my judgment[21]; and I began to reflect more seriously than ever before on the issues and possibilities of my double existence. That part of me which I had the power of projecting, had lately been much exercised and nourished; it had seemed to me of late as though the body of Edward Hyde had grown in stature, as though (when I wore that form) I were conscious of a more generous tide of blood; and I began to spy a danger that, if this were much prolonged, the balance of my nature might be permanently overthrown, the power of voluntary change be forfeited, and the character of Edward Hyde become irrevocably mine. The power of the drug had not been always equally displayed. Once, very early in my career, it had totally failed me; since then I had been obliged on more than one occasion to double, and once, with infinite risk of death, to treble the amount; and these rare uncertainties had cast hitherto the sole shadow on my contentment. Now, however, and in the light of that morning's accident, I was led to remark that whereas, in the beginning, the difficulty had been to throw off the body of Jekyll, it had of late, gradually but decidedly transferred itself to the other side. All things therefore seemed to point to this: that I was slowly losing hold of my original and better self, and becoming slowly incorporated with my second and worse.

Between these two, I now felt I had to choose. My two natures had memory in common, but all other faculties were most unequally shared between them. Jekyll (who was composite) now with the most sensitive apprehensions, now with a greedy gusto, projected and shared in the pleasures and adventures of Hyde; but Hyde was indifferent to Jekyll, or but remembered him as the mountain bandit remembers the cavern in which he conceals himself from pursuit. Jekyll had more than a father's interest; Hyde had more than a son's indifference. To cast in my lot with Jekyll, was to die to those appetites which I had long secretly indulged and had of late begun to pamper. To cast it in with Hyde, was to die to a thousand interests and aspirations, and to become, at a blow and forever, despised and friendless. The bargain might appear unequal; but there was still another consideration in the scales; for while Jekyll would suffer smartingly in the fires of abstinence, Hyde would be not even conscious

21 Refers to the biblical episode in which King Belshazzar of Babylon sees "fingers of a man's hand" writing onto the wall of his palace a mysterious message, which the prophet Daniel reveals to be a sign of God's imminent punishment of Belshazzar for having "lifted" himself "up against the Lord of heaven" (Daniel 5:5 and 5:23).

of all that he had lost. Strange as my circumstances were, the terms of this debate are as old and commonplace as man; much the same inducements and alarms cast the die for any tempted and trembling sinner; and it fell out with me, as it falls with so vast a majority of my fellows, that I chose the better part and was found wanting in the strength to keep to it.

Yes, I preferred the elderly and discontented doctor, surrounded by friends and cherishing honest hopes; and bade a resolute farewell to the liberty, the comparative youth, the light step, leaping impulses and secret pleasures, that I had enjoyed in the disguise of Hyde. I made this choice perhaps with some unconscious reservation, for I neither gave up the house in Soho, nor destroyed the clothes of Edward Hyde, which still lay ready in my cabinet. For two months, however, I was true to my determination; for two months I led a life of such severity as I had never before attained to, and enjoyed the compensations of an approving conscience. But time began at last to obliterate the freshness of my alarm; the praises of conscience began to grow into a thing of course; I began to be tortured with throes and longings, as of Hyde struggling after freedom; and at last, in an hour of moral weakness, I once again compounded and swallowed the transforming draught.

I do not suppose that, when a drunkard reasons with himself upon his vice, he is once out of five hundred times affected by the dangers that he runs through his brutish, physical insensibility; neither had I, long as I had considered my position, made enough allowance for the complete moral insensibility and insensate readiness to evil, which were the leading characters of Edward Hyde. Yet it was by these that I was punished. My devil had been long caged, he came out roaring. I was conscious, even when I took the draught, of a more unbridled, a more furious propensity to ill. It must have been this, I suppose, that stirred in my soul that tempest of impatience with which I listened to the civilities of my unhappy victim; I declare, at least, before God, no man morally sane[22] could have been guilty of that crime upon so pitiful a provocation; and that I struck in no more reasonable spirit than that in which a sick child may break a plaything. But I had voluntarily stripped myself of all those balancing instincts, by which even the worst of us continues to walk

---

22 Moral insanity was proposed as a category of medical diagnosis by Dr. James Prichard in 1835 ("a morbid perversion of the natural feelings, affections, inclinations, temper, habits, moral dispositions, and natural impulses, without any remarkable disorder or defect of the intellect or knowing and reasoning faculties, and particularly without any insane illusion or hallucination") and subsequently was sometimes used in court as a criminal defense plea.

with some degree of steadiness among temptations; and in my case, to be tempted, however slightly, was to fall.

Instantly the spirit of hell awoke in me and raged. With a transport of glee, I mauled the unresisting body, tasting delight from every blow; and it was not till weariness had begun to succeed[23], that I was suddenly, in the top fit of my delirium, struck through the heart by a cold thrill of terror. A mist dispersed; I saw my life to be forfeit; and fled from the scene of these excesses, at once glorying and trembling, my lust of evil gratified and stimulated, my love of life screwed to the topmost peg[24]. I ran to the house in Soho, and (to make assurance doubly sure) destroyed my papers; thence I set out through the lamplit streets, in the same divided ecstasy of mind, gloating on my crime, light-headedly devising others in the future, and yet still hastening and still hearkening in my wake for the steps of the avenger. Hyde had a song upon his lips as he compounded the draught, and as he drank it, pledged the dead man. The pangs of transformation had not done tearing him, before Henry Jekyll, with streaming tears of gratitude and remorse, had fallen upon his knees and lifted his clasped hands to God. The veil of self-indulgence was rent from head to foot, I saw my life as a whole: I followed it up from the days of childhood, when I had walked with my father's hand, and through the self-denying toils of my professional life, to arrive again and again, with the same sense of unreality, at the damned horrors of the evening. I could have screamed aloud; I sought with tears and prayers to smother down the crowd of hideous images and sounds with which my memory swarmed against me; and still, between the petitions, the ugly face of my iniquity stared into my soul. As the acuteness of this remorse began to die away, it was succeeded by a sense of joy. The problem of my conduct was solved. Hyde was thenceforth impossible; whether I would or not, I was now confined to the better part of my existence; and O, how I rejoiced to think it! with what willing humility, I embraced anew the restrictions of natural life! with what sincere renunciation, I locked the door by which I had so often gone and come, and ground the key under my heel!

The next day, came the news that the murder had been overlooked[25], that the guilt of Hyde was patent to the world, and that the victim was a man high in public estimation. It was not only a crime, it had been a tragic folly. I think

---

23 Follow.

24 Raised to its highest pitch (as in tuning a string instrument).

25 Seen from above (by the maidservant at the upstairs window).

I was glad to know it; I think I was glad to have my better impulses thus buttressed and guarded by the terrors of the scaffold. Jekyll was now my city of refuge; let but Hyde peep out an instant, and the hands of all men would be raised to take and slay him[26].

I resolved in my future conduct to redeem the past; and I can say with honesty that my resolve was fruitful of some good. You know yourself how earnestly in the last months of last year, I laboured to relieve suffering; you know that much was done for others, and that the days passed quietly, almost happily for myself. Nor can I truly say that I wearied of this beneficent and innocent life; I think instead that I daily enjoyed it more completely; but I was still cursed with my duality of purpose; and as the first edge of my penitence wore off, the lower side of me, so long indulged, so recently chained down, began to growl for license. Not that I dreamed of resuscitating Hyde; the bare idea of that would startle me to frenzy: no, it was in my own person, that I was once more tempted to trifle with my conscience; and it was as an ordinary secret sinner, that I at last fell before the assaults of temptation. [. . .]

[. . .] I was stepping leisurely across the court after breakfast, drinking the chill of the air with pleasure, when I was seized again with those indescribable sensations that heralded the change; and I had but the time to gain the shelter of my cabinet, before I was once again raging and freezing with the passions of Hyde. It took on this occasion a double dose to recall me to myself; and alas, six hours after, as I sat looking sadly in the fire, the pangs returned, and the drug had to be re-administered. In short, from that day forth it seemed only by a great effort as of gymnastics, and only under the immediate stimulation of the drug, that I was able to wear the countenance of Jekyll. At all hours of the day and night, I would be taken with the premonitory shudder; above all, if I slept, or even dozed for a moment in my chair, it was always as Hyde that I awakened. Under the strain of this continually impending doom and by the sleeplessness to which I now condemned myself, ay, even beyond what I had thought possible to man, I became, in my own person, a creature eaten up and emptied by fever, languidly weak both in body and mind, and solely occupied by one thought: the horror of my other self. But when I slept, or when the virtue of the medicine wore off, I would leap almost without transition (for the

26 City of refuge: in the Bible, a city set aside to provide safe haven for someone guilty of an accidental killing (see Numbers 35:9–34; Deuteronomy 4: 41–43; Joshua 20: 1–9); hands of all men…slay him: echoes the prophecy in Genesis about the "wild man," Ishmael, that "his hand will be against every man, and every man's hand against him" (Genesis 16: 12).

pangs of transformation grew daily less marked) into the possession of a fancy brimming with images of terror, a soul boiling with causeless hatreds, and a body that seemed not strong enough to contain the raging energies of life. The powers of Hyde seemed to have grown with the sickliness of Jekyll. And certainly the hate that now divided them was equal on each side. With Jekyll, it was a thing of vital instinct. He had now seen the full deformity of that creature that shared with him some of the phenomena of consciousness, and was co-heir with him to death: and beyond these links of community, which in themselves made the most poignant part of his distress, he thought of Hyde, for all his energy of life, as of something not only hellish but inorganic. This was the shocking thing; that the slime of the pit seemed to utter cries and voices; that the amorphous dust gesticulated and sinned; that what was dead, and had no shape, should usurp the offices of life[27]. And this again, that that insurgent horror was knit to him closer than a wife, closer than an eye; lay caged in his flesh, where he heard it mutter and felt it struggle to be born; and at every hour of weakness, and in the confidence of slumber, prevailed against him, and deposed him out of life. The hatred of Hyde for Jekyll, was of a different order. His terror of the gallows drove him continually to commit temporary suicide, and return to his subordinate station of a part instead of a person; but he loathed the necessity, he loathed the despondency into which Jekyll was now fallen, and he resented the dislike with which he was himself regarded. Hence the apelike tricks that he would play me, scrawling in my own hand blasphemies on the pages of my books, burning the letters and destroying the portrait of my father; and indeed, had it not been for his fear of death, he would long ago have ruined himself in order to involve me in the ruin. But his love of life is wonderful; I go further: I, who sicken and freeze at the mere thought of him, when I recall the abjection and passion of this attachment, and when I know how he fears my power to cut him off by suicide, I find it in my heart to pity him.

It is useless, and the time awfully fails me, to prolong this description; no one has ever suffered such torments, let that suffice; and yet even to these, habit brought—no, not alleviation—but a certain callousness of soul, a certain

---

27 I.e., functions of life. Jekyll's vision of "amorphous dust" masquerading as life invites comparison with with Genesis 2:7, where "the dust of the ground" is made man only when God gives it shape, breath, and immortal soul. The notion of a godless creation of life from brute matter held painful resonance for a generation struggling to come to terms with the new scientific account of man's origins emerging around the middle of the nineteenth century from the combined findings of geologists and evolutionists, most notably Charles Darwin.

acquiescence of despair; and my punishment might have gone on for years, but for the last calamity which has now fallen, and which has finally severed me from my own face and nature. My provision of the salt, which had never been renewed since the date of the first experiment, began to run low. I sent out for a fresh supply, and mixed the draught; the ebullition followed, and the first change of colour, not the second; I drank it and it was without efficiency. You will learn from Poole how I have had London ransacked; it was in vain; and I am now persuaded that my first supply was impure, and that it was that unknown impurity which lent efficacy to the draught.

About a week has passed, and I am now finishing this statement under the influence of the last of the old powders. This, then, is the last time, short of a miracle, that Henry Jekyll can think his own thoughts or see his own face (now how sadly altered!) in the glass. Nor must I delay too long to bring my writing to an end; for if my narrative has hitherto escaped destruction, it has been by a combination of great prudence and great good luck. Should the throes of change take me in the act of writing it, Hyde will tear it in pieces; but if some time shall have elapsed after I have laid it by, his wonderful selfishness and circumscription to the moment[28] will probably save it once again from the action of his apelike spite. And indeed the doom that is closing on us both, has already changed and crushed him. Half an hour from now, when I shall again and forever reindue[29] that hated personality, I know how I shall sit shuddering and weeping in my chair, or continue, with the most strained and fearstruck ecstasy of listening, to pace up and down this room (my last earthly refuge) and give ear to every sound of menace. Will Hyde die upon the scaffold? or will he find courage to release himself at the last moment? God knows; I am careless; this is my true hour of death, and what is to follow concerns another than myself. Here then, as I lay down the pen and proceed to seal up my confession, I bring the life of that unhappy Henry Jekyll to an end.

---

28 I.e., his astonishing selfishness and limitation of attention to each present moment.
29 Put on again.

Reread the description of Edward Hyde, and then research the concept of deformity and its historical connections to monstrosity or "evil." How does the story connect Hyde's appearance to his evil? How might this concept relate to historical stereotypes about deformity? Utterson also uses the word "troglodytic" in his description of Hyde, and others refer to Hyde as "apelike." As you research deformity, also investigate why Stevenson's Victorian contemporaries were sensitive to connections between humans and apes or troglodytes.

In a small group, discuss the following questions:

- Who is the monster in this story, and why?

- What monstrous attributes does Hyde have?

- What monstrous attributes does Jekyll have?

- Might Jekyll be just as monstrous as Hyde? Why or why not?

Once you've explored these questions, discuss how your answers may have altered your perception of monsters and how they relate to the definitions of "monster" that you had before reading this book?

In this selection from *Jekyll and Hyde*, Jekyll attempts to explain his decisions and justify his actions in regard to the creation and behavior of Hyde. Consider how this explanation differs from other works that only show the monster from an outsider's perspective. Create a visual map of Jekyll's thought process, illustrating both strong and flawed logic. You might use an outline, flow chart, or tree diagram. Accompany the visual with a short essay in which you argue for or against Jekyll's overall logic.

STRANGE TRANSFORMATIONS: JOHN LANDIS'S AN AMERICAN WEREWOLF IN LONDON

By L. Andrew Cooper and Brandy Ball Blake

Film director John Landis might be better known for comedies such as *Animal House* (1978), *The Blues Brothers* (1980), and *Trading Places* (1983), but his take on one of Hollywood's most iconic monsters in *An American Werewolf in London* (1981) nevertheless stands among the most famous and accomplished werewolf stories. Along with his contributions to *Twilight Zone: The Movie* (1983), *American Werewolf* is likely the reason Landis is regarded as a master of the horror genre, a fact recognized by his invitation to contribute two episodes to the cable TV series *Masters of Horror*, "Deer Woman" (2005) and "Family" (2006). Regardless of genre or subject, Landis usually infuses his films with a quirky, offbeat sense of humor.

American Werewolf modernizes the classic film *The Wolf Man* (1941): a stranger in town is attacked by a werewolf and is thus doomed to become one. *American Werewolf*'s monster, however, is much more animalistic than its predecessor, taking on a shape that is almost entirely inhuman and prowling on all fours instead of walking upright. Despite this increased emphasis on the werewolf's animality, the core of *American Werewolf* is still the tragedy of the human who first unwittingly and then unwillingly becomes a ravenous, deadly beast who stalks and kills members of his community. Despite the generally tragic storyline, the film has many darkly humorous moments, often occurring when the wolf man's dead friend Jack appears to him as a spectral rotting corpse and engages in witty dialogue. This unsettling blend of comedy and horror stretches the boundaries of the horror genre and raises questions about the appropriateness and meaning of laughter in the face of monstrosity. These questions are particularly poignant at the end, as a nurse who has fallen in love with the wolf man confronts the creature, which visibly resists the urge to attack her. While some of its behaviors suggest that the wolf runs on pure animal instinct, the creature's refusal to attack the woman standing helpless before him hints that there's more human in the monster than its looks might suggest. Thus neat divisions between man and beast, good and evil threaten to collapse.

As you look over the images here and perhaps see the film itself, think about the film's many oppositions—such as man versus animal, city versus country, American versus British, comedy versus horror—and how they might relate to and reflect on one another.

Figure 12. David Kessler (David Naughton, left) and his friend Jack Goodman (Griffin Dunne, right) are average American students on a backpacking trip through Europe. When they hitchhike deep into the English countryside, they come upon a pub called The Slaughtered Lamb. The people inside want nothing to do with them, but they do give some advice: stick to the road, stay off the moors, and beware the moon. Naturally, the young men soon wander off the road and onto the moors, where by the light of the full moon a werewolf makes them its prey. Jack dies, but the pub denizens come to David's rescue. David is wounded and therefore infected by the wolf, doomed to transform on the next full moon. The film's simple set-up animates the cultural clash suggested by its title. Youthful Americans are clueless as they enter a traditional countryside and become the victims of one of England's rural legends, the werewolf. When David returns to the city and becomes a werewolf, he is doubly out of place: just as an American doesn't really belong in England, a creature from the moors doesn't really belong in London.

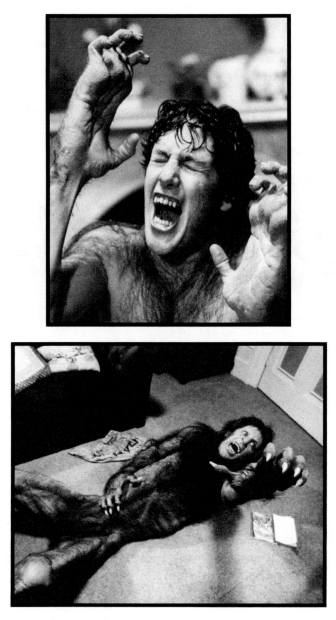

Figure 13. The transformation from man into wolf is a key point in most werewolf stories, and *An American Werewolf in London*'s Oscar-winning transformation sequence set a new standard for monster-makeup effects. The bright lights in which David has his first shape-shifting experience emphasize his agony as well as the details of his body's changes as parts of him twist, swell, shrink, and stretch into the ferocious features of the wolf.

In *American Werewolf*, David's transformation into a wolf appears in graphic detail, showing how aspects of human anatomy might be changed into something more wolfish. Think about the human body and its various parts. One by one, consider what changes to each part would be necessary in order to accomplish a convincing werewolf transformation. As you think about these changes, also consider the changing functions and meanings associated with each part. For example, the human hand allows us to use both simple and complex tools, so hands (arguably) set us apart from the animal kingdom, in which tool use is very limited. As Figure 13 shows, David's werewolf transformation distorts his hands, making them less suitable for using tools and more able to support him as he bolts after his prey. Thus the transformation of this body part provides an opportunity to reflect on how the hand relates to important aspects of human-ness. How might other body parts do the same?

The werewolf is a hairy, snarling monster driven almost entirely by its appetites. The creature's appetites focus mostly on food, but as *American Werewolf* suggests through David and Alex's physical relationship (as well as through scenes in a pornographic movie theater), animal appetites also include sex. Furthermore, *American Werewolf* is not atypical in focusing on a male wolf. Although female werewolves do appear in some films (including *An American Werewolf in Paris*, a sequel released in 1997), they're rare. Perhaps something about these slobbering, hairy beasts makes them more apt as reflections on masculinity. Write an essay in which you take a position on the werewolf's reflections of human sexuality and gender. What does the werewolf suggest about the place of carnal instincts among "civilized" people like London's populace? What roles does animality play in conceptions of the masculine and the feminine?

Compare the shapeshifter of *American Werewolf* with those in *The Strange Case of Dr. Jekyll and Mr. Hyde* and *Twilight*. Consider that David does not choose to become a shapeshifter and is powerless before the werewolf curse. By contrast, Jekyll initially chooses to become Hyde, and Jacob Black's wolf form provides him with power. How do these differences factor into your understandings of these monsters? What moral responsibility does a shapeshifter have for the actions of the darker, animalistic side? How do the choices and powers associated with the transformation affect your sense of the shapeshifters' moral character?

Famous for turning myths and fairy tales upside-down, questioning traditional views of gender and sexuality, and creating vivid landscapes with descriptive language, Angela Carter breaks boundaries in her monster story "The Company of Wolves." Carter's The Bloody Chamber (1979), which includes "The Company of Wolves," presents feminist versions of traditional fairy tales that examine the strengths and weaknesses of female characters as they react to the monstrosity inherent in patriarchal society. "The Company of Wolves" revamps the story of "Little Red Riding Hood," reconstructing a tale that warns against strangers and straying from society's prescribed paths into a more mature examination of werewolves' significance in oral storytelling traditions.

While other werewolf stories explore transformations of humans into animalistic hybrids and emphasize characters who question their own humanity, Carter explores similarities between the werewolf and the wolf, emphasizing the werewolf's animal nature rather than its lost humanity. Vignettes about the victims of both natural wolves and werewolves allow her monsters to remain monstrous, evoking sympathy only in descriptions of the creatures' starvation. However, a twist at the story's end presents victims and monsters in ways that contrast with earlier depictions. As you read, consider the werewolves' monstrous attributes, comparing werewolves to wolves as well as to other hybrids.

THE COMPANY OF WOLVES

BY ANGELA CARTER

One beast and only one howls in the woods by night.

The wolf is carnivore incarnate and he's as cunning as he is ferocious; once he's had a taste of flesh then nothing else will do.

At night, the eyes of wolves shine like candle flames, yellowish, reddish, but that is because the pupils of their eyes fatten on darkness and catch the light from your lantern to flash it back to you—red for danger; if a wolf's eyes reflect only moonlight, then they gleam a cold and unnatural green, a mineral, a piercing colour. If the benighted traveller spies those luminous, terrible sequins stitched suddenly on the black thickets, then he knows he must run, if fear has not struck him stock-still.

But those eyes are all you will be able to glimpse of the forest assassins as they cluster invisibly round your smell of meat as you go through the wood unwisely late. They will be like shadows, they will be like wraiths, grey members of a congregation of nightmare; hark! his long, wavering howl . . . an aria of fear made audible.

The wolfsong is the sound of the rending you will suffer, in itself a murdering.

It is winter and cold weather. In this region of mountain and forest, there is now nothing for the wolves to eat. Goats and sheep are locked up in the byre, the deer departed for the remaining pasturage on the southern slopes— wolves grow lean and famished. There is so little flesh on them that you could count the starveling ribs through their pelts, if they gave you time before they pounced. Those slavering jaws; the lolling tongue; the rime of saliva on the grizzled chops—of all the teeming perils of the night and the forest, ghosts, hobgoblins, ogres that grill babies upon gridirons, witches that fatten their captives in cages for cannibal tables, the wolf is worst for he cannot listen to reason.

You are always in danger in the forest, where no people are. Step between the portals of the great pines where the shaggy branches tangle about you, trapping the unwary traveller in nets as if the vegetation itself were in a plot with the wolves who live there, as though the wicked trees go fishing on behalf of their friends—step between the gateposts of the forest with the greatest trepidation and infinite precautions, for if you stray from the path for one instant, the wolves will eat you. They are grey as famine, they are as unkind as plague.

The grave-eyed children of the sparse villages always carry knives with them when they go out to tend the little flocks of goats that provide the homesteads with acrid milk and rank, maggoty cheeses. Their knives are half as big as they are, the blades are sharpened daily.

But the wolves have ways of arriving at your own hearthside. We try and try but sometimes we cannot keep them out. There is no winter's night the cottager does not fear to see a lean, grey, famished snout questing under the door, and there was a woman once bitten in her own kitchen as she was straining the macaroni.

Fear and flee the wolf; for, worst of all, the wolf may be more than he seems.

There was a hunter once, near here, that trapped a wolf in a pit. This wolf had massacred the sheep and goats; eaten up a mad old man who used to live by himself in a hut halfway up the mountain and sing to Jesus all day; pounced on a girl looking after the sheep, but she made such a commotion that men came with rifles and scared him away and tried to track him into the forest but he was cunning and easily gave them the slip. So this hunter dug a pit and put a duck in it, for bait, all alive-oh; and he covered the pit with straw smeared with wolf dung. Quack, quack! went the duck and a wolf came slinking out of the forest, a big one, a heavy one, he weighed as much as a grown man and the straw gave way beneath him—into the pit he tumbled. The hunter jumped down after him, slit his throat, cut off all his paws for a trophy.

And then no wolf at all lay in front of the hunter but the bloody trunk of a man, headless, footless, dying, dead.

A witch from up the valley once turned an entire wedding party into wolves because the groom had settled on another girl. She used to order them to visit her, at night, from spite, as they would sit and howl around her cottage for her, serenading her with their misery.

Not so very long ago, a young woman in our village married a man who vanished clean away on her wedding night. The bed was made with new sheets and the bride lay down in it; the groom said he was going out to relieve himself, insisted on it, for the sake of decency, and she drew the coverlet up to her chin and she lay there. And she waited and she waited and then she waited again—surely he's been gone a long time? Until she jumps up in bed and shrieks to hear a howling, coming on the wind from the forest.

That long-drawn, wavering howl has, for all its fearful resonance, some inherent sadness in it, as if the beasts would love to be less beastly if only they knew how and never cease to mourn their own condition. There is a vast melancholy in the canticles of the wolves, melancholy infinite as the forest, endless as these long nights of winter and yet that ghastly sadness, that mourning for their own, irremediable appetites, can never move the heart for not one phrase in it hints at the possibility of redemption; grace could not come to the wolf from its own despair, only through some external mediator, so that, sometimes, the beast will look as if he half welcomes the knife that despatches him.

The young woman's brothers searched the outhouses and the haystacks but never found any remains so the sensible girl dried her eyes and found herself another husband not too shy to piss into a pot who spent the nights indoors. She gave him a pair of bonny babies and all went right as a trivet until, one freezing night, the night of the solstice, the hinge of the year when things do not fit together as well as they should, the longest night, her first good man came home again.

A great thump on the door announced him as she was stirring the soup for the father of her children and she knew him the moment she lifted the latch to him although it was years since she'd worn black for him and now he was in rags and his hair hung down his back and never saw a comb, alive with lice.

'Here I am again, missus,' he said. 'Get me my bowl of cabbage and be quick about it.'

Then her second husband came in with wood for the fire and when the first one saw she'd slept with another man and, worse, clapped his red eyes on her little children who'd crept into the kitchen to see what all the din was about, he shouted: 'I wish I were a wolf again, to teach this whore a lesson!' So a wolf he instantly became and tore off the eldest boy's left foot before he was chopped up with the hatchet they used for chopping logs. But when the wolf lay bleeding and gasping its last, the pelt peeled off again and he was just as he had been, years ago, when he ran away from his marriage bed, so that she wept and her second husband beat her.

They say there's an ointment the Devil gives you that turns you into a wolf the minute you rub it on. Or, that he was born feet first and had a wolf for his father and his torso is a man's but his legs and genitals are a wolf's. And he has a wolf's heart.

Seven years is a werewolf's natural span but if you burn his human clothing you condemn him to wolfishness for the rest of his life, so old wives hereabouts think it some protection to throw a hat or an apron at the werewolf, as if clothes made the man. Yet by the eyes, those phosphorescent eyes, you know him in all his shapes; the eyes alone unchanged by metamorphosis.

Before he can become a wolf, the lycanthrope strips stark naked. If you spy a naked man among the pines, you must run as if the Devil were after you.

It is midwinter and the robin, the friend of man, sits on the handle of the gardener's spade and sings. It is the worst time in all the year for wolves but this strong-minded child insists she will go off through the wood. She is quite sure the wild beasts cannot harm her although, well-warned, she lays a carving knife in the basket her mother has packed with cheeses. There is a bottle of harsh liquor distilled from brambles; a batch of flat oatcakes baked on the hearthstone; a pot or two of jam. The flaxen-haired girl will take these delicious gifts to a reclusive grandmother so old the burden of her years is crushing her to death. Granny lives two hours' trudge through the winter woods; the child wraps herself up in her thick shawl, draws it over her head. She steps into her stout wooden shoes; she is dressed and ready and it is Christmas Eve. The malign door of the solstice still swings upon its hinges but she has been too much loved ever to feel scared.

Children do not stay young for long in this savage country. There are no toys for them to play with so they work hard and grow wise but this one, so pretty and the youngest of her family, a little late-comer, had been indulged by her mother and the grandmother who'd knitted her the red shawl that, today, has the ominous if brilliant look of blood on snow. Her breasts have just begun to swell; her hair is like lint, so fair it hardly makes a shadow on her pale forehead; her cheeks are an emblematic scarlet and white as she just started her woman's bleeding, the clock inside her that will strike, henceforward, once a month.

She stands and moves within the invisible pentacle of her own virginity. She is an unbroken egg; she is a sealed vessel; she has inside her a magic space the entrance to which is shut tight with a plug of membrane; she is a closed system; she does not know how to shiver. She has her knife and she is afraid of nothing.

Her father might forbid her, if he were home, but he is away in the forest, gathering wood, and her mother cannot deny her.

The forest closed upon her like a pair of jaws.

There is always something to look at in the forest, even in the middle of winter—the huddled mounds of birds, succumbed to the lethargy of the season, heaped on the creaking boughs and too forlorn to sing; the bright frills of the winter fungi on the blotched trunks of the trees; the cuneiform slots of rabbits and deer, the herringbone tracks of the birds, a hare as lean as a rasher of bacon streaking across the path where the thin sunlight dapples the russet brakes of last year's bracken.

When she heard the freezing howl of a distant wolf, her practised hand sprang to the handle of her knife, but she saw no sign of a wolf at all, nor of a naked man, neither, but then she heard a clattering among the brushwood and there sprang on to the path a fully clothed one, a very handsome young one, in the green coat and wideawake hat of a hunter, laden with carcasses of game birds. She had her hand on her knife at the first rustle of twigs but he laughed with a flash of white teeth when he saw her and made her a comic yet flattering little bow; she'd never seen such a fine fellow before, not among the rustic clowns of her native village. So on they went together, through the thickening light of the afternoon.

Soon they were laughing and joking like old friends. When he offered to carry her basket, she gave it to him although her knife was in it because he told her his rifle would protect them. As the day darkened, it began to snow again; she felt the first flakes settle on her eyelashes but now there was only half a mile to go and there would be a fire, and hot tea, and a welcome, a warm one, surely, for the dashing huntsman as well as for herself.

This young man had a remarkable object in his pocket. It was a compass. She looked at the little round glass face in the palm of his hand and watched the wavering needle with a vague wonder. He assured her this compass had taken him safely through the wood on his hunting trip because the needle always told him with perfect accuracy where the north was. She did not believe it; she knew she should never leave the path on the way through the wood or else she would be lost instantly. He laughed at her again; gleaming trails of spittle clung to his teeth. He said, if he plunged off the path into the forest that surrounded them, he could guarantee to arrive at her grandmother's house a good quarter of an hour before she did, plotting his way through the undergrowth with his compass, while she trudged the long way, along the winding path.

I don't believe you. Besides, aren't you afraid of the wolves?

He only tapped the gleaming butt of his rifle and grinned.

Is it a bet? he asked her. Shall we make a game of it? What will you give me if I get to your grandmother's house before you?

What would you like? she asked disingenuously.

A kiss.

Commonplaces of a rustic seduction; she lowered her eyes and blushed.

He went through the undergrowth and took her basket with him but she forgot to be afraid of the beasts, although now the moon was rising, for she wanted to dawdle on her way to make sure the handsome gentleman would win his wager.

Grandmother's house stood by itself a little way out of the village. The freshly falling snow blew in eddies about the kitchen garden and the young man stepped delicately up the snowy path to the door as if he were reluctant to get his feet wet, swinging his bundle of game and the girl's basket and humming a little tune to himself.

There is a faint trace of blood on his chin; he has been snacking on his catch.

He rapped upon the panels with his knuckles.

Aged and frail, granny is three-quarters succumbed to the mortality the ache in her bones promises her and almost ready to give in entirely. A boy came out from the village to build up her hearth for the night an hour ago and the kitchen crackles with busy firelight. She has her Bible for company, she is a pious old woman. She is propped up on several pillows in the bed set into the wall peasant-fashion, wrapped up in the patchwork quilt she made before she was married, more years ago than she cares to remember. Two china spaniels with liver-coloured blotches on their coats and black noses sit on either side of the fireplace. There is a bright rug of woven rags on the pantiles. The grandfather clock ticks away her eroding time.

We keep the wolves outside by living well.

He rapped upon the panels with his hairy knuckles.

It is your granddaughter, he mimicked in a high soprano.

Lift up the latch and walk in, my darling.

You can tell them by their eyes, eyes of a beast of prey, nocturnal, devastating eyes as red as a wound; you can hurl your Bible at him and your apron after, granny, you thought that was a sure prophylactic against these infernal vermin . . . now call on Christ and his mother and all the angels in heaven to protect you but it won't do you any good.

His feral muzzle is sharp as a knife; he drops his golden burden of gnawed pheasant on the table and puts down your dear girl's basket, too. Oh, my God, what have you done with her?

Off with his disguise, that coat of forest-coloured cloth, the hat with the feather tucked into the ribbon; his matted hair streams down his white shirt and she can see the lice moving in it. The sticks in the hearth shift and hiss; night and the forest have come into the kitchen with darkness tangled in its hair.

He strips off his shirt. His skin is the colour and texture of vellum. A crisp stripe of hair runs down his belly, his nipples are ripe and dark as poison fruit but he's so thin you could count the ribs under his skin if only he gave you the time. He strips off his trousers and she can see how hairy his legs are. His genitals, huge. Ah! huge.

The last thing the old lady saw in all this world was a young man, eyes like cinders, naked as stone, approaching her bed.

The wolf is carnivore incarnate.

When he had finished with her, he licked his chops and quickly dressed himself again, until he was just as he had been when he came through her door. He burned the inedible hair in the fireplace and he wrapped the bones up in a napkin that he hid away under the bed in the wooden chest in which he found a clean pair of sheets. These he carefully put on the bed instead of the tell-tale stained ones he stowed away in the laundry basket. He plumped up the pillows and shook out the patchwork quilt, he picked up the Bible from the floor, closed it and laid it on the table. All was as it had been before except that grandmother was gone. The sticks twitched in the grate, the clock ticked and the young man sat patiently, deceitfully beside the bed in the granny's nightcap.

Rat-a-tap-tap.

Who's there, he quavers in granny's antique falsetto.

Only your granddaughter.

So she came in, bringing with her a flurry of snow that melted in tears on the tiles, and perhaps she was a little disappointed to see only her grandmother sitting beside the fire. But then he flung off the blanket and sprang to the door, pressing his back against it so that she could not get out again.

The girl looked round the room and saw there was not even the indentation of a head on the smooth cheek of the pillow and how, for the first time she'd seen it so, the Bible lay closed on the table. The tick of the clock cracked like a whip. She wanted her knife from her basket but she did not dare reach for it because his eyes were fixed upon her—huge eyes that now seemed to shine with a unique, interior light, eyes the size of saucers, saucers full of Greek fire, diabolic phosphorescence.

What big eyes you have.

All the better to see you with.

No trace at all of the old woman except for a tuft of white hair that had caught in the bark of an unburned log. When the girl saw that, she knew she was in danger of death.

Where is my grandmother?

There is nobody here but we two, my darling.

Now a great howling rose up all around them, near, very near, as close as the kitchen garden, the howling of a multitude of wolves; she knew the worst wolves are hairy on the inside and she shivered, in spite of the scarlet shawl she pulled more closely round herself as if it could protect her although it was as red as the blood she must spill.

Who has come to sing us carols, she said.

Those are the voices of my brothers, darling; I love the company of wolves. Look out of the window and you'll see them.

Snow half-caked the lattice and she opened it to look into the garden. It was a white night of moon and snow; the blizzard whirled around the gaunt, grey beasts who squatted on their haunches among the rows of winter cabbage, pointing their sharp snouts to the moon and howling as if their hearts would break. Ten wolves; twenty wolves—so many wolves she could not count them, howling in concert as if demented or deranged. Their eyes reflected the light from the kitchen and shone like a hundred candles.

It is very cold, poor things, she said; no wonder they howl so.

She closed the window on the wolves' threnody and took off her scarlet shawl, the colour of poppies, the colour of sacrifices, the colour of her menses, and, since her fear did her no good, she ceased to be afraid.

What shall I do with my shawl?

Throw it on the fire, dear one. You won't need it again.

She bundled up her shawl and threw it on the blaze, which instantly consumed it. Then she drew her blouse over her head; her small breasts gleamed as if the snow had invaded the room.

What shall I do with my blouse?

Into the fire with it, too, my pet.

The thin muslin went flaring up the chimney like a magic bird and now off came her skirt, her woollen stockings, her shoes, and on to the fire they went, too, and were gone for good. The firelight shone through the edges of her skin; now she was clothed only in her untouched integument of flesh. This dazzling, naked she combed out her hair with her fingers; her hair looked white as the snow outside. Then went directly to the man with red eyes in whose unkempt mane the lice moved; she stood up on tiptoe and unbuttoned the collar of his shirt.

What big arms you have.

All the better to hug you with.

Every wolf in the world now howled a prothalamion outside the window as she freely gave the kiss she owed him.

What big teeth you have!

She saw how his jaw began to slaver and the room was full of the clamour of the forest's Liebestod but the wise child never flinched, even when he answered:

All the better to eat you with.

The girl burst out laughing; she knew she was nobody's meat. She laughed at him full in the face, she ripped off his shirt for him and flung it into the fire, in the fiery wake of her own discarded clothing. The flames danced like dead souls on Walpurgisnacht and the old bones under the bed set up a terrible clattering but she did not pay them any heed.

Carnivore incarnate, only immaculate flesh appeases him.

She will lay his fearful head on her lap and she will pick out the lice from his pelt and perhaps she will put the lice into her mouth and eat them, as he will bid her, as she would do in a savage marriage ceremony.

The blizzard will die down.

The blizzard died down, leaving the mountains as randomly covered with snow as if a blind woman had thrown a sheet over them, the upper branches of the forest pines limed, creaking, swollen with the fall.

Snowlight, moonlight, a confusion of paw-prints.

All silent, all still.

Midnight; and the clock strikes. It is Christmas Day, the werewolves' birthday, the door of the solstice stands wide open; let them all sink through.

See! sweet and sound she sleeps in granny's bed, between the paws of the tender wolf.

Like monsters, fairy tales have been adapted and revised throughout history, reflecting the cultures from which variants originate. Research a variant of "Little Red Riding Hood" (such as "The Story of Grandmother," Charles Perrault's "Little Red Riding Hood," the Grimm Brothers' "Little Red Cap"). How does this variant compare to your memories of the "Red Riding Hood" story? To Carter's story? How does Carter's monster reflect the culture and time period when Carter wrote?

Consider the turbulent relationship between women and monsters in literature and movies. While often monsters' prey, women in modern horror stories sometimes take on the roles of both victim and heroine. What is the relationship between Carter's wolf, usually depicted as a predator, and Red Riding Hood, usually depicted as prey? How does this Red Riding Hood compare to female victims in other monster stories? To female heroines? How would you classify her role? How does she compare to the female protagonists of movies such as *Halloween*, A *Nightmare on Elm Street*, or *The Texas Chainsaw Massacre*? To Bella Swan in *Twilight*?

Carter uses language to create vivid visual and auditory imagery—descriptions of the forest and of the wolves eyes, comparisons to opera, etc. In small groups, use Carter's descriptions as a guide to recreate a scene from the story in a manner that conveys analytical insights about the story's monster(s). Use both images and sound in your recreation, producing a video, short performance piece, or slideshow. Then write a brief explanation of your recreation's analytical insights.

Author, journalist, drama critic, and theater manager—Bram Stoker had a diverse professional life long before writing Dracula (1897), and through the course of these careers, he met numerous authors of Gothic works, including Oscar Wilde and Sheridan Le Fanu. While Dracula is his most famous novel, Stoker also wrote several other Gothic works, including The Jewel of Seven Stars (1903), The Lady of the Shroud (1909), and The Lair of the White Worm (1911).

In "Monster Culture (Seven Theses)," Jeffrey Jerome Cohen asserts that "monstrous difference tends to be cultural, political, racial, economic, sexual." The vampire, and Dracula in particular, has been interpreted as representing all of these categories of difference, making it one of the most multifaceted and controversial monsters in literature. As you read the selections from Dracula, consider ways that Dracula and the other vampires of the story could represent difference. In addition, reflect on how these vampires compare to or deviate from modern representations of vampires.

excerpts from

DRACULA

BY BRAM STOKER

[. . .] By this time I had finished my supper, and by my host's desire had drawn up a chair by the fire and begun to smoke a cigar which he offered me, at the same time excusing himself that he did not smoke. I had now an opportunity of observing him, and found him of a very marked physiognomy.

His face was a strong—a very strong—aquiline[1], with high bridge of the thin nose and peculiarly arched nostrils, with lofty domed forehead, and hair growing scantily round the temples, but profusely elsewhere. His eyebrows were very massive, almost meeting over the nose, and with bushy hair that seemed to curl in its own profusion. The mouth, so far as I could see it under the heavy moustache, was fixed and rather cruel-looking, with peculiarly sharp white teeth; these protruded over the lips, whose remarkable ruddiness showed astonishing vitality in a man of his years. For the rest, his ears were pale, and at the tops extremely pointed; the chin was broad and strong, and the cheeks firm though thin. The general effect was one of extraordinary pallor.

1 That is, a curve like that of an eagle's beak.

Figure 14. Dracula, played by Bela Lugosi in Tod Browning's 1931 film *Dracula*, welcomes Renfield to the castle. Despite his refined appearance, Lugosi's slow movements and intense expressions make him a frightening figure. Lugosi's outfit is now a stereotypical model for vampire Halloween costumes.

Hitherto I had noticed the backs of his hands as they lay on his knees in the firelight, and they had seemed rather white and fine; but seeing them now close to me, I could not but notice that they were rather coarse—broad, with squat fingers. Strange to say, there were hairs in the centre of the palm. The nails were long and fine, and cut to a sharp point. As the Count leaned over me and his hands touched me, I could not repress a shudder. It may have been that his breath was rank, but a horrible feeling of nausea came over me, which, do what I would, I could not conceal. The Count, evidently noticing it, drew back; and with a grim sort of smile, which showed more than he had yet done his protuberant teeth, sat himself down again on his own side of the fireplace. We were both silent for a while, and as I looked towards the window I saw the first dim streak of the coming dawn. There seemed a strange stillness over everything; but as I listened I heard as if from down below in the valley the howling of many wolves. The Count's eyes gleamed, and he said:—

'Listen to them—the children of the night. What music they make!'
Seeing, I suppose, some expression in my face strange to him, he added: —

'Ah, sir, you dwellers in the city cannot enter into the feelings of the hunter.' Then he rose and said:—

'But you must be tired. Your bedroom is all ready, and tomorrow you shall sleep as late as you will. I have to be away till the afternoon; so sleep well and dream well!' With a courteous bow, he opened for me himself the door to the octagonal room, and I entered my bedroom.

I am all in a sea of wonders. I doubt; I fear; I think strange things which I dare not confess to my own soul. God keep me, if only for the sake of those dear to me! [. . .]

[. . .] When he left me I went to my room. After a little while, not hearing any sound, I came out and went up the stone stair to where I could look out towards the south. There was some sense of freedom in the vast expanse, inaccessible though it was to me, as compared with the narrow darkness of the courtyard. Looking out on this, I felt that I was indeed in prison, and I seemed to want a breath of fresh air, though it were of the night. I am beginning to feel this nocturnal existence tell on me. It is destroying my nerve. I start at my own shadow, and am full of all sorts of horrible imaginings. God knows that there is ground for my terrible fear in this accursed place! I looked out over the beautiful expanse, bathed in soft yellow moonlight till it was almost as light as day. In the soft light the distant hills became melted, and the shadows in the valleys and gorges of velvety blackness. The mere beauty seemed to cheer me. There was peace and comfort in every breath I drew. As I leaned from the window my eye was caught by something moving a storey below me, and somewhat to my left, where I imagined, from the order of the rooms, that the windows of the Count's own room would look out. The window at which I stood was tall and deep, stone-mullioned, and though weather-worn, was still complete; but it was evidently many a day since the case had been there. I drew back behind the stonework, and looked carefully out.

What I saw was the Count's head coming out from the window. I did not see the face, but I knew the man by the neck and the movement of his back and arms. In any case I could not mistake the hands which I had had so many opportunities of studying. I was at first interested and somewhat amused, for it is wonderful how small a matter will interest and amuse a man when he is a prisoner. But my very feelings changed to repulsion and terror when I saw the whole man slowly emerge from the window and begin to crawl down the castle wall over the dreadful abyss, *face down* with his cloak spreading out around him like great wings. At first I could not believe my eyes. I thought it was some trick of the moonlight, some weird effect of shadow; but I kept looking, and it could be no delusion. I saw the fingers and toes grasp the corners of the stones, worn clear of the mortar by the stress of years, and by thus using every projection and inequality move downwards with considerable speed, just as a lizard moves along a wall.

What manner of man is this, or what manner of creature, is it in the semblance of man? I feel the dread of this horrible place overpowering me; I am in fear—in awful fear—and there is no escape for me; I am encompassed about with terrors that I dare not think of. . . [. . .]

Figure 15. In Freddie Francis's 1968 *Dracula Has Risen from the Grave*, a woman falls prey to Dracula's mesmerizing power. This is one of Christopher Lee's many appearances as Dracula; his interpretation of the character amplifies the vampire's sexuality.

[. . .] Here I am, sitting at a little oak table where in old times possibly some fair lady sat to pen, with much thought and many blushes, her ill-spelt love letter, and writing in my diary in shorthand all that has happened since I closed it last. It is nineteenth century up-to-date with a vengeance. And yet, unless my senses deceive me, the old centuries had, and have, powers of their own which mere 'modernity' cannot kill.

Later: The morning of 16 May.—God preserve my sanity, for to this I am reduced. Safety and the assurance of safety are things of the past. Whilst I live on here there is but one thing to hope for: that I may not go mad, if, indeed, I be not mad already. If I be sane, then surely it is maddening to think that of all the foul things that lurk in this hateful place the Count is the least dreadful to me; that to him alone I can look for safety, even though this be only whilst I can serve his purpose. Great God! merciful God! Let me be calm, for out of that way lies madness indeed. I begin to get new lights on certain things which have puzzled me. Up to now I never quite knew what Shakespeare meant when he made Hamlet say: —

> My tablets! quick, my tablets!
> 'Tis meet that I put it down, etc.,[2]

---

2 Misquotation of *Hamlet*

for now, feeling as though my own brain were unhinged or as if the shock had come which must end in its undoing, I turn to my diary for repose. The habit of entering accurately must help to soothe me.

The Count's mysterious warning frightened me at the time; it frightens me more not when I think of it, for in the future he has a fearful hold upon me. I shall fear to doubt what he may say!

When I had written in my diary and had fortunately replaced the book and pen in my pocket I felt sleepy. The Count's warning came into my mind, but I took pleasure in disobeying it. The sense of sleep was upon me, and with it the obstinacy which sleep brings as outrider. The soft moonlight soothed, and the wide expanse without gave a sense of freedom which refreshed me. I determined not to return tonight to the gloom-haunted rooms, but to sleep here, where of old ladies had sat and sung and lived sweet lives whilst their gentle breasts were sad for their menfolk away in the midst of remorseless wars. I drew a great couch out of its place near the corner, so that, as I lay, I could look at the lovely view to east and south, and unthinking of and uncaring for the dust, composed myself for sleep.

Figure 16. After drinking blood in Francis Ford Coppola's *Dracula* (1992), Dracula transforms from an old man into a young man both to integrate himself into English society and to regain his lost love, embodied by Mina Harker—a plotline that does not appear in the original novel. This transformation allows him to conceal himself and his purpose.

I suppose I must have fallen asleep; I hope so, but I fear, for all that followed was startlingly real—so real that now sitting here in the broad, full sunlight of the morning, I cannot in the least believe that it was all sleep.

I was not alone. The room was the same, unchanged in any way since I came into it; I could see along the floor, in the brilliant moonlight, my own footsteps marked where I had disturbed the long accumulation of dust. In the moonlight opposite me were three young women, ladies by their dress and manner. I thought at the time that I must be dreaming when I saw them, for, they threw no shadow on the floor. They came close to me, and looked at me for some time, and then whispered together. Two were dark, and had high aquiline noses, like the Count, and great dark, piercing eyes, that seemed to be almost red when contrasted with the pale yellow moon. The other was fair, as fair as can be, with great masses of golden hair and eyes like pale sapphires. I seemed somehow to know her face, and to know it in connection with some dreamy fear, but I could not recollect at the moment how or where. All three had brilliant white teeth that shone like pearls against the ruby of their voluptuous lips. There was something about them that made me uneasy, some longing and at the same time some deadly fear. I felt in my heart a wicked, burning desire that they would kiss me with those red lips. It is not good to note this down, lest some day it should meet Mina's eyes and cause her pain; but it is the truth. They whispered together, and then they all three laughed— such a silvery, musical laugh, but as hard as though the sound never could have come through the softness of human lips. It was like the intolerable, tingling sweetness of water-glasses when played on by a cunning hand. The fair girl shook her head coquettishly, and the other two urged her on. One said: —

'Go on! You are first, and we shall follow; yours is the right to begin.'
The other added:—

'He is young and strong; there are kisses for us all.' I lay quiet, looking out from under my eyelashes in an agony of delightful anticipation. The fair girl advanced and bent over me till I could feel the movement of her breath upon me. Sweet it was in one sense, honey-sweet, and sent the same tingling through the nerves as her voice, but with a bitter underlying the sweet, a bitter offensiveness, as one smells in blood.

I was afraid to raise my eyelids, but looked out and saw perfectly under the lashes. The girl went on her knees, and bent over me, fairly gloating. There was a deliberate voluptuousness which was both thrilling and repulsive, and as she arched her neck she actually licked her lips like an animal, till I could see in the moonlight the moisture shining on the scarlet lips and on the red tongue as it lapped the white sharp teeth. Lower and lower went her head as the lips went below the range of my mouth and chin and seemed to fasten on my throat. Then she paused, and I could hear the churning sound of her tongue as it licked her teeth and lips, and I could feel the hot breath on my neck. Then the skin of my throat began to tingle as one's flesh does when the hand that is to tickle it approaches nearer—nearer. I could feel the soft, shivering touch of the lips on the super sensitive skin of my throat, and the hard dents of two sharp teeth, just touching and pausing there. I closed my eyes in languorous ecstasy and waited—waited with beating heart.

But at that instant, another sensation swept through me as quick as lightning. I was conscious of the presence of the Count, and of his being as if lapped in a storm of fury. As my eyes opened involuntarily I saw his strong hand grasp the slender neck of the fair woman and with giant's power draw it back, the blue eyes transformed with fury, the white teeth champing with rage, and the fair cheeks blazing red with passion. But the Count! Never did I imagine such wrath and fury, even to the demons of the pit. His eyes were positively blazing. The red light in them was lurid, as if the flames of hell fire blazed behind them. His face was deathly pale, and the lines of it were hard like drawn wires; the thick eyebrows that met over the nose now seemed like a heaving bar of white-hot metal. With a fierce sweep of his arm, he hurled the woman from him, and then motioned to

Figure 17. In Coppola's film, Dracula also transforms into a hybrid bat form, which contradicts the humanity manifested in his young self and the love he has for Mina.

the others, as though he were beating them back; it was the same imperious gesture that I had seen used to the wolves. In a voice which, though low and

almost in a whisper, seemed to cut through the air and then ring in the room
he said:—

> 'How dare you touch him, any of you? How dare you cast eyes on
> him when I had forbidden it? Back, I tell you all! This man belongs
> to me! Beware how you meddle with him, or you'll have to deal
> with me.' The fair girl, with a laugh of ribald coquetry, turned to
> answer him:—

> 'You yourself never loved; you never love!' On this the other women
> joined, and such a mirthless, hard, soulless laughter rang through
> the room that it almost made me faint to hear; it seemed like the
> pleasure of fiends. Then the Count turned, after looking at my face
> attentively, and said in a soft whisper:—

> 'Yes, I too can love; you yourselves can tell it from the past. Is it
> not so? Well, now I promise you that when I am done with him
> you shall kiss him at your will. Now go! go! I must awaken him, for
> there is work to be done.'

> 'Are we to have nothing tonight?' said one of them, with a low laugh,
> as she pointed to the bag which he had thrown upon the floor, and
> which moved as though there were some living thing within it. For
> answer he nodded his head. One of the women jumped forward and
> opened it. If my ears did not deceive me there was a gasp and a
> low wail, as of a half-smothered child. The women closed round,
> whilst I was aghast with horror; but as I looked they disappeared,
> and with them the dreadful bag. There was no door near them, and
> they could not have passed me without my noticing. They simply
> seemed to fade into the rays of the moonlight and pass out through
> the window, for I could see outside the dim, shadowy forms for a
> moment before they entirely faded away.

Then the horror overcame me, and I sank down unconscious. [. . .]

Research one of the following two concepts: (1) Physiognomy and criminality in the Victorian period or (2) Anti-semitism in the Victorian period. How do the details of Jonathan Harker's description of Dracula connect to these concepts?

As with *Frankenstein*, *Dracula* has been adapted to film numerous times. Each time, the Count looks different. Examine the pictures included in the selection, and, if possible, watch one of *Dracula's* film adaptations. In small groups discuss the various representations of Dracula. What elements of his appearance are consistent? Which are unique to particular adaptations? Does the vampire's appearance stay true to the cultural and historical context of Stoker's novel (late Victorian England), or does the context in which the movie was made influence Dracula's physical characteristics and mannerisms? Consider clothing, makeup, body language, posture, facial expressions, and any other physical features. After considering these features, prepare a short presentation in which you use one of the images above or another image of a movie vampire to support an interpretation of Dracula's appearance.

Bram Stoker's *Dracula* sometimes appears to be a very inhuman monster, as when he climbs lizard-like down the castle wall. However, many film adaptations of Dracula make him seem more human. Why would films make this change? Brainstorm a list that compares the representations of Dracula's humanity and monstrosity to the representations of Frankenstein's creature in the novel and subsequent film adaptations. In what ways do the films make these characters seem more monstrous? More human?

The werewolf, which is most commonly male, may be a reflection on masculinity, but what about the vampire? How does *Dracula* corroborate or challenge masculinity and masculine sexual norms? Alternately, while Count Dracula is the primary monster of Stoker's story, many audiences have found the female vampires more monstrous than the Count. How do the "Weird Sisters" reflect on concepts of femininity? In what ways do Dracula and the Weird Sisters invert their gender roles? Write a research paper that makes an argument about the connection between gender roles and monstrosity in this novel. You may want to research such concepts as sexual inversion, the Flaneur, the Angel in the House, the Fallen Woman, and the New Woman.

The following article comes from the introductory chapter to Skin Shows: An Introduction to Gothic Monstrosity. *Its author, Judith Halberstam, is a professor of English who specializes in gender studies. Since its publication in 1995,* Skin Shows *has had a strong influence over how scholars think about both novels and films that feature monsters. It has also contributed important ideas to an area of study known as queer theory. Instead of treating sexuality and gender as universal concepts, queer theory approaches ideas such as "heterosexual" and "homosexual" as well as "male" and "female" as labels that convey the assumptions and prejudices of particular cultural and historical contexts. Halberstam's book isn't written for a general audience: it presents academic arguments that rely both implicitly and explicitly on concepts familiar to scholars who study literature, film, and queer theory. Parts of it are therefore likely to be difficult for readers who are new to such study, but the difficulty pays off with a sophisticated understanding of monsters' social significance.*

Although Halberstam's work makes important claims about the ways monsters both reflect on and help to shape social constructions of human sexuality, it doesn't consider sexuality in a vacuum. Like the work by Jeffrey Jerome Cohen included in this book, it focuses on ways monsters represent Otherness, "the deviant subjectivities opposite which the normal, the healthy, and the pure can be known." According to Halberstam, monsters "can represent gender, race, nationality, class, and sexuality in one body... Monsters have to be everything the human is not and, in producing the negative of human, [they] make way for the invention of the human as white, male, middle class, and heterosexual." In other words, representations of inhuman monstrosity include many aspects of human identity, and in doing so, they mark certain categories of people as inhuman. Only straight white men with money—arguably the most powerful category of people in the English-speaking world—end up looking fully human. As you read, pay particular attention to Halberstam's discussion of "how sexuality became the dominant mark of otherness" rather than marks of otherness such as gender, race, nationality, and class.

PARASITES AND PERVERTS
AN INTRODUCTION TO GOTHIC MONSTROSITY

BY JUDITH HALBERSTAM

So many monsters; so little time.
—promotional slogan for HELLRAISER

SKIN SHOWS

In *The Silence of the Lambs* (1991) by Jonathan Demme, one of many modern adaptations of *Frankenstein*, a serial killer known as Buffalo Bill collects women in order to flay them and use their skins to construct a "woman suit."

Sitting in his basement sewing hides, Buffalo Bill makes his monster a sutured beast, a patchwork of gender, sex, and sexuality. Skin, in this morbid scene, represents the monstrosity of surfaces and as Buffalo Bill dresses up in his suit and prances in front of the mirror, he becomes a layered body, a body of many surfaces laid one upon the other. Depth and essence dissolve in this mirror dance and identity and humanity become skin deep.

My subject is monsters and I begin in Buffalo Bill's basement, his "filthy workshop of creation," because it dramatizes precisely the distance traveled between current representations of monstrosity and their genesis in nineteenth-century Gothic fiction. Where the monsters of the nineteenth century metamorphized modern subjectivity as a balancing act between inside/outside, female/male, body/mind, native/foreign, proletarian/aristocrat, monstrosity in postmodern horror films finds its place in what Baudrillard has called the obscenity of "immediate visibility"[1] and what Linda Williams has dubbed "the frenzy of the visible."[2] The immediate visibility of a Buffalo Bill, the way in which he makes the surface itself monstrous transforms the cavernous monstrosity of Jekyll/Hyde, Dorian Gray, or Dracula into a beast who is all body and no soul.

Victorian monsters produced and were produced by an emergent conception of the self as a body which enveloped a soul, as a body, indeed, enthralled to its soul. Michel Foucault writes in *Discipline and Punish* that "the soul is the prison of the body" and he proposes a genealogy of the soul that will show it to be born out of "methods of punishment, supervision and constraint."[3] Foucault also claims that, as modern forms of discipline shifted their gaze from the body to the soul, crime literature moved from confession or gallows speeches or the cataloguing of famous criminals to the detective fiction obsessed with identifying criminality and investigating crime. The hero of such literature was now the middle- or upper-class schemer whose crime became a virtuoso performance of skill and enterprise.

There are many congruities between Gothic fiction and detective fiction but in the Gothic, crime is embodied within a specifically deviant form—the monster—that announces itself (de-monstrates) as the place of corruption. Furthermore, just as the detective character appears across genres in many different kinds of fiction (in the sensation novel, in Dickens), so Gothic infiltrates the Victorian novel as a symptomatic moment in which boundaries between good and evil, health and perversity, crime and punishment, truth and deception, inside and outside, dissolve and threaten the integrity of the narrative itself. While many literary histories, therefore, have relegated Gothic to a subordinate status in relation to realism, I will be arguing that nineteenth-century literary tradition *is* a Gothic tradition and that this has everything to do with the changing technologies of subjectivity that Foucault describes.

Gothic fiction is a technology of subjectivity, one which produces the deviant subjectivities opposite which the normal, the healthy, and the pure can be known. Gothic, within my analysis, may be loosely defined as the rhetorical style and narrative structure designed to produce fear and desire within the reader. The production of fear in a literary text (as opposed to a cinematic text) emanates from a vertiginous excess of meaning. Gothic, in a way, refers to an ornamental excess (think of Gothic architecture—gargoyles and crazy loops and spirals), a rhetorical extravagance that produces, quite simply, too much. Within Gothic novels, I argue, multiple interpretations are embedded in the text and part of the experience of horror comes from the realization that meaning itself runs riot. Gothic novels produce a symbol for this interpretive mayhem in the body of the monster. The monster always becomes a primary focus of interpretation and its monstrosity seems available for any number of meanings.

Within the nineteenth-century Gothic, authors mixed and matched a wide variety of signifiers of difference to fabricate the deviant body—Dracula, Jekyll/Hyde, and even Frankenstein's monster before them are lumpen bodies, bodies pieced together out of the fabric of race, class, gender, and sexuality. In the modern period and with the advent of cinematic body horror, the shift from the literary Gothic to the visual Gothic was accompanied by a narrowing rather than a broadening of the scope of horror. One might expect to find that cinema multiplies the possibilities for monstrosity but in fact, the visual register can only imagine the dreadful spectacle of the monster and so its monstrosity is limited only by the reader's imagination; in the horror film, the monster must always fail to be monstrous enough and horror therefore depends upon the explicit violation of female bodies as opposed to simply the sight of the monster.

Furthermore, as I noted, while nineteenth-century Gothic monstrosity was a combination of the features of deviant race, class, and gender, within contemporary horror, the monster, for various reasons, tends to show clearly the markings of deviant sexualities and gendering but less clearly the signs of class or race. Buffalo Bill in *The Silence of the Lambs*, for example, leads one to suppose that the monstrous body is a sexed or gendered body only, but this particular body, a borrowed skin, is also clearly inscribed with a narrative of class conflict. To give just one example of deviant class in this film, the heroine, Clarice Starling, is identified by Hannibal Lecter as a woman trying to hide her working-class roots behind "bad perfume" and cheap leather shoes. Given the emphasis in this film upon skins and hides, it is all too significant that cheap leather gives Starling away. Poor skin, in this film, literally signifies poverty, or the trace of it. As we will see, however, the narrative of monstrous class identity has been almost completely subsumed within *The Silence of the Lambs* by monstrous sexuality and gender.

The discourse of racialized monstrosity within the modern horror film proves to be a discursive minefield. Perhaps because race has been so successfully Gothicized within our recent history, filmmakers and screenplay writers tend not to want to make a monster who is defined by a deviant racial identity. European anti-Semitism and American racism towards black Americans are precisely Gothic discourses given over to the making monstrous of particular kinds of bodies.

To give an example of what I am arguing here, one can look at a contemporary horror film, *Candyman* (1990), and the way it merges monstrosity and race.

In *Candyman* two female graduate students in anthropology at the University of Illinois at Chicago are researching urban legends when they run across the story of Candyman, the ghost of a murdered black man who haunts the Cabrini Green projects. Candyman was the son of a former slave who made good by inventing a procedure for the mass production of shoes. Despite his wealth, Candyman still ran into trouble with the white community by falling in love with a white woman. He was chased by white men to Cabrini Green where they caught him, cut his right hand off, and drove a hook into the bloody stump. Next Candyman was covered in honey and taken to an apiary where the bees killed him. Now, the urban myth goes, Candyman responds to all who call him. The two researchers, a white woman and a black woman, go to Cabrini Green to hunt for information on Candyman. Naturally, the black woman, Bernadette, is killed by Candyman, and the white woman, Helen, is seduced by him. While the film on some level attempts to direct all kinds of social criticisms at urban planners, historians, and racist white homeowners, ultimately the horror stabilizes in the ghastly body of the black man whose monstrosity turns upon his desire for the white woman and his murderous intentions towards black women.

No amount of elaborate framing within this film can prevent it from confirming racist assumptions about black male aggression towards white female bodies. Monstrosity, in this tired narrative, never becomes mobile; rather, it remains anchored by the weight of racist narratives. The film contains some clever visual moves, like a shot of Helen going through the back of a mirror into a derelict apartment. She next passes through a graffiti painting of a black man's face. She stops for a moment in the mouth of the black man and this startling image hints at the various forms of oral transmissions that the film circulates. Is Helen contained by the oral history of the Candyman or is she the articulate voice of the academy that disrupts its transmission and brings violence to the surface? Inevitably, Helen's character stabilizes under the sign of the white woman victim and Candyman's horror becomes a static signifier of black male violence. If race in nineteenth-century Gothic was one of many clashing surfaces of monstrosity, in the context of twentieth-century Gothic, race becomes a master signifier of monstrosity and when invoked, it blocks out all other possibilities of monstrous identity.

The fact that monstrosity within contemporary horror seems to have stabilized into an amalgam of sex and gender demonstrates the need to read a history of otherness into and out of the history of Gothic fiction. Gothic fiction of the nineteenth century specifically used the body of the monster to produce race, class, gender, and sexuality within narratives about the relation between subjectivities and certain bodies.

Monstrosity (and the fear it gives rise to) is historically conditioned rather than a psychological universal. While the horror within *Frankenstein* seemed to depend upon the monster's actual hideous physical aspect, his status as anomaly, and his essential foreignness, the threat of Buffalo Bill depends upon the violence of his identity crisis, a crisis that will exact a price in female flesh. Buffalo Bill's identity crisis is precisely that, a crisis of knowledge, a "category crisis"[4]; but it no longer takes the form of the anomaly—now a category crisis indicates a crisis of sexual identity.

It is in the realm of sexuality, however, that Buffalo Bill and Frankenstein's monster seem to share traits and it is here that we may be inclined to read Buffalo Bill as a reincarnation of many of the features of nineteenth-century monstrosity. As a sexual being, Frankenstein's monster is foreign and as an outsider to the community, his foreign sexuality is monstrous and threatens miscegenation. Frankenstein's lonely monster is driven out of town by the mob when he threatens to reproduce. Similarly, Buffalo Bill threatens the community with his indeterminate gender and sexuality. Indeed, sexuality and its uneasy relation to gender identity creates Buffalo Bill's monstrosity. But much ground has been traveled between the stitched monstrosity of Frankenstein and the sutured gender horror of Buffalo Bill; while both monsters have been sewn into skin bodysuits and while both want to jump out of their skins, the nineteenth-century monster is marked by racial or species violation while Buffalo Bill seems to be all gender. If we measure one skin job against the other, we can read transitions between various signifying systems of identity.

Skin, becomes a kind of metonym for the human; and its color, its pallor, its shape mean everything within a semiotic of monstrosity. Skin might be too tight (Frankenstein's creature), too dark (Hyde), too pale (Dracula), too superficial (Dorian Gray's canvas), too loose (Leatherface), or too sexed (Buffalo Bill). Skin houses the body and it is figured in Gothic as the ultimate boundary, the material that divides the insides from the outside. The vampire will puncture and mark the skin with his fangs, Mr. Hyde will covet white skin, Dorian Gray will desire his own canvas, Buffalo Bill will covet female skin, Leatherface will wear his victim's skin as a trophy and recycle his flesh as food. Slowly but surely the outside becomes the inside and the hide no longer conceals or contains, it offers itself up as a text, as body, as monster. The Gothic text, whether novel or film, plays out an elaborate skin show.

How sexuality became the dominant mark of otherness is a question that we may begin to answer by deconstructing Victorian Gothic monsters and examining the constitutive features of the horror they represent. If, for example, many nineteenth-century monsters seem to produce fears more clearly related to racial identity than gender identity, how is it that we as modern readers have been unable to discern these more intricate contours of difference? Obviously, the answer to such a question and many others like it lies in a history of sexuality, a history introduced by Michel Foucault and continued by recent studies which link Foucault's work to a history of the novel.[5]

Where sexuality becomes an identity, other "others" become invisible and the multiple features of monstrosity seem to degenerate back into a primeval sexual slime. Class, race, and nation are subsumed, in other words, within the monstrous sexual body; accordingly, Dracula's bite drains pleasure rather than capital, Mr. Hyde symbolizes repression rather than the production of self, and both figure foreign aspect as a threat to domestic security.

The body that scares and appalls changes over time, as do the individual characteristics that add up to monstrosity, as do the preferred interpretations of that monstrosity. Within the traits that make a body monstrous—that is, frightening or ugly, abnormal or disgusting—we may read the difference between an other and a self, a pervert and a normal person, a foreigner and a native.

GOTHIC GNOMES

In her 1832 introduction to *Frankenstein*, Shelley writes, "I bid my hideous progeny go forth and prosper."[7] Shelley's "hideous progeny" was not merely her novel but the nineteenth-century Gothic novel itself. The Gothic, of course, did indeed prosper and thrive through the century. It grew in popularity until, by the turn of the century, its readership was massive enough that a writer could actually make a living from the sale of his Gothic works. In 1891, for example, Robert Louis Stevenson loosed his "shilling shocker," *Dr. Jekyll and Mr. Hyde*, upon the reading public hoping for commercial returns. Stevenson described his novella as a "Gothic gnome" and worried that he had produced a gross distortion of literature.[8] Such an anxiety marked Gothic itself as a monstrous form in relation to its popularity and its improper subject matter. The appellation "Gothic gnome" labeled the genre as a mutation or hybrid form of true art and genteel literature.

But monsters do indeed sell books and books sell monsters and the very popularity of the Gothic suggests that readers and writers collaborate in the production of the features of monstrosity. Gothic novels, in fact, thematize the monstrous aspects of both production and consumption—*Frankenstein* is, after all, an allegory about a production that refuses to submit to its author and *Dracula* is a novel about an arch-consumer, the vampire, who feeds upon middle-class women and then turns them into vampires by forcing them to feed upon him. The Gothic, in fact, like the vampire itself, creates a public who consumes monstrosity, who revels in it, and who then surveys its individual members for signs of deviance or monstrosity, excess or violence.

Anxiety about the effects of consuming popular literature revealed itself in England in the 1890s in the form of essays and books which denounced certain works as "degenerate" (a label defined by Max Nordau's book *Degeneration*).[9] Although Gothic fiction obviously fell into this category, the censors missed the mark in denouncing such works. Rather than condoning the perversity they recorded, Gothic authors, in fact, seemed quite scrupulous about taking a moral stand against the unnatural acts that produce monstrosity. Long sentimental sermons on truth and purity punctuate many a gruesome tale and leave few doubts as to its morality by the narrative's end. Bram Stoker, for example, sermonizes both in his novels and in an essay printed in the journal *The Nineteenth Century* called "The Censorship of Fiction." In this essay, Stoker calls for stricter surveillance of popular fiction and drama. Stoker thinks censorship would combat human weakness on two levels, namely, "the weakness of the great mass of people who form audiences, and of those who are content to do base things in the way of catering for these base appetites." Obviously, Stoker did not expect his own writing to be received as a work that "catered to base appetites"[10] because, presumably, it used perverse sexuality to identify what or who threatened the dominant class.

Similarly, Oscar Wilde was shocked by the critics who called *The Picture of Dorian Gray* "poisonous" and "heavy with the mephitic odours of moral and spiritual putrefecation." Wilde's novel, after all, tells the story of a young man seduced by a poisonous book and punished soundly for his corruptions. Wilde defends his work by saying, "It was necessary, sir, for the dramatic development of this story to surround Dorian Gray with an atmosphere of moral corruption." He continues, "Each man sees his own sin in Dorian Gray."[11]

Producing and consuming monsters and monstrous fictions, we might say, adds up to what Eve Sedgwick has called, in her study of Gothic conventions, "an aesthetic of pleasurable fear."[12] The Gothic, in other words, inspires fear and desire at the same time—fear of and desire for the other, fear of and desire for the possibly latent perversity lurking within the reader herself. But fear and desire within the same body produce a disciplinary effect. In other words, a Victorian public could consume Gothic novels in vast quantities without regarding such a material as debased because Gothic gave readers the thrill of reading about so-called perverse activities while identifying aberrant sexuality as a condition of otherness and as an essential trait of foreign bodies. The monster, of course, marks the distance between the perverse and the supposedly disciplined sexuality of a reader. Also, the signifiers of "normal" sexuality maintain a kind of hegemonic power by remaining invisible.

So, the aesthetic of pleasurable fear that Sedgwick refers to makes pleasure possible only by fixing horror elsewhere, in an obviously and literally foreign body, and by then articulating the need to expel the foreign body. Thus, both Dracula and Hyde are characters with markedly foreign physiognomies; they are dark and venal, foreign in both aspect and behavior. Dracula, for example, is described by Harker as an angular figure with a strong face notable for "peculiarly arched nostrils . . . a lofty domed forehead," bushy hair and eyebrows, "sharp white teeth," and ears pointed at the tops.[13] Hyde is described as small and deformed, "pale and dwarfish . . . troglodytic."[14] By making monstrosity so obviously a physical condition and by linking it to sexual corruption, such fictions bind foreign aspects to perverse activities.

The most telling example I can find of a monstrous foreigner in Gothic is Bram Stoker's Count Dracula who obviously comes to England from a distant "elsewhere" in search of English blood. Critics have discussed at length the perverse and dangerous sexuality exhibited by the vampire but, with a few exceptions, criticism has not connected Dracula's sexual attacks with the threat of the foreign. Dracula, I argue in my fourth chapter, condenses the xenophobia of Gothic fiction into a very specific horror—the vampire embodies and exhibits all the stereotyping of nineteenth-century anti-Semitism. The anatomy of the vampire, for example, compares remarkably to anti-Semitic studies of Jewish physiognomy—peculiar nose, pointed ears, sharp teeth, claw-like hands—and furthermore, in Stoker's novel, blood and money (central facets in anti-Semitism) mark the corruption of the vampire. The vampire merges Jewishness and monstrosity and represents this hybrid monster as a threat to Englishness and English womanhood in particular. In the Jew, then, Gothic fiction finds a monster versatile enough to represent fears about race, nation, and sexuality, a monster who combines in one body fears of the foreign and the perverse.

PERVERSION AND PARASITISM

Within nineteenth-century anti-Semitism, the Jew was marked as a threat to capital, to masculinity, and to nationhood. Jews in England at the turn of the century were the objects of an internal colonization. While the black African became the threatening other abroad, it was closer to home that people focused their real fears about the collapse of the nation through a desire for racial homogeneity.[15] Jews were referred to as "degenerate," the bearers of syphilis, hysterical, neurotic, as blood-suckers and, on a more practical level, Jews were viewed as middlemen in business.[16] Not all Gothic novels are as explicit as *Dracula* about their identification of monster and Jew. In some works we can read a more generalized code of fear which links horror to the Oriental[17] and in others we must interpret a bodily semiotic that marks monsters as symbols of a diseased culture. But to understand better how the history of the Gothic novel charges the entanglement of race, nation, and sexuality in productions of otherness, we might consider the Gothic monster as the antithesis of "Englishness."

Benedict Anderson has written about the cultural roots of the nation in terms of "imagined communities" which are "conceived in language, not in blood."[18] By linking the development of a print industry, particularly the popularization of novels and newspapers, to the spread of nationalism, Anderson pays close attention to the ways in which a shared conception of what constitutes "nation-ness" is written and read across certain communities. If the nation, therefore, is a textual production which creates national community in terms of an inside and an outside and then makes those categories indispensable, Gothic becomes one place to look for a fiction of the foreign, a narrative of who and what is not-English and not-native. The racism that becomes a mark of nineteenth-century Gothic arises out of the attempt within horror fiction to give form to what terrifies the national community. Gothic monsters are defined both as other than the imagined community and as the being that cannot be imagined as community.

"Racism and anti-Semitism," Anderson writes, "manifest themselves, not across national boundaries, but within them. In other words, they justify not so much foreign ward as domestic oppression and domination" (136). The racism and anti-Semitism that I have identified as a hallmark of nineteenth-century Gothic literature certainly direct themselves towards a domestic rather than a foreign scene. Gothic in the 1890s, as represented by the works of Robert Louis Stevenson, Bram Stoker, and Oscar Wilde, takes place in the backstreets of London in laboratories and asylums, in old abandoned houses and decaying city streets, in hospitals and bedrooms, in homes and gardens.

The monster, such a narrative suggests, will find you in the intimacy of your own home; indeed, it will make your home its home (or you its home) and alter forever the comfort of domestic privacy. The monster peeps through the window, enters through the back door, and sits beside you in the parlor; the monster is always invited in but never asked to stay. The racism that seems to inhere to the nineteenth-century Gothic monster, then, may be drawn from imperialistic or colonialist fantasies of other lands and peoples, but it concentrates its imaginative force upon the other peoples in "our" lands, the monsters at home. The figure of the parasite becomes paramount within Gothic precisely because it is an internal not an external danger that Gothic identifies and attempts to dispel.

The Gothic novel, I have been arguing, establishes the terms of monstrosity that were to be, and indeed were in the process of being, projected onto all who threatened the interests of a dwindling English nationalism. As the English empire stretched over oceans and continents, the need to define an essential English character became more and more pressing. Non-nationals, like Jews, for example, but also like the Irish or Gypsies, came to be increasingly identified by their alien natures and the concept of "foreign" became ever more closely associated with a kind of parasitical monstrosity, a non-reproductive sexuality, and an anti-English character. Gothic monsters in the 1880s and 1890s made parasitism—vampirism—the defining characteristic of horror. The parasitical nature of the beast might be quite literal, as in Stoker's vampire, or it might be a more indirect trait, as suggested by the creeping and homeless Hyde; it might be defined by a homoerotic influence, as exerted by Dorian Gray. Parasitism, especially with regards to the vampire, represents a bad or pathological sexuality, non-reproductive sexuality, a sexuality that exhausts and wastes and exists prior to and outside of the marriage contract.

The ability of race ideology and sexology to create a new elite to replace the aristocracy also allows for the staging of historical battles within the body. This suggests how Gothic monstrosity may intersect with, participate in, and resist the production of a theory of racial superiority. The Gothic monster—Frankenstein's creature, Hyde, Dorian Gray, and Dracula—represents the dramatization of the race question and of sexology in their many different incarnations. If Frankenstein's monster articulates the injustice of demonizing one's own productions, Hyde suggests that the most respectable bodies may be contaminated by bad blood; and if Dorian Gray's portrait makes an essential connection between the homosexual and the uncanny, Dracula embodies once and for all the danger of the hybrid race and the perverse sexuality within the form of the vampire.

THE POWER OF HORROR

In Gothic, as in many areas of Victorian culture, sexual material was not repressed but produced on a massive scale, as Michel Foucault has argued.[19] The narrative, then, that professed outrage at acts of sexual perversion (the nightly wanderings of Hyde, for example, or Dracula's midnight feasts) in fact produced a catalogue of perverse sexuality by first showcasing the temptations of the flesh in glorious technicolor and then by depicting so-called normal sex as a sickly enterprise devoid of all passion. One has only to think of the contrast between Mina Harker's encounter with Count Dracula—she is found lapping at blood from his breast—and her sexually neutral, maternal relations with her husband.

The production of sexuality as identity and as the inversion of identity (perversion—a turning away from identity) in Gothic novels consolidates normal sexuality by defining it in contrast to its monstrous manifestations. Horror, I have suggested, exercises power even as it incites pleasure and/or disgust. Horror, indeed, has a power closely related to its pleasure-producing function and the twin mechanism of pleasure-power perhaps explains how it is that Gothic may empower some readers even as it disables others. An example of how Gothic appeals differently to readers may be found in contemporary slasher movies like *The Texas Chainsaw Massacre* (1974) and *Halloween* (1978). Critics generally argue that these films inspire potency in a male viewer and incredible vulnerability in a female viewer. However, the mechanisms of Gothic narrative never turn so neatly around gender identifications. A male viewer of the slasher film, like a male reader of the nineteenth-century Gothic, may find himself on the receiving end of countless acts of degradation in relation to monstrosity and its powers while the female reader and spectator may be able to access a surprising source of power through monstrous forms and monstrous genres.

In her psychoanalytic study of fear, *Powers of Horror*, Julia Kristeva defines horror in terms of "abjection." The abject, she writes, is "something rejected from which one does not part, from which one does not protect oneself as from an object. Imaginary uncanniness and real threat, it beckons to us and ends up engulfing us."[20] In a chapter on the writings of Celine, Kristeva goes on to identify abjection with the Jew of anti-Semitic discourse. Anti-Semitic fantasy, she suggests, elevates Jewishness to both mastery and weakness, to "sex tinged with femininity and death" (185).

The Jew, for Kristeva, anchors abjection within a body, a foreign body that retains a certain familiarity and that therefore confuses the boundary between self and other. The connection that Kristeva makes between psychological categories and socio-political processes leads her to claim that anti-Semitism functions as a receptacle for all kinds of fears—sexual, political, national, cultural, economic. This insight is important to the kinds of arguments that I am making about the economic function of the Gothic monster. The Jew in general within anti-Semitism is Gothicized or transformed into a figure of almost universal loathing who haunts the community and represents its worst fears. By making the Jew supernatural, Gothic anti-Semitism actually makes Jews into spooks and Jew-hating into a psychological inevitability. The power of literary horror, indeed, lies in its ability to transform political struggles into psychological conditions and then to blur the distinction between the two. Literary horror, or Gothic, I suggest, uses the language of race hatred (most obviously anti-Semitism) to characterize monstrosity as a representation of psychological disorder. To understand the way monster may be equated with Jew or foreigner or non-English national, we need to historicize Gothic metaphors like vampire and parasite. We also have to read the effacement of the connection between monster and foreigner alongside the articulation of monster as a sexual category.

THE RETURN OF THE REPRESSED

In an introduction to *Studies on Hysteria* written in 1893, Freud identifies the repressed itself as a foreign body. Noting that hysterical symptoms replay some original trauma in response to an accident, Freud explains that the memory of trauma "acts like a foreign body which, long after its entry, must continue to be regarded as an agent that is still at work."[21] In other words, until an original site of trauma reveals itself in therapy, it remains foreign to body and mind but active in both. The repressed, then, figures as a sexual secret that the body keeps from itself and it figures as foreign because what disturbs the body goes unrecognized in the mind.

The fiction that Freud tells about the foreign body as the repressed connects remarkably with the fiction Gothic tells us about monsters as foreigners. Texts, like bodies, store up memories of past fears, of distant traumas. "Hysterics," writes Freud, "suffer mainly from reminiscences" (7). History, personal and social, haunts hysterics and the repressed always takes on an uncanny life of its own. Freud here has described the landscape of his own science—foreignness is repressed into the depths of an unconscious, a kind of cesspool of forgotten memories, and it rises to the surface as a sexual disturbance. Psychoanalysis gothicizes sexuality; that is to say, it creates a body haunted by a monstrous sexuality and forced into repressing its Gothic secrets. Psychoanalysis, in the Freudian scenario, is a sexual science able to account for and perhaps cure Gothic sexualities. Gothicization in this formula, then, is the identification of bodies in terms of what they are not. A Gothic other stabilizes sameness, a gothicized body is one that disrupts the surface-depth relationship between the body and the mind. It is the body that must be spoken, identified, or eliminated.

THE TECHNOLOGY OF MONSTERS

Monsters are meaning machines. They can represent gender, race, nationality, class, and sexuality in one body. And even within these divisions of identity, the monster can still be broken down. Dracula, for example, can be read as an aristocrat, a symbol of the masses; he is predator and yet feminine, he is consumer and producer, he is parasite and host, he is homosexual and heterosexual, he is even a lesbian. Monsters and the Gothic fiction that creates them are therefore technologies, narrative technologies that produce the perfect figure for negative identity. Monsters have to be everything the human is not and, in producing the negative of human, these novels make way for the invention of human as white, male, middle class, and heterosexual.

The monster always represents the disruption of categories, the destruction of boundaries, and the presence of impurities and so we need monsters to recognize and celebrate our own monstrosities. [. . .]

Notes

1. Jean Baudrillard, "The Ecstasy of Communication," in *The Anti-Aesthetic: Essays on Postmodern Culture*, ed. Hal Foster (Port Townsend, Wash.: Bay Press, 1983), 130. Baudrillard writes: "Obscenity begins precisely when there is no more spectacle, no more

scene when all becomes transparence and immediate visibility, when everything is exposed to the harsh and inexorable light of information and communication."

2. Linda Williams, *Hard Core: Power, Pleasure and the "Frenzy of the Visible"* (Berkeley and Los Angeles: University of California Press, 1989).

3. Michel Foucault, *Discipline and Punish: The Birth of the Prison*, trans. Alan Sheridan (New York: Vintage, 1979), 30, 29.

4. This term is coined by Marjorie Garber in Vested Interests: Cross-Dressing and Cultural Anxiety (New York: Routledge, 1992), 16. In this study of transvestism, Garber suggests that the cross-dresser and the transsexual provoke category crises that are displaced onto the place of gender and ambiguity. This argument is useful to the claim that I make that all difference in modernity has been subsumed under the aegis of sexual difference.

5. Most notable, for my purposes, among such studies are Nancy Armstrong's *Desire and Domestic Fiction: A Political History of the Novel* (New York and Oxford: Oxford University Press, 1987) and David A. Miller's *The Novel and the Police* (Berkeley and Los Angeles: University of California Press, 1988).

6. Claire Kahane, "Gothic Mirrors and Feminine Identity," *The Centennial Review* 24 (1980): 43–64.

7. Mary Shelley, *Frankenstein or The Modern Prometheus* (1831; reprint, ed. M. K. Joseph, New York and Oxford: Oxford University Press, 1980), 10.

8. See Patrick Brantlinger and Richard Boyle, "The Education of Edward Hyde: Stevenson's 'Gothic Gnome' and the Mass Readership of Late Victorian England," in *100 Years of Dr. Jekyll and Mr. Hyde*, ed. Gordon Hirsch and William Veeder (Chicago: University of Chicago Press, 1988).

9. Max Simon Nordau, *Degeneration* (New York: D. Appleton and Co., 1895).

10. Bram Stoker, "The Censorship of Fiction" *The Nineteenth Century* (September 1908): 4810.

11. See the introduction to Oscar Wilde, *The Picture of Dorian Gray* (1891; reprint, ed. and with an introduction by Isobel Murray, Oxford and New York: Oxford University Press, 1981).

12. Eve Kosofsky Sedgwick, *The Coherence of Gothic Conventions* (New York and London: Methuen, 1986), vi.

13. Bram Stoker, *Dracula* (1897; reprint, New York: Bantam, 1981), 18.

14. Robert Louis Stevenson, *The Strange Case of Dr. Jekyll and Mr. Hyde* (1886; reprint, New York: Bantam, 1981), 18.

15. In an article on the influence of Spanish models of nationhood upon English debates of "the Jewish question," Michel Ragussis looks at nineteenth-century novels like *Ivanhoe* and their positioning of questions of nationhood alongside calls for Jewish assimilation: "By depicting the persecution of the Jews at a critical moment in history—the founding of the English nation-state—*Ivanhoe* located 'the Jewish question' at the heart of English national identity" (478). See "The Birth of a Nation in Victorian Culture: The Spanish

Inquisition, the Converted Daughter, and the 'Secret Race,'" *Critical Inquiry* 20 (spring 1994): 477–508.

16. See, for example, Henry Arthur Jones, "Middlemen and Parasites," *The New Review* 8 (June 1893): 645–54; and "The Dread of the Jew," *The Spectator* 83 (September 9, 1899): 338–39, where the author discusses references made in popular periodicals of the time to Jews as "a parasitical race with no ideals beyond precious metals." "Parasite" and "degenerate" became coded synonyms for Jews in such literature.

17. See, for example, Richard Marsh, *The Beetle* (1897), in *Victorian Villainies*, ed. Graham Greene and Sir Hugh Greene (New York: Penguin, 1984). For an excellent article on this little-known Gothic text, see Kelly Hurley, "'The Inner Chambers of All Nameless Sin': *The Beetle*, Gothic Female Sexuality and Oriental Barbarism," in *Virginal Sexuality and Textuality in Victorian Literature*, ed. Lloyd Davis (Albany: State University of New York Press, 1993), 193–213.

18. Benedict Anderson, *Imagined Communities: Reflections on the Origin and Spread of Nationalism* (London and New York: Verso, 1983), 133.

19. Michel Foucault, *The History of Sexuality*, vol. 1, *An Introduction*, trans. Robert Hurley (New York: Vintage, 1980).

20. Julia Kristeva, *Powers of Horror: An Essay on Abjection*, trans. Leon S. Roudiez (New York: Columbia University Press, 1982), 4.

21. Sigmund Freud and Josef Brauer, *Studies on Hysteria* (1893; reprint, trans. and ed. James Strachey, New York: Basic, 1987), 6.

Halberstam argues that "the signifiers of 'normal' sexuality maintain a kind of hegemonic power by remaining invisible." First, use your library's resources and/or the Internet to find two or three definitions of "hegemonic" (alternately, "hegemony"). In your own words, what is "hegemonic power?" How could sexuality have this kind of power? Next, consider the ways "normal" sexuality can be invisible by searching the Internet for novels and films, some that feature gay characters and some that feature straight characters. How often do your results refer to straight characters or the stories they're in explicitly as "straight" or "heterosexual?" How often do your results refer to gay characters or the stories they're in *explicitly* as "gay" or "homosexual?" How do you explain the differences you discover? With your discoveries in mind, make a list of novels and films that you might classify as "straight." What difference does applying this label make in the ways people might perceive those texts?

Because "Parasites and Perverts" is the introduction of a book-length argument, most of the evidence for Halberstam's claims doesn't appear here. However, the history of monster stories offers much evidence that you might use to support her claims. Consider Halberstam's claim that "The Gothic text, whether novel or film, plays out an elaborate skin show" in which skin is "a kind of metonym for the human." First, what is a "metonym," and how is skin a "metonym for the human"? Next, brainstorm your own list of evidence that shows the significance of skin in monster stories. Finally, using what you've learned so far about monsters in novels and films, consider examples where skin is shown, discussed, or otherwise emphasized. What do these examples specifically reveal about the relationships among skin, monstrosity, and humanity?

Join a small group of students to discuss the many claims about monsters in "Parasites and Perverts." Individually, each group member should list at least three claims from the chapter that either were difficult to understand or would benefit from further explanation. As a group, compare your lists. If a claim appears on someone else's list that isn't on yours, elaborate, in your own words, on what that claim means. Similarly, your collaborators should explain ideas on your list that aren't on theirs. For claims that appear on everyone's lists, use library and Internet sources to look up any unfamiliar words, authors, or texts mentioned near where the claims appear in the chapter. Together, your group should finish with a much fuller understanding of Halberstam's argument.

"Parasites and Perverts" comments on many of the novels and films represented in this book, including the classic Gothic novels *Frankenstein, The Strange Case of Dr. Jekyll and Mr. Hyde,* and *Dracula* as well as the movies *Candyman* and *The Texas Chainsaw Massacre.* After considering the monsters in these texts and many others, Halberstam concludes, "The monster always represents the disruption of categories, the destruction of boundaries, and the presence of impurities and so we need monsters and need to recognize and celebrate our own monstrosities." Choose a monster from one of the novels or films with which you are now familiar, and write a short essay about something useful in the way the monster disrupts categories. Craft a thesis with a very specific claim about why we need this monster, and cite both the monster's original text and "Parasites and Perverts" as you demonstrate how the monster disrupts categories and why that disruption is valuable.

L. Andrew Cooper, an expert on Gothic fiction and horror films, is the author of Gothic Realities: The Impact of Horror Fiction on Modern Culture (2010), which traces the impacts of media violence from eighteenth-century print fictions through twenty-first century films. He also has a forthcoming book called Dario Argento, about the titular maestro of Italian horror. In addition to his focus on horror, Cooper writes and teaches about film studies, gender studies, and queer theory.

The following selection from Gothic Realities, which focuses on The Texas Chainsaw Massacre 2 and Buffy the Vampire Slayer, responds to questions about sexuality raised in texts such as Frankenstein, The Strange Case of Dr. Jekyll and Mr. Hyde, and Dracula as well as J. Sheridan LeFanu's Carmilla and Oscar Wilde's The Picture of Dorian Gray. Cooper argues that these texts participated in associating specific types of monstrosity with homosexuality, which became "a category that allowed defenders of the status quo to identify and attack communities that threatened to destroy established norms with their illicit sexual behavior." As a result, homosexuals were vilified by an equation that grew out of nineteenth century fiction and persists today: MONSTER = HOMOSEXUAL. As you read this selection, pay attention to ways in which Cooper engages with other writers who connect monstrosity and sexuality.

---

excerpt from

GOTHIC REALITIES: THE IMPACT OF HORROR FICTION ON MODERN CULTURE

BY L. ANDREW COOPER

ROMPS IN THE CLOSET

The Persistence of Nineteenth-Century Notions in Contemporary Pop Culture

THE TROUBLE WITH REVERSE DISCOURSE

The formula MONSTER = HOMOSEXUAL is a metaphor that merely visualizes the monstrosity already built into homosexuality as a social construct. Conceived as a pathological category, "homosexual" stigmatizes the people it names; with or without vampire fangs, an image or person labeled "homosexual" is implicitly monstrous. Of course, the meanings associated with any term are negotiable. When people adopt the label "homosexual" for themselves, they have the power to make it signify differently, to make it say something other than *monster*. Foucault explains:

> There is no question that the appearance in nineteenth-century psychiatry, jurisprudence, and literature of a whole series of discourses on the species and subspecies of homosexuality, inversion, pederasty, and "psychic hermaphrodism" made possible a strong advance of social controls into this area of "perversity"; but it also made possible the formation of a "reverse" discourse: homosexuality began to speak on its own behalf, to demand that its legitimacy or "naturality" be acknowledged, often in the same vocabulary, using the same categories by which it was medically disqualified.[1]

Cultural, legal, and scientific discourses of the nineteenth century constructed homosexuality as a pathology in order to identify and control it, but in doing so they created a language of selfhood that enabled people to understand, justify, and defend their desires.

Without such terms as "homosexual" and "gay," there could be no homophile and gay rights movements. The "queer theory" championed by Judith Halberstam, Lee Edelman, and others relies on a more recent instance of reverse discourse: once hurled as an insult meaning "abnormal," the label "queer" now functions as a starting point for attacks on the construction of normality and the insidious operations of heteronormativity. The term "heteronormativity" reflects a set of social norms that valorize opposite-sex relations by vilifying same-sex relations. A person (or subject) in heteronormative culture knows her- or himself not according to what she or he *is* but according to what she or he *isn't*. To be a straight, normal heterosexual is not *to have sex* with someone who has different genitalia; it is *to not have sex* with someone who has similar genitalia. Thus the heterosexual knows her- or himself through what Julia Kristeva describes as abjection, a process through which a person knows who "I" is by contrasting her or himself with the abject, which "has only one quality of the object—that of being opposed to *I*. According to this frightfully circular logic, the homosexual is the heterosexual's opposite, its abject, and the forces of heteronormativity (embodied in their extreme by the Traditional Values Coalition and the American Family Association) ensure that good heterosexual subjects define themselves as anything but homosexual and define the homosexual as anything but *I*.[2] Those who use "queer" as a position of empowered subjectivity, then, reverse the form of abjectification that constitutes the heterosexual/homosexual binary, making the heterosexual as "not I" and the queer as the subject defined as "*not* not-I." The queer "not not-I" takes a position that exposes and critiques the threats that heteronormativity poses to the queer social self.

Reverse discourses like queer theory function as interventions in history, redirections of the currents of historical meaning. They can resignify historical terminology, but they cannot erase history. The survival of pejorative meanings in "queer," "homosexual," and "gay" is manifest every time a tittering child on the animated television show *South Park* (or on the real-life playgrounds that the show lampoons) condemns something by saying "That's gay!" Reclaiming the queer,

the homosexual, and the monstrous as a viable and valorized category of identity isn't a simple, finite act. Queer theory has been celebrating queerness for decades, but the same queer celebrated in rarefied (and rare) academic circles faces a very real physical threat on Main Street U.S.A. A reverse discourse is a competing discourse, certainly, but its embrace of marginality is by definition distinct from the dominant discourse. When critics and artists try to elevate same-sex sexual relations through retrograde participation in the discourse of monstrosity, then, they risk reinforcing that monstrosity in mainstream culture. Harry M. Benshoff sums up this predicament in his study *Monsters in the Closet*:

> For example, some lesbians find *Basic Instinct*'s killer queer to be an empowering figure, rather than merely a negative stereotype . . . Ultimately, however, I would argue that the resultant connotative and cumulative effect of such images on non-queer spectators remains retrogressive . . . And even when the films themselves problematize these figures by linking them to social oppression . . .

they nonetheless still reaffirm for uncritical audiences the semiotic overlap of homosexual and violent killer.[3]

In other words, while a minority celebrates the powerful queerness embodied by cinematic monsters like the killer lesbians of *Basic Instinct*, the majority sees its fears and discrimination justified.

MONSTROUS EQUATIONS FROM DORIAN GRAY TO JEFFREY DAHMER

As Benshoff suggests, the primary obstacle confronting those who want to celebrate queer monsters in fiction and film is the monsters' lamentable tendency to kill people. Claiming that these monsters are good unfortunately implies that killing people is good. Oscar Wilde was already grappling with this problem when he wrote *The Picture of Dorian Gray*. If Dorian is, as countless critics have argued, homosexual, he is a homosexual monster, a debaucher of boys and the murderer of his artist-friend Basil. While Carmilla and Jekyll/Hyde's monstrosity appears on their bodies, Dorian's appears on his portrait. After having been kept from the portrait for a long time, Dorian's friend Basil sees it and remarks that it has developed "the face of a satyr" and "the eyes of a devil." The portrait becomes the outward manifestation of Dorian's inward monstrosity; Dorian explicitly identifies it as the "conscience" he denies and would "destroy."[4] The portrait therefore represents Dorian to himself and to Basil as the monster he believes his actions have made him. Haunted by his portrait-conscience, Dorian spirals into darkness, seeming to approach what Elaine Showalter calls "the only form of narrative closure thought appropriate to the Gay Gothic:" suicide.[5]

However, instead of turning his violence against himself, at the end of Wilde's novel Dorian attacks his portrait. Though the effort kills him, this attack on the portrait differs significantly from a suicide because, instead of trying to destroy the person (himself) whom society as judged a monster, he tries to destroy monstrosity's *image*. As Edward S. Brinkley argues, "the attack on the portrait . . . cannot be read as judgment on Dorian or as a suicide per se" but rather as an attack on "the realm in which the moral judgments made against Dorian *obtain*."[6] *Dorian Gray* represents the moral judgments of society in the portrait: if, as the interpretation offered by Wilde's prosecutors suggests, the portrait's pathological corruption represents "homosexuality" as the Victorians understood it, it does *not* represent the homosexual as someone with an intrinsically corrupted soul. The portrait, as an externalization of

Dorian's conscience, reflects Dorian's internalization of society's judgment, an internalization of what the twenty-first century would call homophobia. Dorian's attack on the portrait reflects a desire to purge the self-hatred imposed by Victorian culture. The culture proves more powerful, and Dorian dies in the attack.

Fighting against the pathological associations of homosexuality at the very moment of the concept's emergence, Dorian Gray could be interpreted as a homosexual monster/hero, someone whose supernatural pathology carries with it a perverse righteousness. Through it might help to account for why a novel about a putatively homosexual murderer holds a place of reverence in gay culture, this liberationist reading of Wilde's work presents a major problem: though the portrait my very well represent homosexuality, the "loathsome red dew" that appears on the portrait's hand after Dorian kills Basil also represents murder. At first glance, the blood on the portrait's hand may not seem problematic. The portrait's hand isn't Dorian's hand; if the portrait represents the culture's condemnation of Dorian, then the dewy blood is more directly on the culture's hand. Following this logic, the novel blames the culture for shelling out the shame that drives Dorian to murder Basil, for the murder only occurs after a look at the picture that Basil created fills him with "an uncontrollable feeling of hatred." In placing blame for Dorian's actions on the culturally-inflected portrait that inspires him, *Dorian Gray* does not remove all the blame from its (anti)hero. Dorian's culpability becomes visible when, after he dies, his body takes on the portrait's appearance.[7] Dorian's assumption in death of his portrait's visage inscribes the culture's crimes into his identity; it figures a retroactive justification of society's judgment. Through his murderous acts, Dorian reveals himself to be what society suspected him of being all along. Murder is therefore inextricable from the pattern of queer associations in Dorian's portrait and in Wilde's novel. Unless reverse discourse goes so far as to remove murder from ethical condemnation, the murderous queer monster is reprehensible even if his sexual aberration is, to some, heroic.

The real-life fate of a serial murderer and homosexual—Jeffrey Dahmer—offers a parallel to the fictional fate of Dorian Gray. Though an actual killer rather than a figure from Gothic fiction, Dahmer quickly entered the mythology with which American culture surrounds its madmen, taking the part of a Gothic villain. Just as Wilde's novel suggests that Dorian murders Basil because he has internalized his culture's homophobia, several analysts of Dahmer's case have suggested that Dahmer's string of homicides was a product of homophobia.[8] However, media coverage of the Dahmer case did not raise a public outcry against homophobia, but as Diana Fuss claims, "in the case of Jeffrey Dahmer, the 'homosexual-murderer-necrophilic-cannibal' equation . . . proved particularly fertile ground in the late twentieth century for activating old phobias and breeding new justifications for the recriminalization and repathologization of gay identity."[9] This paradoxical response—strengthening homophobia to combat homophobia's negative effects—indicates the intractability of the MONSTER = HOMOSEXUAL formula as well as its reflective corollary, HOMOSEXUAL = MONSTER. People who experience same-sex desire can work to reverse the pathologizing tendencies of "queer" and "homosexual" by taking on the labels in acts of resignification, but the dominant culture retains the power to resignify the resignifiers; in the mythologizing of Jeffrey Dahmer, "we see . . . a continuation of the colonizing of homosexuality by heterosexual culture, the conflation of heterosexuality with civilization and homosexuality with savagery."[10] The cultural response to Jeffrey Dahmer, the murderer and monster who had the misfortune to inherit the legacy of *Dorian Gray* a century later, demonstrates how reverse discourse ends up reinforcing the pathologies it seeks to undermine.

JUDITH HALBERSTAM'S *SKIN SHOWS* AND JOSS WHEDON'S *BUFFY THE VAMPIRE SLAYER*

Even the most well-meaning of cultural texts can fall victim to the intractability of the MONSTER = HOMOSEXUAL formula. The first book of a foundational queer theorist, Judith Halberstam's *Skin Shows* is very canny about how Gothic texts participate in the articulation of homosexuality, arguing that "monsters are meaning machines," and demonstrating, for example, how medical discourse "produces perversion in exactly the process that Jekyll uses to produce Hyde."[11] Halberstam's work exemplifies literary criticism's potential for denaturalizing homosexuality's negative associations in many ways, but in a reading of the 1986 film *The Texas Chainsaw Massacre 2*, it applies MONSTER = HOMOSEXUAL in order to make a larger point about the horror film and, in the process, reinforces the very association that it would undo.

The heroine of *Texas Chainsaw 2*, Stretch, goes through quite an ordeal. She survives several attacks by multiple maniacs, including a few unwelcome sexual advances from the film's eponymous chainsaw-wielding madman, Leatherface. She witnesses horror after horror: in one scene, she watches a good friend get skinned alive and then has to wear his face in order to avoid being butchered herself. At the end of the film, the only surviving maniac, Chop-Top, chases her through a massive labyrinth until, at the top of a tower-like structure, she discovers the rotten corpse of the maniacs' grandmother. Conveniently, this corpse has a chainsaw between her legs that Stretch is able to pick up and use to defend herself, which she does successfully, dispatching Chop-Top with a whirl of the roaring blade. Leatherface's use of the chainsaw repeatedly identifies it as a phallic symbol—at one point, he rubs an inactive saw between Stretch's legs and becomes sexually excited. When Stretch seizes the mother's chainsaw, she seizes a female phallus and fights the maniacs with a phallic power of her own.[12]

Halberstam accurately represents the film's storyline and its figuration of the chainsaw as a phallic power that women can seize to overcome their male persecutors, but she misrepresents the film's final image. After defeating Chop-Top, Stretch spins around madly, waving the chainsaw over her head in a fashion that exactly duplicates gestures that Leatherface makes throughout the *Texas Chainsaw* series. Halberstam reads this as a positive image of empowerment: "The chain saw has been sutured and grafted onto the female body, rendering it a queer body of violence and power, a monstrous body that has blades, makes noise, and refuses to splatter."[13] The chain saw does become an extension of Stretch's body, creating a phallic woman, but the film consistently associates phallic power with madness: the film's vigilante hero, Lefty (portrayed by Dennis Hopper, who has a tendency to play madmen), wields a chainsaw, behaves as insanely as the killers he hunts, and ultimately fails to accomplish anything. Representations of chainsaw-wielding maniacs throughout the film critique the dangers of violent, uncontrolled masculinity, and the female body that incorporates pathological masculine power shares in the pathology. Stretch is indeed empowered by seizing the phallus, but her empowerment is emphatically negative.

Stretch's traumatic ordeal drives her insane, causing her to identify with her attackers. She becomes a monstrous phallic woman, but the phallic woman in *Texas Chainsaw* is not necessarily a phallic lesbian. Stretch's monstrous body does not combine monstrosity with a "queer," or non-normative sexuality. No scene in the film suggests that she is attracted to women, and there are no verbal or visual cues that indicate that she might identify with lesbianism or any other non-normative sexual category. If "queer" identity is a category for those who refuse normative categories, affirming "not not-I" as an (anti)identity, Stretch never offers such a refusal or accepts such an (anti) identification. The only thing that might mark her as queer is the fact that, like Carmilla, she wields the phallus: Halberstam, not the text, attaches the queer label to her phallic transformation. While many representations from the nineteenth century forward associate deranged phallic women with lesbians and queers, this film, on its own, does nothing to duplicate or reinforce such associations. Halberstam claims that one of the purposes of her book is to imagine "a posthuman monstrosity that is partial, compromised, messy, and queer."[14] By forcing such a reading on *Texas Chainsaw 2*, Halberstam seems to want to reclaim "monstrosity" and relate it to queerness in a kind of valorizing reverse discourse. Because the film only associates pathology with its images of monstrosity, the monstrosity that Halberstam would reclaim is far from valorous. Halberstam's reading of *Texas Chainsaw Massacre 2* merely repeats the negative, homophobic association between non-normative sexuality and monstrosity.

Halberstam's treatment of *Texas Chainsaw 2* shows how attempts to resignify "monster" along with "queer" within the context of Gothic horror are significantly more vexed than attempts to resignify "queer" alone. Resignification of "queer" has succeeded in some quarters because it valorizes the abnormality that the word denotes, reversing the normal/abnormal hierarchy. It changes meanings by shifting the value of abnormal from bad to good. Accomplishing similar shifts, recent films such as those in the *Shrek* series, which is about a lovable and misunderstood ogre, make "good guys" out of creatures who look like monsters but do not behave monstrously.[15] However, *Shrek* isn't a horror movie. The resignification of an abject figure—such as an ogre or a queer—typically succeeds by removing that figure from abjection, from the status of vilified other to valorized self. When monstrosity leaves abjection and ceases to horrify, it ceases to be Gothic. As Halberstam points out, the Gothic monster "can represent any *horrible* trait," and a "monster functions as a monster . . . when it is able to condense as many *fear-producing* traits as possible into one body" (emphasis added).[16] Queer abnormality is not necessarily horrific, but Gothic monstrosity is. Valorizing Gothic monsters means valorizing homicidal maniacs, creatures, human and otherwise, who literally destroy life. If Dorian Gray found the secret to immortality and then did nothing but make friends, Wilde's novel would have no place in this study. If Stretch from *Texas Chainsaw 2* took the phallic chainsaw and went on a picnic, Halberstam's reading of her as a queer-positive figure would be unproblematic. But she doesn't—instead, Stretch kills someone and spins around like a lunatic, and thus her story's ending is true to its genre, and her monstrosity remains pathological.

The hugely popular Gothic television show *Buffy the Vampire Slayer*, which aired in the U.S. from 1997 to 2003, offers an example of an artifact from contemporary popular culture that, like Halberstam's academic treatment of *Texas Chainsaw 2*, tries and fails to resignify Gothic monstrosity. In the series' fourth season, the episode "New Moon Rising" involves parallel storylines that serve as a commentary on diverse sexualities. Willow, one of the show's main characters, is involved in a sexual relationship with another woman for the first time in her life, and she has not yet identified herself to her friends as lesbian. At the beginning of the episode, Willow's ex-boyfriend Oz, who abandoned her abruptly and mysteriously earlier in the season, comes back to town. Oz is a werewolf, but he is not a villain. Buffy, the show's vampire-slaying lead character and Willow's best friend, has gotten a new boyfriend, Riley, since Oz left, and Riley does not know about Oz's hidden, monstrous identity. A member of a monster-hunting military organization called the Initiative, Riley is displeased by what he learns about Willow's past. He shares his displeasure with Buffy:

> RILEY: I didn't know Willow as the kind of girl . . . into dangerous guys . . . she seemed smarter than that.
>
> BUFFY: Oz is not dangerous . . . Something happened to him; it wasn't his fault. God, I never knew you were such a bigot.
>
> RILEY: . . . It's a little weird to date someone who tries to eat you once a month.
>
> BUFFY: Love isn't logical, Riley. It's not like you can be Mr. Joe Sensible about it all the time. God knows I haven't been.[17]

Though Buffy doesn't explain what she means by her own lack of sensibleness in matters of love until the end of the episode, the long-time viewer knows that she is referring to her own non-normative sexual history: she had an extended, sexual relationship with a male vampire named Angel. Riley's reference to Willow as the "kind of girl" who likes "weird" relationships, combined with the way Buffy defends Oz by claiming his condition is not his "fault," echoes the sort of conversation two straight people might have when trying to make sense of the experience of finding out one of their best friends is gay. The fact that Willow does indeed come out to Buffy later in the episode, which pushes the usually articulate Buffy into a condition of shocked babbling, turns these echoes into deafening screams. Willow's relationship with a werewolf, Buffy's relationship with a vampire, and Willow's relationship with another woman all parallel and inform characters' understandings of themselves and one another.

The show's message is ultimately about how people shouldn't judge people just because they are unconventional: it encourages toleration and acceptance of difference. At the end of the episode, Riley explains to Buffy that he has learned his lesson:

> RILEY: I was wrong about Oz. I was being a bigot.
>
> BUFFY: . . . You found out that Willow was in a sort of unconventional relationship, and it gave you the wiggins. It happens.
>
> RILEY: Still, I was in a totally black and white space, people versus monsters, and it ain't like that. Especially when it comes to love.
>
> BUFFY: I have to tell you some stuff . . . about my past . . . and it's not all stuff you're gonna like.

Riley has seen that Oz is a good person, so he knows that his prejudice was unfounded. He rejects the "black and white" binary opposition "people versus monsters." Buffy has also learned to understand her boyfriend's difficulty with revelations about unconventional relationships because she had the same sort of difficulty when Willow came out to her. After hearing Willow come out about her unconventionality, Buffy is now ready to face such difficulty and tell the truth about herself.

If anything could resignify the negativity of associating homosexuality with monstrosity, this show's handling of the werewolf/vampire/lesbian parallels might, but the negativity inherent in the horrors of lycanthropy and vampirism ultimately thwarts resignification. As Buffy's description of Oz's lycanthropy indicates, being a werewolf means Oz has contracted a disease; it was "something that happened to him." Similarly, Angel's vampirism was something that happened to him, an invasion of his body by a demon. The conditions that the show parallels with lesbianism are pathological conditions— conditions that bring no culpability but are nonetheless a horrible "fault." Several episodes of the series focus on the horrors of what could happen if Oz or Angel ever loses control of his monstrous nature: if the werewolf's or the vampire's desires for the flesh and blood of his fellow man take over, he will murder people.

In addition to being a lesbian, Willow is a witch. The association of lesbians with monstrous witches is older and more prevalent than even the association of lesbians with phallic vampires. Though this association might seem to make Willow's witchcraft another indicator of her monstrous lesbianism in itself, in "New Moon Rising" it doesn't in any overt way. Up until this point, the series has gone to great lengths to show that, despite the occasional bad witch, witches and witchcraft are parts of valid religious traditions and are usually forces of good. This positive meaning ascribed to lesbian witchiness fades by the show's sixth season. Near the end of the season, Willow's girlfriend, Tara, is shot and killed. In the episode "Villains," Willow goes into a rage, turns her hair and eyes black, and starts hunting her girlfriend's murderer, Warren. Warren is a stereotypical nerd who has become a misogynistic killer; even after Willow has mystically lashed his arms to two trees, he continues to spout gynophobic slurs, calling the first girl he killed a "bitch" and making fun of Willow's grief. Willow takes a bullet and uses magic to make it slowly penetrate Warren's skin. Then she flays him and burns him to cinders.[18]

Willow's rage-driven spree of mystical violence continues until, in the season finale, she tries to destroy the entire world, and Buffy and her friends must oppose her or perish. Her male friend, Xander, a simple carpenter, talks her down by saying he loves her.[19] Thus a man calms lesbian rage and lulls the monstrous lesbian back into the proper social order. *Buffy* falls into the same trap that many well-meaning representations of lesbian witches fall into, as Paulina Palmer observes:

> [Such representations] illustrate, in this respect, the difficulties that confront the writer who attempts parodically to rework the grotesque images which patriarchal culture projects upon women.

Rather than redefining the boundaries of the abject, she may end up reinforcing them and perpetuating, unchanged and unchallenged, existing prejudices.[20]

Repetition of gyno- and homophobic images perpetuates the negativity of the associations the repetition would resignify. That *Buffy* succumbs to an overtly homophobic representation of lesbian monstrosity reflects the negativity inherent in monstrosity, a negativity that the show never managed to evade fully in the first place.

Notes

1. Foucault, *History of Sexuality*, vol. 1: *An Introduction*, 101.

2. Julia Kristeva, *Powers of Horror: An Essay on Abjection*, trans. Leon S. Roudiez (New York: Columbia University Press, 1982), 2.

3. Harry M. Benshoff, *Monsters in the Closet: Homosexuality and the Horror Film* (New York: Manchester University Press, 1997), 232.

4. Wilde, *The Picture of Dorian Gray*, 121–122, 166.

5. Showalter, *Sexual Anarchy*, 113.

6. Edward S. Brinkley, "Homosexuality as (Anti)Illness: Oscar Wilde's *The Picture of Dorian Gray* and Gabriele D'Annunzio's *Il Piacere*," *Studies in Twentieth Century Literature* 22.1 (1998), 73.

7. Wilde, *The Picture of Dorian Gray*, 133, 122, 167.

8. Philip Jenkins, *Using Murder: The Social Construction of Serial Homicide* (New York: Aldine de Gruyter, 1994), 1–2.

9. Diana Fuss, *Identification Papers: Readings on Psychoanalysis, Sexuality, and Culture* (New York: Routledge, 1995), 98.

10. Richard Tithecott, *Of Men and Monsters: Jeffrey Dahmer and the Construction of the Serial Killer* (Madison: University of Wisconson Press, 1997), 81.

11. Judith Halberstam, *Skin Shows*, 21, 69.

12. *Texas Chainsaw Massacre 2*, DVD, directed by Tobe Hooper (1986; Los Angeles: MGM-UA, 2000).

13. Halberstam, *Skin Shows*, 160.

14. Ibid., 188.

15. *Shrek*, directed by Vicky Jenson and Andrew Adamson (2001; Los Angeles: Dreamworks SKG). For a compelling account of how classic monsters become kid-friendly, see Harvey Roy Greenberg, "Heimlich Manuevers: On a Certain Tendency of Horror and Speculative

Cinema," in *Horror Film and Psychoanalysis*, reprint, ed. Steven Jay Schneider (New York: Cambridge University Press, 2009), 122–141.

16. Halberstam, *Skin Shows*, 21.

17. "New Moon Rising," *Buffy the Vampire Slayer: The Complete Fourth Season*, DVD, created by Joss Whedon (1999; Los Angeles: Twentieth Century–Fox Home Video, 2003).

18. *Buffy the Vampire Slayer: The Complete Sixth Season*, DVD, created by Joss Whedon (2001; Los Angeles: Twentieth Century–Fox Home Video, 2004).

19. Willow is also Jewish, making the scene read eerily like a straight Christ reclaiming a wayward lesbian Jew through his unwavering love and forgiveness.

20. Paulina Palmer, *Lesbian Gothic: Transgressive Fictions* (New York: Cassell: 1999), 40.

Cooper explains that the practice of taking historically negative language and concepts and using them in a positive way is sometimes known as reverse discourse, and he uses the common example of the word "queer," which has historically been an insult to sexual minorities but is now often a term of empowerment. Cooper focuses on Judith Halberstam's interpretation of *The Texas Chainsaw Massacre 2* and Joss Whedon's *Buffy the Vampire Slayer* as examples of attempts at reverse discourse that end up reinforcing the negative pattern of associating homosexuality with monstrosity. Brainstorm other attempts to use reverse discourse in film, books, music, and video games that have instead reinforced negative patterns. Do you think that reverse discourse could ever be entirely successful? Why or why not?

Cooper approaches identity as a process of negation—people figure out who they are by making claims about what they *are not*. Thus a heterosexual is someone who is not homosexual, i.e., a person who does not have sex "with someone who has similar genitalia." In a group of classmates, discuss other examples of human identity that rely on negation. Examples might relate to race, ethnicity, gender, nationality, or age and could be fictional or nonfictional, historical or contemporary. What exactly is negated in your examples, and what are the social consequences?

In his discussion of the equation MONSTER = HOMOSEXUAL, Cooper directly addresses ideas taken up by other authors that appear in selections from this book, including Judith Halberstam, Mary Shelley, Robert Louis Stevenson, and Bram Stoker. Write an essay in which you either apply Cooper's ideas to one of these selections or argue that the selections point toward conclusions that contradict Cooper's claims.

Natalie Wilson, an expert in gender studies, feminist theory, and popular culture, teaches literature and women's studies. While her book Seduced by Twilight (2011) examines Stephenie Meyer's Twilight saga and its resulting phenomenon through a critical feminist lens, her essay "Civilized Vampires versus Savage Werewolves" focuses instead on race. This essay appears in the collection Bitten by Twilight (2010), which includes scholarship on Stephenie Meyer's books as well as Twilight fandom and the franchise that has grown around the books.

While the specific characteristics of Meyer's vampires (particularly glittering in the sun) differ from those of traditional monsters, the popularity of the books rests largely in the relationships between Bella Swan and Edward Cullen (a vampire) and between Bella and Jacob Black (a werewolf), reflecting today's value on physical beauty as well as female desire for sensitive-but-dangerous men. These relationships, the crux of the series, raises questions about the possibility of love between "good" monsters and a human. While the Cullen family remains as dangerous as any vampires, the novel presents them as "civilized" monsters who feed on animals rather than humans, and though Jacob Black may be a werewolf, the books emphasize his human qualities more than his monstrous ones.

"Civilized Vampires versus Savage Werewolves" addresses important stereotypes that appear in Meyer's Twilight novels. Not only does the article illustrate the tension between vampires and werewolves, it details how these two monsters represent the social constructs of race and class that are so integrated into our culture—to a point that they often go unnoticed. As you read this essay, consider how often you notice racial or class divisions in popular books and movies.

CIVILIZED VAMPIRES VERSUS SAVAGE WEREWOLVES: RACE AND ETHNICITY IN THE *TWILIGHT* SERIES

By Natalie Wilson

While the cultural phenomenon surrounding *Twilight* now boasts several million devoted fans, the series' representation of race is rarely a topic of discussion. This chapter interrogates the unexamined white privilege permeating the *Twilight* texts, arguing the saga upholds dominant ideas about race that associate whiteness with civility, beauty, and intellect on the one hand, and indigenous people with animality and primitivism on the other.

The series relies on a structural divide between humans, vampires, and werewolves. Indeed, it is the relationships and tensions between these groups that ground the narrative. The story begins with Bella Swan, an average white human teenage girl, moving to Forks, Washington, and falling in love with Edward Cullen, a beautiful and talented white vampire. Bella also finds friendship with Jacob Black, a Quileute, who later in the series becomes a shape-shifting werewolf tasked with protecting his people from vampires. Jacob falls in love with Bella, but Bella ultimately chooses Edward. This love triangle is echoed by the larger struggle between the Cullens (Edward's vampire family) and the Quileutes (a Native American tribe), who view each other as enemies. Read as a racial allegory, a white, working class human chooses between an ultra-white, ultra-privileged vampire and a far less privileged wolf of color.

The story thus echoes older tales of conquest and imperialism, though instead of the white cowboys and Native Americans who populated western films, we now have vampires and werewolves vying over borders as well as women. Although the saga depicts the animosity between the Cullens and the Quileute as hinging on vampire and werewolf affiliation, the vampires and humans are predominantly presented as white while the werewolves are presented as native. The love triangle at the series' core is also imbued with racial connotations, with a white vampire in competition with a Native American shape-shifter. Their characters are contrasted using various binaries that equate Edward with whiteness (and its associations with civility, wealth, and intellect) and Jacob with the indigenous (and its associations with animals, primitivism, and savagery). Like Bella, readers are encouraged to choose between these two different racialized suitors.

Examining *Twilight* representations of race reveals the ways in which racial identities continue to be constructed in media texts. In keeping with dominant conception of white/non-white, *Twilight* constructs race using a binary frame. Whiteness in the texts is idealized in its racial associations. Edward is constructed as a white, godlike vampire, and the color white is associated with purity, beauty, and heroism. The non-white is rendered inferior, with the Quileute shape-shifting werewolves portrayed as not as good or heroic as the white vampires, and their russet-colored skin, black hair, and dark eyes are associated with violence, danger and savagery. Even the heroic Cullens are presented as more dangerous when their eyes turn black, suggestion that those who are "white and delightsome" are also susceptible to evil.[1] This black/white, dark/light symbolism of the book echoes long-standing media associations of whiteness with goodness, heroism, and superiority.

GOT VAMPIRE PRIVILEGE?

In the series, being a vampire accords one all sorts of privileges that echo real-world white privilege, or the social capital afforded to those with white skin. For example, the Cullens' beauty, wealth, and intellect are linked to their whiteness. When Bella first sees them, she is unable to stop staring, noting, "Every one of them was chalky pale . . . Paler than me, the albino" (Meyer, 2005, p. 18). She goes on to relate that they were all "devastatingly, inhumanely beautiful" (p. 19) describing their faces as ones "you never expected to see except perhaps on the airbrushed pages of a fashion magazine, or painted by an old master as the face of an angel" (p. 19). Although Bella never uses the word white in this description, the references to models, classical art, and angels link the Cullens to images that are associated with whiteness in the U.S. culture. As the series progresses, Cullen beauty continues to be linked to whiteness, from their pale skin to the clothes they wear to the white mansion they reside in. Edward, in particular, is associated with white perfection, He has a "perfect" body that is "white, cool, and polished as marble" (Meyer, 2008, p. 25).

Yet, the whiteness of the Cullens is never explicitly linked to their privilege in the texts. This accords with white privilege in the real world, which functions as an unmarked, naturalized category conferring superiority on those with white skin. Much like in the real world, such privilege is not recognized but serves as an unexamined and desirable norm. In one of the most influential essays examining such privilege, "Unpacking the Invisible Knapsack," McIntosh (2009) argues whiteness works as a hidden system of advantage in our world. Yet, as McIntosh notes, the majority of whites do not recognize the unearned privilege their whiteness confers upon them. She explains:

> I have come to see white privilege as an invisible package of unearned assets that I can count on cashing in each day, but about which I was "meant" to remain oblivious . . . whites are taught to think of their lives as morally neutral, normative, and average, and also ideal. (p. 78)

Dyer (1997) similarly notes that whites do not acknowledge their whiteness. This in itself is a function of power. He argues that whites are represented as "just human," or as the norm, noting "this assumption that white people are just people, which is not far off from saying that whites are people whereas other colours are something else, is endemic to white culture" (p. 10). Asserting that in Western culture whites play predominant roles, Dyer maintains that "at the level of representation . . . whites are not of a certain race, they're just the human race" (p. 11).

In *Twilight*, Bella never names Edward as racially white nor does she consider the mixed race connotations of her friendship and possible romance with Jacob. She does not, in effect, *see* race, including her own. This failure is in itself a trapping of white privilege. While her acceptance of others and diversity is laudable, her failure to recognize her own racially based privileges results in a text that renders white privilege invisible. In kind, young readers of the series are not encouraged to examine the racial power dynamics that shape their own lives; rather, they are given the facile message that race does not really matter, that we should all just focus on getting along (or on nabbing ourselves a super cute vampire boyfriend).

The fact that the Cullens carry what McIntosh (2009) refers to as "an invisible weightless knapsack of special provisions, maps, passports, codebooks, visas, clothes, tools, and blank checks" is key to their power and success (p. 79). In the final book of the series, Bella is able to draw on this "knapsack" to prepare a bevy of provisions for her daughter Renesmee. Fearing her new vampire family may lose their battle with the Volturi (a powerful vampire coven), Bella is able to secure falsified birth certificates, passports, and a driver's license so that Renesmee can escape to safety if necessary. Packing these in a small black leather backpack along with "twice the yearly income from the average American household" (Meyer, 2008, p. 672) in cash, Bella literally packs a knapsack of special provisions that would not be possible without her white vampire privilege.

WHITENESS AND/AS WEALTH

The metaphor used by Wise (2005) relating whiteness to money in the bank is particularly apt in relation to the representation of privilege in Meyer's series. Wise writes, "the virtual invisibility that whiteness affords those of us who have it is like psychological money in the bank, the proceeds of which we cash in every day while others are in a state of perpetual overdraft" (p. 120). As mentioned above, Bella cashes in on these privileges in *Breaking Dawn* in various ways, using her "proceeds" to draw on important networks, secure documents, and withdraw cash.

This strand of the text reveals the links between white privilege and class privilege. Yet, readers are not encouraged to question such unearned privileges, but to desire them. The Cullens are presented as living the good life and their activities and tastes tend toward those things associated with high culture: they like classical music, appreciate art, value education, like to travel, and have sophisticated fashion and home décor know-how. The description of the home office of Carlisle Cullen (Edward's vampire father) captures this representation. Bella remarks that Carlisle's "towering bookshelves" represent "more books than I'd ever seen outside a library" (Meyer, 2005, p. 335) and notes that his desk looks like a college dean's. Carlisle is framed as the originator of the vegetarian vampire philosophy and his ability to resist drinking human blood is represented as a marker of civilized restraint. Bella's father, Charlie Swan, refers to Carlisle as "an asset to the community" (p. 36) commenting that his children are "well behaved and polite" (p. 36). The rest of the Cullen brood are similarly civilized, with a fondness for fine things, education and European travel. As Bella details, they all dress "exceptionally well" (p. 32) with clothes hinting of "designer origins" (p. 32). Their home is depicted as opulent, decked out in white and gold with an accompanying garage populated with luxury cars. Isle Esme (an island off the coast of Rio de Janeiro owned by Edward's vampire mother, Esme Cullen) carries on the white opulent theme with a master bedroom that Bella dubs "the white room" (Meyer, 2008, p. 100). Edward is similarly associated with wealth, as when he gives Bella a five carat diamond and casually remarks, "I inherited quite a few bobbles like this" (Meyer, 2007, p. 43). His gold eyes and hair, as well as the gold bed in his room and his shiny Volvo, associate him with riches.

In contrast, Jacob's house resembles "a tiny barn" (Meyer, 2006, p. 131) and his garage consists of "a couple of preformed sheds that had been bolted together with their walls knocked out" (p. 133). Rather than luxury cars and designer duds, he has an '86 Rabbit and wears sweats or "ragged, grease smeared jeans" (Meyer, 2007, p. 77). Edward has multiple college degrees and composes symphonic lullabies, whereas Jacob fixes cars and has to be reminded by Bella to do his homework. Here, the differing class levels, as well as the way whiteness is associated with wealth and intelligence and non-whiteness with physicality and manual labor, contributes to the racial divide.

Bella, though she has white skin privilege, is economically more in line with Jacob. Referring to the "scarcity of my funds," she details her "decrepit computer" (Meyer, 2005, p. 5) and refers to her dad's small two bedroom house with its "shabby" (Meyer, 2007, p. 43) chairs and lack of dishwasher. Bella reveals she lived in a "lower-income neighborhood" (Meyer, 2005, p. 14) back in Arizona and is relieved when she sees that most of the cars in the Forks high school parking lot "were older like mine" (p. 14). Later in the series, Jacob suggests Bella is attracted to Edward's wealth, but she denies this. Although she is represented as not initially liking being the recipient of the Cullens' gifts, by the series end she has enjoyed parties, a designer wedding dress, a luxury vacation to Isle Esme, and boasts a fancy cottage complete with a new closet full of designer clothing. When Bella chooses Edward at the series close, she also chooses wealth and all the privileges it brings.

LIGHT VERSUS DARK, CIVILIZED VERSUS SAVAGE

In addition to associating whiteness with wealth, the saga relies on a number of key binaries that further associate whiteness (and white vampires) with rationality, culture, and progress. Contrastingly, indigenous culture tends to be associated with irrationality, nature, savagery, and the past. As Dyer (1997) notes, whiteness is particularly associated with godliness. Referring to the "whitening of the image of Christ," Dyer argues that constructing god as white has perpetuated notions of white superiority, framing whites as more spiritual and godly than raced people (p. 17).[2] This framing relates particularly to Edward, whom Bella repeatedly refers to as god-like and angelic. She claims he has "the face of an angel" (Meyer, 2005, p. 19), "the voice of an archangel" (p. 311) and, relates that "I couldn't imagine how an angel could be any more glorious" (p. 241). She also refers to him as "my perpetual savior" (p. 166), as a "godlike creature" (p. 292), and notes he "looked like a god" (p. 65).

Contrastingly, when Bella first sees Jacob and his friends at La Push, she notices the "straight black hair and copper skin of the newcomers" (Meyer, 2005, p. 117). She describes them as "all tall and russet-skinned, black hair cropped short" (Meyer, 2006, p. 263) with "strikingly similar hostility in every pair of eyes" (p. 323). As the series continues, the Quileutes' dark faces are emphasized repeatedly in a fashion reminiscent of the notion that all raced people look the same. While Edward's eyes and hair are gold, Jacob's are dark. His last name is Black, and he, like other Quileute characters, is associated with a lack of light—his house has "narrow windows" (p. 130) and he has "long, glossy black hair" that hangs "like black satin curtains on either side of his broad face" (p. 131). These descriptions may suggest that his vision is shrouded, that he does not see things clearly. Edward, in contrast, is like an all-knowing god. Significantly, his mind-reading skills are shown as a benevolent power that he uses to protect Bella.

While Edward's whiteness is portrayed as next to godliness in the texts, Jacob and other Quileute characters' russet-colored skin and black hair are associated with animality. In general, the Quileute characters are less glowingly described than the white Cullens. For example, Billy is depicted as "heavyset" with black eyes, flaring nostrils, and "a face that overflowed, the cheeks resting against his shoulders, with creases running through the russet skin like an old

Figure 18. This movie poster from *Twilight: Eclipse* depicts a close-up of Edward Cullen's paleness (top left) in stark contrast with Jacob Black's darker tones (bottom left). Edward's nice clothes and calm expression suggest his nobility, while Jacob's bare, tattooed skin and menacing glare suggest his savagery.

leather jacket" (Meyer, 2005, pp. 234–235). Emily, whom Bella calls "wolf girl" (Meyer, 2006, p. 332), has "satiny copper skin and long, straight, crow-black hair" (p. 331), and Leah is described as "beautiful in an exotic way" (p. 149) with "perfect copper skin, glistening black hair, eyelashes like feather dusters" (p. 149). Here, words such as "crow-black" and "feather" again associate the Quileute with animals.

Kim, another Quileute female, is depicted as having "a wide face, mostly cheekbones, with eyes too small to balance them out. Her nose and mouth were too broad for traditional beauty. Her flat black hair was thin and wispy" (Meyer, 2007, p. 242). In keeping with dominant media representations of indigenous peoples, *Twilight* depicts the Quileute characters as "exotic" rather than traditionally beautiful. Their non-Eurocentric features are then further associated with a lack of light (e.g., both Jacob's and Emily's houses are focused on for their tiny windows), a propensity for violence (e.g., Jacob sexually assaults Bella in *Eclipse*, and Sam, the wolf pack leader, disfigures his fiancée Emily), and as outside civil society (via their representation as a "pack" that shuns clothing and lives across the border in La Push).

In addition to its depictions of the Quileute characters as literally and figuratively darker, the series also features a number of other characters whose villainy is either associated with non-white skin and/or their black hair and clothing. One of Bella's would-be killers in *New Moon*, Laurent, for example, is described as having olive skin and glossy black hair in the book and is played by an African American actor in the films. The evil Volturi, their name redolent of black vultures, are repeatedly associated with their long black capes and "dark ruby eyes" (Meyer, 2008, p. 118). Felix and Demetri, two of the Volturi guard, have an "olive complexion" (Meyer, 2006, p. 463), and Aro has jet black hair. In the film adaptation of *New Moon*, these evil characters are visually associated with darkness and savagery: Laurent tries to eat Bella in the meadow, and the Volturi make lunch of a group of unsuspecting human tourists.

Even the raced vampire allies are portrayed as more savage than their white counterparts. In *Breaking Dawn*, the animal-skin-wearing Amazonian vampires are depicted as "feline" (Meyer, 2008, p. 612) with "long black braids" (p. 612). Bella observes, "It wasn't just their eccentric clothes that made them seem wild but everything about them" (p. 612). Noting their "restless" eyes (p. 612), "darting movements," and "fierce appearance," she relates, "I'd never met any vampires less civilized" (p. 613). The Brazilian workers featured earlier in the book on Isle Esme during Edward and Bella's honeymoon are similarly associated with darkness. The "tiny coffee-skinned woman" with "dark eyes" is "superstitious" (p. 114) and speaks in what Bella describes as an "alien tongue" (p. 136).

Additionally, the wolves are depicted as less civilized than the vampires. In keeping with stereotypical view of native Others, they function according to a pack mentality and group think. Their transformation into wolf form is "an involuntary reaction" (Meyer, 2007, p. 63); they are unable to exercise free will. While the Cullens are associated with civility, the wolves are referred to as "mutant canines" (p. 31) by Edward and "big idiot wolf boys" by Bella (p. 231). They are also characterized as not keeping their word. Sam goes "back on every promise he'd ever made" (p. 123), and Jacob breaks promises to the pack as well as to Bella. More generally, they are voracious, animal-like eaters, chomping down plates of eggs and multiple hot dogs—at one point, Bella jokes that Jacob could eat an entire cow (p. 243). And, at the series close, Aro notes the wolves would be exceedingly good guard dogs (Meyer, 2008, p. 700). This reference emphasizes they are more like obedient animals than cognizant humans. While the wolves are presented as a pack, the Cullens are presented as regal peacekeepers. This animal/human divide is echoed by the fact the Quileute are referred to as the "wolf pack" and the Cullens as a "clan" by fans and in the media, with "pack" being far less civilized a designation than "clan."

When Edward shares with Bella that Carlisle is responsible for the truce between the Cullen vampires and the Quileutes, he presents his family as the noble clan of benevolent rulers who act as a civilizing force. In the final book of the series, *Breaking Dawn*, this view is further promoted when the Cullens introduce "culture" to Jacob, inviting him into their home. Sleeping and eating outside at first, in various states of undress, he is gradually "civilized" and moves inside the house, or into the white world. Esme feeds and clothes the wayward wolf-boy, offering him shelter and sustenance.

Thus, Jacob alternates from being noble to being savage. As Hall (1995) reveals, this dual-sided representation of native characters is common. He writes, "The good side of this figure is portrayed in a certain primitive nobility and simple dignity. The bad side is portrayed in terms of cheating and cunning, and, further out, savagery and barbarism" (p. 21). Bird (1996) similarly argues that media portrayals of Native American males "have alternated between two main images: the ignoble savage (Indian as wild, marauding beast) and the noble savage (Indian as close to the land, spiritual, heroic, virtuous—and doomed)" for over a century (p. 245). In *Twilight*, Jacob's "good side" is brave, dedicated, protective, and loyal. His "bad side" is temperamental, vindictive, violent, and undomesticated. Intriguingly, his good aspects are often rendered in animal-like terms which present him not so much as a savage beast, but as a loyal dog. These depictions, despite having positive associations with "man's best friend," nevertheless portray Jacob and the wolves as more animal-like than human, a portrayal that has historically been used in relation to Native Americans. Tellingly, when Edward is associated with animality, he is characterized as a lion, the king of the jungle (2005, p. 215). Jacob, on the other hand, is depicted as a loyal dog, a savage wolf, and, at one point, a sure-footed mountain goat (2007, p. 475).

EDWARD AS MIND, JACOB AS BODY

Twilight can also be read as upholding traditional ideas of mind versus body and culture versus nature. Edward (and the Cullens) are associated with the mind and culture, while Jacob, the Quileute, the wolves, and other raced characters are associated with the body and nature. As Larson (2006) argues, most representations of Native Americans in media texts are negative. Even when such characters are positively depicted, their power derives not form their intellect but from their bodies or their closeness to nature. She writes, "Native American characters are provided with power either because they are 'one with nature' or because they are 'beasts.' Both images draw on a 'physical versus mental' dichotomy, positioning Indians as inferior to whites" (p. 56).

Twilight draws on this mind/body binary, positioning Edward as mind. He has various graduate degrees, is well-spoken and well-read, and is distanced from his ice-cold body. As a mind reader, he lives not only through his own mind, but by reading the thoughts of others. Jacob, in contrast, is grounded in corporeality—his bodily size, color, and temperature are constantly focused on in the books. His russet-colored skin is contrasted to Edward's marble-whiteness. Further, as a werewolf, Jacob and other Quileute characters are associated in various ways with the unruly body. The wolves' bodies run hot and their physical anger cannot be contained. For example, in *New Moon*, Paul, a wolf pack member, cannot control his anger and erupts into wolf form to fight Jacob. And Sam, the wolf pack leader, reportedly lost control and attacked his fiancée, Emily, permanently disfiguring her face and body. More generally, the werewolves' lack of clothing further emphasizes their status *as* bodies.

In contrast, Edward is depicted as a restrained, civilizing mind. His "impossibly selfless" (Meyer, 2007, p. 49) nature is proven when he does not try to prevent Bella's continuing friendship with Jacob as well as through his politeness and magnanimity when dealing with the wolves. He is represented as always thinking about Bella, as having her best interests at heart. He is a good influence who encourages her to pursue college. And, he denies his own bodily desires in various capacities. As a vegetarian vampire, he controls his bloodlust; as a 106-year-old virgin he controls his sexual desire.

On the other hand, Jacob, a modern-day Tonto, is the trusty fun-loving sidekick—fixing Bella's motorbike, holding her hand, cheering her up—but never capturing her heart or conquering with his mind. Readers, like Bella, are encouraged to see Edward as the hero and Jacob as the best friend. In this capacity, Jacob also functions as a rebel, encouraging Bella in her efforts to court danger. He rides into town on his motorbike, threatening the civility of Forks.

Furthering the emphasis of the mind/body binary is the sexualization of the wolf body. Echoing traditional representations of colonized peoples, the series presents Jacob (and the other wolves) as perpetually in a state of undress. Their bodies are sexualized more overtly than other bodies in the saga. This, too, is in keeping with historical representations. As van Lent (1996) argues in "Her Beautiful Savage," sexuality pervaded captivity narratives with native men framed as dangerous yet desirable noble savages and warriors. Analyzing the popularity of "Indian Romances," van Lent suggests that turning the native male into a romantic hero both renders his supposed violence sexy and ameliorates the history of colonization. "Loving him," van Lent writes, "a minority and a victim of much we regret—makes American dominant culture feel less guilty" (p. 226). This is why, according to van Lent, native men are often hypersexualized.

In relation to *Twilight*, the sexualization of Jacob became even more apparent with the film adaptations wherein an often shirtless Taylor Lautner, the actor who plays Jacob Black, flexes his muscles for the camera. The texts offer a precedent for this representation, though, focusing as they do on Jacob's (and the other wolves') lack of clothing. As van Lent (1996) notes, "The representation of Native Americans without clothes is a very old tradition" (p. 217). This tradition began with early narratives as sketches and continued through to modern films, where indigenous peoples seem to be in a permanent state of undress. In *Twilight*, this nakedness is justified via the transformation from wolf to human and is so ubiquitous that Bella asks him, "Is it really so impossible to wear clothes, Jacob?" (Meyer, 2007, p. 215).

The focus on Jacob's nudity is in keeping with a history of white representations of native men as more bodily, more brute, and more animalistic than white men. Although Bella obsesses over Edward's attractiveness too, it is most often his eyes that she fixates on. The traditional notion of eyes as "windows to the soul" is key here. While Bella most often concentrates on Edward's head—his hair, eyes, and mouth, she appreciates Jacob's warm skin and muscled torso. Once again, Edward is rendered as mind, Jacob as body. In these various representations, Jacob is associated with bodily activities and desires. Through his mechanic work, his excessive need for sleep, his hot temperature, and his hot-headedness, he is grounded in his body—and, significantly, a body he cannot control.

Taken together, these representations in *Twilight*, in which whiteness is associated with intellect, morality, and regality and darkness with animality, savagery, and evil, communicates to readers rather disturbing messages about race.

COLONIZING THE WOLF

The history of werewolf lore, which Frost (2003) claims is rooted in the "bestial instincts lurking beneath our civilized exteriors," can be read in relation to the racial divide the *Twilight* series enacts. Just as werewolves are traditionally depicted as cunning, swift, ferocious, and cruel, so too have native peoples been associated with "a lower or more primitive state" (p. 28). The term "werewolf," literally meaning man-wolf, connotes beastliness and irrationality, attributes that were also associated with those "in need" of colonization.

In the series, the white Cullen vampires represent a colonizing force whose worldview and actions impinge on the lives of the Quileute. As the lore Jacob relates conveys, the "cold ones" threatened the lives and the culture of the Quileute, and thus the werewolves were born. Further, the representation of the wolves as less civilized, as closer to nature, and as running in packs all accords with the historical justifications that argued colonization was necessary to tame savage peoples. Bella adopts this view in *New Moon*, by assuming the wolves are savage killers.

Twilight can be read as informed by a colonial viewpoint that results in the Quileute being depicted in stereotypical fashion. As Larson argues (2006), most media representations of native characters accord to three main stereotypes: the "good Indian" who is brave, calm, a friend to nature, and nice to whites; the "bad Indian" who is brutal, cruel, savage, superstitious, gets in way of white people, and does not fight fair; and the "degraded Indian" who succumbs to various vices, is infantilized, and dehumanized (p. 47). In the series, the representation of the Quileute concurs with these stereotypes. In particular, Jacob's character, as a mixture of all three types, perpetuates the dominant racial ideology which constructs the indigenous as "Other."

First, he functions as a "good Indian" via his bravery, his friendship with Bella, and his associations with the forest and La Push. Jacob, as the "good Indian" of the story, tells Bella his cultural "legends" but does not

Figure 19. This image from *Twilight: New Moon* presents Jacob's wolf pack. The pack's purpose in the film is to protect Bella from the vampires who want to kill her, and their body language in this poster confirms their dangerous, animalistic natures.

place much stock in them, characterizing Quileutes as overly superstitious. Before his turn to wolf, he is very critical of the "La Push gag," calling it a cult and mocking the fact they are "all about *our* land and *tribe pride*" (Meyer, 2006, p. 173). Referring to what is happening as "like a bad western" (p. 174), Jacob has adopted a white, Westernized view of his culture and heritage. When he asks Bella, "So do you think we're a bunch of superstitious natives, or what?" with "a hint of worry" in his voice, he emphasizes his own fear that this is indeed the case (Meyer, 2005, p. 126). His Westernized view, or colonial viewpoint, results in negative views of himself and other tribe members. His turn to wolf is redolent of forced colonization—a turn caused, significantly, by the presence of the white Cullen vampires.

Once he does turn wolf, he resents the change, likening it to being drafted into a war he does not want to fight (Meyer, 2007, p. 484). He refers to being a shape-shifter as a "life sentence" (Meyer, 2006, p. 287) and characterizes himself as a "time bomb" (Meyer, 2007, p. 345) that almost ripped his father's face off the first time he transitioned into a wolf. And, while he is especially reluctant to serve his wolf-mates and follow Sam's orders, he, in keeping with the colonial viewpoint the text enacts, seems happy to be at the beck and call of the white girl he has fallen in love with, reminding Bella, "I offered eternal servitude, remember, I'm your slave for life" (p. 321). We might read Jacob's forced turn to wolf in relation to white conquest—he does not want to fight, to be an animal, but the Cullen intrusion forces him to do so. However, as the texts portray his mistrust of the Cullens as unfounded, Jacob's rage is rendered less sympathetic.

Rather than a justified warrior hero, he is presented as "a monster who might hurt somebody" (Meyer, 2006, p. 345). He is a "bad Indian," one who is prejudiced against vampires, suspects Edward's motives, loses his temper easily, and gets in the way of Bella and Edward's relationship. Throughout the series, his intrusions interrupt many markers of civilized life, from proms, to weddings, to pregnancies. He is, in effect, the dark horse that keeps threatening to sully Bella's union with Edward. He is depicted as very vocal in his dislike for vampires, saying "vampires don't count as people" (Meyer, 2006, p. 310). He blames "bloodsuckers" (p. 267) for his shape-shifting fate, failing to take any personal responsibility for his volatility. And, as depicted in the film version of *New Moon*, Jacob is a seething muscle-mass of anger. In the film, his anger is writ large as he lashes out not only at Edward, but at Bella, Paul, Mike Newton (a human friend of Bella's), and Alice Cullen (Edward's vampire sister).

Jacob is a "degraded Indian" in that he is infantilized as a wolf-boy, with his demonstrated immaturity and Bella continually reminding him how young he is. At the close of the book, we learn Jacob can be bribed easily when he tells Bella his dad paid him $20 to come to the prom and warn Bella about the vampires. His unscrupulous nature is further revealed when he breaks the treaty by telling Bella about his shape-shifting ancestry. Moreover, he forces Bella to kiss him in *New Moon* and then threatens suicide in order to get her to kiss him again in *Eclipse*. And, though Jacob repeatedly promises he will never hurt Bella, he purposefully puts her in very hot water with Charlie by leaving her motorbike in the driveway, an action which Bella characterizes as "petty and just plain *mean*" (Meyer, 2006, p. 554). Moreover, he is dehumanized, quite literally, in his transition to a shape-shifting wolf.

Compared to the high-culture Edward, who fittingly looks like a classically beautiful statue, Jacob is childlike, irrational, temperamental, impulsive, and beastly (especially in *Eclipse*, when he forces Bella to kiss him and laughs when, with her retaliating punch to his jaw, she breaks her hand). This contrasting depiction of Bella's suitors, with the white vampire as gentleman-hero and the native werewolf as an aggressive cad, accords to racialized stereotypes of white versus non-white behavior.

The fact that Bella chooses Edward over Jacob at the series close and that this choice is framed as a "happy ending" implies that what Edward represents—whiteness, civility, wealth, and intellect—is the better choice. Bella has rejected "the less-mature, more-reckless Bella who could laugh it off with Jacob" (Meyer, 2007, p. 231) and chosen the Cullen vampire life, a life that brings with it a knapsack full of privileges. This choice, read in the context of the racial ideologies that shape U.S. society, reinforces messages of white superiority. These ideologies, or "chain of meanings," often function at an unconscious level (Hall, 1995, p. 18). This is especially true of the dominant ideology of white privilege. As Hall argues, "Since (like gender) race appears to be 'given' by Nature, racism is one of the most profoundly 'naturalised' of existing ideologies" (p. 19). Thus, a key site in which we need to render such hierarchies visible is via the extermination of cultural texts.

CONCLUSION

Twilight, as a series that has captured the public imagination, needs to be examined in terms of the dominant ideology of race that shapes the U.S. culture. Particularly as *Twilight* is marketed as a young adult series, it is imperative that we continue to interrogate how media construct definitions of race for young audiences. While claims that we live in a post-racial world have become increasingly common following Obama's election in the 2008 U.S. presidential race (see Schorr, 2008), young readers, especially if they are not white, likely regularly experience or witness racial discrimination. *Twilight*, turning racial strife into a problem of vampire, werewolf, and human interaction, reflects the fact that racial divides are still prevalent. However, by perpetuating ideas of whites as civilized and indigenous peoples as savages, it simultaneously naturalizes and perpetuates age-old racial divides.

Such depictions, even when situated in a fantasy, do contribute to dominant notions of race shaping U.S. culture. And, because so many young people are reading the series, it is even more crucial to remember that the fantasies portrayed in media texts are often held up as ideal. Gunshot westerns were largely fantasy too, and think of the lasting legacy they have left us with in terms of Native Americans being seen as angry warriors who scalp too often and drink too much. Further, the fact that the series depicts a real group of indigenous people is problematic, especially given the failure to mention Native American realities of poverty, unemployment, and social disenfranchisement. Instead, *Twilight* relies on stereotypical representation of race, focuses on falsified legends, and leaves out any consideration of the lasting effects of colonization. While the texts are indeed fictional, we cannot discount the power such fiction holds over our lives, over the socialization of young readers, and we need to, even as fans, be critical about some of the more delimiting messages the series offers about race.

Notes

1. The *Book of Mormon* in 2 Nephi 30:6 reads ". . . their scales of darkness shall begin to fall from their eyes; and many generations shall not pass away among them, save they shall be a white and a delightsome people." This phrase is thought to reflect the belief that the darker-skinned Lamanites (or Native Americans according to Mormon doctrine) would become *whiter* once they embraced Mormon belief. For a discussion of the history of this belief and phrase, see the Mormonism Research Ministry at http://www.mrm.org/white-and-delightsome.

2. Here, I use the term "raced" in keeping with Shannon Winnubst's (2003) conceptualization of the term in order to trouble the white/non-white binary and to emphasize whiteness as the unmasked, normative racial category.

Bibliography

Bird, S. E. (1996). Not my fantasy: The persistence of Indian imagery in *Dr. Quinn, Medicine Woman*. In E. S. Bird (Ed.), *Dressing in feathers: The construction of the Indian in American popular culture* (pp. 245–261). Oxford: Westview Press.

Dyer, R. (1997). *White*. London: Routledge.

Frost, B. J. (2003). *The essential guide to werewolf literature*. Madison, WI: The University of Wisconsin Press.

Hall, S. (1995). The whites of their eyes: Racist ideologies and the media. In G. Dines and J. M. Humez (Eds.), *Gender, race, and class in media* (pp. 18–22). Thousand Oaks, CA: Sage.

Larson, S. G. (2006). Native Americans in film and television entertainment. In S. G. Larson, *Media and minorities: The politics of race in news and entertainment.* (pp. 45–56). Lanham, MD: Rowman and Littlefield.

McIntosh, P. (2009). White privilege: Unpacking the invisible knapsack. In E. Disch (Ed.), *Reconstructing gender* (5th ed.), (pp. 78–83). Boston, MA: McGraw Hill.

Meyer, S. (2005). *Twilight.* New York: Little, Brown, and Company.

— (2006). *New Moon.* New York: Little, Brown, and Company.

— (2007). *Eclipse.* New York: Little, Brown, and Company.

— (2008). *Breaking Dawn.* New York: Little, Brown, and Company.

Schorr, D. (2008, January 28). A new, 'post-racial' political era in America. National Public Radio. Retrieved December 29, 2009, from http://www.npr.org/templates/story/story.php?storyId=18489466.

van Lent, P. (1996). 'Her Beautiful Savage': The current sexual image of the Native American male. In E. S. Bird (Ed.), *Dressing in feathers: The construction of the Indian in American popular culture* (pp. 211–227). Oxford: Westview Press.

Winnubst, S. (2003). V*ampires, anxieties, and dreams: Race and sex in the contemporary United States,* Hypatia, 18, 1–20.

Wise, T. (2005). Membership has its privileges: Thoughts on acknowledging and challenging. In P. S. Rothenberg (Ed.), *White privilege: Essential readings on the other side of racism* (pp. 119–122). New York: Worth Publishers.

Research the *Twilight* phenomenon. What are fans' perceptions of the books' monsters? Pay particular attention to information about "Team Jacob" and "Team Edward," the labels given to the fan preferences for either Jacob Black or Edward Cullen. Examine the comments made by fans.

- Do fans choose their "team" based on preferences for vampires or for werewolves? What comments lead you to believe this?

- What attributes of vampires and werewolves lead to this choice? Alternately, do fans choose their "team" based on race or class?

- If fans don't seem to make obvious, conscious choices based on such factors, do you see any language in fan comments that leads you to believe that some choices are unconsciously based on race or class?

In groups, look at the images of Jacob Black and Edward Cullen from *Twilight: Eclipse* (page 161) and *Twilight: New Moon* (page 167), movie adaptations of the *Twilight* books, and debate the following questions:

- How "monstrous" do the characters seem?

- What attributes make the characters different from humans? Similar to them?

- What do their appearances convey about changing perspectives on monsters in American culture? Of the meaning of monsters (vampires and werewolves in particular) in American culture?

- How do these monsters and their cultural meanings differ from Dracula? From other monsters in this book?

On the internet, find additional posters from the *Twilight* movie series and write a short paper that uses details from them to confirm or refute Wilson's assessment of race and class in *Twilight*. How do race and/or class come across in these images? How do they connect to the monstrosity of Edward and Jacob?

THE HORRORS OF RACE AND AMERICAN HISTORY: *CANDYMAN*

BY L. ANDREW COOPER AND BRANDY BALL BLAKE

Although mainstream feature films are collaborative efforts that sometimes involve hundreds of people in their creation, critics sometimes treat a film's director as its author, at least when referring to a film's lone creator is useful or expedient. Bernard Rose, director of *Candyman* (1992), certainly deserves recognition for his contributions to the film. As the director behind more "respectable" films such as *Immortal Beloved* (1994), he likely gave *Candyman* some of its high-production finesse. As writer and actor, he also created the screenplay and performed as one of the film's more memorable minor characters, the arrogant and overbearing Professor Archie Walsh. Nevertheless, *Candyman* is best known as Clive Barker's *Candyman*, as the film is based on the famous British horror novelist's short story "The Forbidden," and Barker's name was used heavily in the film's marketing. Barker achieved his greatest notoriety by adapting his short novel *The Hellbound Heart* into the movie *Hellraiser* (1987), which has spawned numerous sequels featuring the much-loved (and feared) monster Pinhead. In addition to directing *Hellraiser*, Barker wrote and directed *Nightbreed* (1990), in which supernatural monsters are a force of good against human monsters, and *Lord of Illusions* (1995), which explores a link between monstrosity and magic.

The titular monster of *Candyman* comes from an urban legend, the story of a deranged killer who has a hook for a hand. This familiar tale blends with another urban legend, often known as "Bloody Mary," the story of a ghost who appears if someone says her name enough times in front of a mirror. The

173

legend of Candyman suggests that saying "Candyman" five times in front of a mirror will make the hook-man appear. White graduate student Helen Lyle (Virginia Madsen) comes across the story while doing research on urban legends. She discovers that people in an impoverished African American community in Chicago's Cabrini Green area have come to believe that the legend is true. Helen and her friend Bernadette investigate, discovering that the leader of a gang has been using Candyman's name to help cover up his illegal activities. When Helen and Bernadette expose the ruse, Helen gets the attention of the real Candyman: the vengeful spirit of Daniel Robitaille, an African-American former slave who was lynched for having a romantic relationship with a white woman. Candyman returns because Helen's exposure of the gang leader as a fraud has damaged the faith of Candyman's followers, and he needs people to believe in him. However, the film's clever use of perspective creates uncertainty about whether Candyman might be a figment of Helen's imagination. As Helen and Candyman develop a subtly sadomasochistic connection that mirrors the relationship that got Daniel Robitaille killed, the murders of Helen's friends and the kidnapping of a baby in Cabrini Green draw suspicion on her. In the end, the existence of Candyman remains uncertain, but Helen herself has become a part of Candyman's legend as well as a legend on her own.

Questions about America's history of racial and economic injustice lie at the heart of *Candyman*. Candyman haunts Cabrini Green just as the horrors of slavery haunt American memories, but in what on the surface seems like an irony, he haunts other African Americans, not the descendants of the white people responsible for slavery and for lynching Daniel Robitaille. The poverty of Cabrini Green offers a parallel manifestation of this haunting: the ghost of slavery is not literal bondage but continuing entrapment of African American people in the nightmarish conditions of the urban poor. That Candyman/Robitaille was lynched for having a relationship with a white woman is no coincidence: in the years following the abolition of slavery in America, claims about uncontrollable black male sexuality raised the specter of rape, and the alleged need to protect white women from rape at the hands of black men helped to justify, at least in some people's minds, the written and unwritten laws known as "Jim Crow" that segregated African American people and helped to keep generations from being able to climb out of poverty. Thus the torments of Helen at Candyman's hands evoke historically fraught fears surrounding black male sexuality. The legend of Candyman *is* the legend of predatory black male sexuality; the threats of their phallic hooks are one and the same.

Candyman's reflections on this history of oppression are inherently problematic. By telling the story of a black male monster who menaces a white woman, a story that reflects on the injustices supported by stories of black male monsters who menace white women, the film repeats and becomes part of the very history that it reflects, perpetuating the fear of black male sexuality. Is *Candyman*, then, a racist film? Some critics say yes, and some say no. Whether the film is or isn't racist, it introduces a monster laden with significance, a monster scary enough to inspire two film sequels and to become one of the great icons of modern monster-movie history.

Figure 20. *Candyman's* opening credits show titles over images of city streets, and they culminate in a shot of bees that swarm over Chicago's skyline. The white mob that lynched Daniel Robitaille, creating Candyman, sawed off his hand (which the monster replaces with a hook), covered his naked body with honey, and forced him into an apiary, where bees stung him to death. Because of their role in this history, bees become a harbinger of Candyman's presence and a symbol of his power. As they spread through the city like a shadow, they symbolize Candyman's haunting presence and establish his identity as a distinctly urban monster. When Helen and Bernadette investigate the Candyman legend, they come across candy that hides razor blades, a symbol that, like the bees, combines sweetness with a dangerous sting. This association of pleasure and danger resonates with the specter of black sexuality at the heart of the Candyman story.

Figure 21. When Helen (Virginia Madsen) investigates the legend of Candyman in Cabrini Green, she comes across graffiti that combines images of the monster himself with references to his story. In this image, Helen stands in front of one of those layered references: "Sweets to the Sweet." The reference to sweetness alludes to the "candy" in Candyman's name, which is itself an allusion to cultural ties among drugs, candy, and criminality that ultimately associate pleasure with death. The graffiti is written in excrement, which imbues the phrase with nasty irony. Finally, "Sweets to the Sweet" is a quote of Shakespeare's Hamlet, Act 5, Scene 1, in which Hamlet's mother mourns the suicide of Hamlet's intended bride by scattering flowers (sweets) on the grave of the young woman (the sweet).

Figure 22. When Candyman (Tony Todd) first appears to Helen, he approaches her calmly, hypnotizing her with his supernatural voice and presence as he explains, "I am the writing on the wall, the whisper in the classroom— without these things, I am nothing, so now I must shed innocent blood." As Candyman opens his arms to her, a shot / reverse shot editing pattern establishes their connection to each other, showing that Helen is in his thrall. This erotically tinged thrall, similar to Dracula's, arguably relates to the power of storytelling, which enthralls listeners and viewers.

Figure 23. After being blamed for crimes she believes Candyman committed, Helen seeks Candyman out in order to rescue the kidnapped baby. Helen makes a deal: she must willingly give herself up to him as a victim, and the baby will go free. Giving herself up involves a kiss that transfers a swarm of bees from him to her. Before and after their union, Helen sees graffiti on a wall that says, "It was always Helen." This graffiti suggests that Helen—and perhaps Daniel Robitaille's lover, of whom she might be an avatar, and perhaps, by extension, the sexuality of white women in general—has always been an integral part of Candyman's story. The graffiti also gives credence to what Candyman says as he seduces her into his embrace, "Our names will be written on a thousand walls, our crimes told and retold by our faithful believers. We shall die together in front of their very eyes, and give them something to be haunted by. Come with me, and be immortal."

You have probably been exposed to urban legends before. In the United States, common urban legends involve crocodiles in sewers, dogs getting "dried off" in microwave ovens, and the killer in a car's backseat whose attack is thwarted by a following car's high beams, just to name a few. Brainstorm about urban legends: what stories have you heard or read that either are or *might* be urban legends? Are any of those stories connected to monsters or monstrous figures like Candyman? If so, what characteristics distinguish the monsters of urban legends from other monsters? What sort of urban (or suburban, or rural) legend would be appropriate for your area? Make notes about your answers to these questions, and come to class ready to tell one or more of your stories.

Candyman is faithful to Clive Barker's short story "The Forbidden" in many ways, but it changes the setting from the U.K. to the U.S. Thus a film that is in some ways fundamentally about the haunting of American history is based on material that is not American at all. In a group of students, discuss how you might adapt the basic story of *Candyman* for another setting. Fill in the following table, describing aspects of the setting and characters and considering the significance of your descriptions for the story. How must factors such as plot and character development change because of your choices? How do these changes affect the meanings you see in the film?

Variable	Description	Significance
Geography		
Population		
Race		
Sex/Gender		
Affluence		

Share your group's table with the class, entering a discussion of all of your adaptations and creating a composite table. What conclusions can you draw about the relationship of each variable to the fundamentals of storytelling?

Candyman uses a stereotypical story about dangerous black male sexuality in a way that reflects on the nature and power of that stereotype. Nevertheless, by using the stereotype, the film risks perpetuating it, and thus it might be perceived as racist and could potentially result in the continuation of racial injustice. Write an essay that analyzes the film in order to take a position on whether it is fundamentally racist. Be sure to use specific images and dialogue, either the images and quotes provided here or other evidence you acquire on your own.

Setting aside rare exceptions such as *Blacula* (1972), *A Vampire in Brooklyn* (1995), and *Snoop Dogg's Hood of Horror* (2006), mainstream American horror films rarely involve major roles for African American men. *Night of the Living Dead* and *Candyman*, both described in this book, are among the rare exceptions, and coincidentally or not, they both associate their leading African American men with violence and rage. Compare and contrast Ben from *Night of the Living Dead* with Candyman from *Candyman*. Are there similarities beyond the superficial? If so, what is their significance?

Sigmund Freud is the father of psychoanalysis and one of the chief architects of modern psychology. Although present-day psychologists in the United States have abandoned most of Freud's theories as frameworks for scientific inquiry, critics and theorists continue to use Freudian concepts as frameworks for understanding literature, film, and the arts. Freud's best-known books include The Interpretation of Dreams *(1900),* Three Essays on the Theory of Sexuality *(1905),* Beyond the Pleasure Principle *(1920),* The Ego and the Id *(1923), and* Civilization and Its Discontents *(1930).*

In "The Uncanny," Freud explores E.T.A. Hoffmann's short story "The Sand-Man." Freud argues that the feeling of uncanniness arises from experiencing something that is both familiar and unfamiliar at the same time. Ultimately, he concludes that the feeling stems from the return of disturbing emotions that were repressed (often called "the return of the repressed"), and the ultimate source of repressed emotion is the process of what he calls oedipalization, especially the feeling of castration anxiety that it can cause. To illustrate his theory, Freud draws on Hoffmann's depiction of Nathaniel's encounter with the monstrous Coppelius, whose threat to remove Nathaniel's eyes is a figurative threat of castration. Considering Freud's explanation of the uncanny in a broader context, most monsters can cause the uncanny feeling because they are born from fears that individuals—and sometimes entire societies—try to repress. As you read "The Uncanny," pay attention to the ways Freud situates his own theory in relation to the ideas of others. Also note the distinctions Freud makes between the uncanny in literature and the uncanny in real life.

excerpts from

THE UNCANNY (1919)

By Sigmund Freud

I

The subject of the "uncanny" is undoubtedly related to all that is terrible—to all that arouses dread and creeping horror; it is equally certain, too, that the word is not always used in a clearly definable sense, so that it tends to coincide with whatever excites dread. Yet we may expect that it implies some intrinsic quality which justifies the use of a special name. One is curious to know what this peculiar quality is which allows us to distinguish as "uncanny" certain things within the boundaries of what is "fearful."

As good as nothing is to be found upon this subject in elaborate treatises on aesthetics, which in general prefer to concern themselves with what is beautiful, attractive and sublime, that is with feelings of a positive nature, with the circumstances and the objects that call them forth, rather than with the opposite feelings of unpleasantness and repulsion. I know of only one attempt in medico-psychological literature, a fertile but not exhaustive paper by E. Jentsch.[1] [...]

[...] Two courses are open to us at the start. Either we can find out what meaning has come to be attached to the word "uncanny" in the course of its history; or we can collect all those properties of persons, things, sensations, experiences and situations which arouse in us the feeling of uncanniness, and then infer the unknown nature of the uncanny from what they all have in common. I will say at once that both courses lead to the same result: the "uncanny" is that class of the terrifying which leads back to something long known to us, once very familiar. How this is possible, in what circumstances the familiar can become uncanny and frightening, I shall show in what follows. Let me also add that my investigation was actually begun by collecting a number of individual cases, and only later received confirmation after I had examined what language could tell us. In this discussion, however, I shall follow the opposite course.

The German word *unheimlich*[2] is obviously the opposite of *heimlich, heimisch,* meaning "familiar," "native," "belonging to the home"; and we are tempted to conclude that what is "uncanny" is frightening precisely because it is *not* known and familiar. Naturally not everything which is new and unfamiliar is frightening, however; the relation cannot be inverted. We can only say that what is novel can easily become frightening and uncanny; some new things are frightening but not by any means all. Something has to be added to what is novel and unfamiliar to make it uncanny. [...]

[...] *Heimlich,* adj. belonging to the house, not strange, familiar, tame, intimate, comfortable, homely, etc.

II. Concealed, kept from sight, so that others do not get to know about it, withheld from others.

---

1 "Zur Psychologic des Unheimlichen."

2 [Throughout this paper "uncanny" is used as the English translation *of "unheimlich,"* literally "unhomely" —Trans.]

What interests us most is to find that among its different shades of meaning the word *heimlich* exhibits one which is identical with its opposite, *unheimlich*. What *is heimlich* thus comes to be *unheimlich*. In general we are reminded that the word *heimlich* is not unambiguous, but belongs to two sets of ideas, which without being contradictory are yet very different: on the one hand, it means that which is familiar and congenial, and on the other, that which is concealed and kept out of sight. [...]

[...] Thus *heimlich* is a word the meaning of which develops towards an ambivalence, until it finally coincides with its opposite, *unheimlich*. *Unheimlich* is in some way or other a sub-species of *heimlich*. Let us retain this discovery, which we do not yet properly understand, alongside of Schelling's definition of the "uncanny." Then if we examine individual instances of uncanniness, these indications will become comprehensible to us.

II

In proceeding to review those things, persons, impressions, events and situations which are able to arouse in us a feeling of the uncanny in a very forcible and definite form, the first requirement is obviously to select a suitable example to start upon. Jentsch has taken as a very good instance "doubts whether an apparently animate being is really alive; or conversely, whether a lifeless object might not be in fact animate"; and he refers in this connection to the impression made by wax-work figures, artificial dolls and automatons. He adds to this class the uncanny effect of epileptic seizures and the manifestations of insanity, because these excite in the spectator the feeling that automatic, mechanical processes are at work, concealed beneath the ordinary appearance of animation. Without entirely accepting the author's view, we will take it as a starting-point for our investigation because it leads us on to consider a writer who has succeeded better than anyone else in producing uncanny effects.

Jentsch says: "In telling a story, one of the most successful devices for easily creating uncanny effects is to leave the reader in uncertainty whether a particular figure in the story is a human being or an automaton; and to do it in such a way that his attention is not directly focused upon his uncertainty, so that he may not be urged to go into the matter and clear it up immediately, since that, as we have said, would quickly dissipate the peculiar emotional effect of the thing. Hoffmann has repeatedly employed this psychological artifice with success in his fantastic narratives."

This observation, undoubtedly a correct one, refers primarily to the story of "The Sand-Man" in Hoffmann's *Nachtstücken*,[3] which contains the original of Olympia, the doll in the first act of Offenbach's opera, *Tales of Hoffmann*. But I cannot think—and I hope that most readers of the story will agree with me—that the theme of the doll, Olympia, who is to all appearances a living being, is by any means the only element to be held responsible for the quite unparalleled atmosphere of uncanniness which the story evokes; or, indeed, that it is the most important among them. Nor is this effect of the story heightened by the fact that the author himself treats the episode of Olympia with a faint touch of satire and uses it to make fun of the young man's idealization of his mistress. The main theme of the story is, on the contrary, something different, something which gives its name to the story, and which is always re-introduced at the critical moment: it is the theme of the "Sand-Man" who tears out children's eyes.

The feeling of something uncanny is directly attached to the figure of the Sand-Man, that is, to the idea of being robbed of one's eyes; and that Jentsch's point of an intellectual uncertainty has nothing to do with this effect. Uncertainty whether an object is living or inanimate, which we must admit in regard to the doll Olympia, is quite irrelevant in connection with this other, more striking instance of uncanniness. It is true that the writer creates a kind of uncertainty in us in the beginning by not letting us know, no doubt purposely, whether he is taking us into the real world or into a purely fantastic one of his own creation. He has admitted the right to do either; and if he chooses to stage his action in a world peopled with spirits, demons and ghosts, as Shakespeare does in *Hamlet*, in *Macbeth* and, in a different sense, in *The Tempest* and *A Midsummer-Night's Dream*, we must bow to his decision and treat his setting as though it were real for as long as we put ourselves into his hands. But this uncertainty disappears in the course of Hoffmann's story, and we perceive that he means to make us, too, look through the fell Coppola's glasses—perhaps, indeed, that he himself once gazed through such an instrument. For the conclusion of the story makes it quite clear that Coppola the optician really is the lawyer Coppelius and thus also the Sand-Man.

---

3 [From Haus=house; Häuslichkeit=domestic life.—Trans.]

There is no question, therefore, of any "intellectual uncertainty"; we know now that we are not supposed to be looking on at the products of a madman's imagination behind which we, with the superiority of rational minds, are able to detect the sober truth; and yet this knowledge does not lessen the impression of uncanniness in the least degree. The theory of "intellectual uncertainty" is thus incapable of explaining that impression.

We know from psychoanalytic experience, however, that this fear of damaging or losing one's eyes is a terrible fear of childhood. Many adults still retain their apprehensiveness in this respect, and no bodily injury is so much dreaded by them as an injury to the eye. We are accustomed to say, too, that we will treasure a thing as the apple of our eye. A study of dreams, phantasies and myths has taught us that a morbid anxiety connected with the eyes and with going blind is often enough a substitute for the dread of castration. In blinding himself, Oedipus, that mythical law-breaker, was simply carrying out a mitigated form of the punishment of castration—the only punishment that according to the *lex talionis* was fitted for him. We may try to reject the derivation of fears about the eye from the fear of castration on rationalistic grounds, and say that it is very natural that so precious an organ as the eye should be guarded by a proportionate dread; indeed, we might go further and say that the fear of castration itself contains no other significance and no deeper secret than a justifiable dread of this kind. But this view does not account adequately for the substitutive relation between the eye and the male member which is seen to exist in dreams and myths and phantasies; nor can it dispel the impression one gains that it is the threat of being castrated in especial which excites a peculiarly violent and obscure emotion, and that this emotion is what first gives the idea of losing other organs its intense colouring. All further doubts are removed when we get the details of their "castration-complex" from the analyses of neurotic patients, and realize its immense importance in their mental life.

Moreover, I would not recommend any opponent of the psychoanalytic view to select precisely the story of the Sand-Man upon which to build his case that morbid anxiety about the eyes has nothing to do with the castration-complex. For why does Hoffmann bring the anxiety about eyes into such intimate connection with the father's death? And why does the Sand-Man appear each time in order to interfere with love? He divides the unfortunate Nathaniel from his betrothed and from her brother, his best friend; he destroys his second object of love, Olympia, the lovely doll; and he drives him into suicide at the moment when he has won back his Clara and is about to be happily united to her. Things like these and many more seem arbitrary and meaningless in the story so long as we deny all connection between fears about the eye and castration; but they become intelligible as soon as we replace the Sand-Man by the dreaded father at whose hands castration is awaited.[4]

---

4 In fact, Hoffmann's imaginative treatment of his material has not played such havoc with its elements that we cannot reconstruct their original arrangement. In the story from Nathaniel's childhood, the figures of his father and Coppelius represent the two opposites into which the father-imago is split by the ambivalence of the child's feeling; whereas the one threatens to blind him, that is, to castrate him, the other, the loving father, intercedes for his sight. That part of the complex which is most strongly repressed, the death-wish against the father, finds expression in the death of the good father, and Coppelius is made answerable for it. Later, in his student days, Professor Spalanzani and Coppola the optician reproduce this double representation of the father-imago, the Professor as a member of the father-series, Coppola openly identified with the lawyer Coppelius. Just as before they used to work together over the fire, so now they have jointly created the doll Olympia; the Professor is even called the father of Olympia This second occurrence of work in common shows that the optician and the mechanician are also components of the father-imago, that is, both are Nathaniel's father as well as Olympia's. I ought to have added that in the terrifying scene in childhood, Coppelius, after sparing Nathaniel's eyes, had screwed off his arms and legs as an experiment; that is, he had experimented on him as a mechanician would on a doll. This singular feature, which seems quite out of perspective in the picture of the Sand-Man, introduces a new castration-equivalent; but it also emphasizes the identity of Coppelius and his later counterpart, Spalanzani the mechanician, and helps us to understand who Olympia is. She, the automatic doll, can be nothing else than a personification of Nathaniel's feminine attitude towards his father in his infancy. The father of both, Spalanzani and Coppola, are, as we know, new editions, reincarnations of Nathaniel's "two" fathers. Now Spalanzani's otherwise incomprehensible statement that the optician has stolen Nathaniel's eyes so as to set them in the doll becomes significant and supplies fresh evidence for the identity of Olympia and Nathaniel. Olympia is, as it were, a dissociated complex of Nathaniel's which confronts him as a person, and Nathaniel's enslavement to this complex is expressed in his senseless obsessive love for Olympia. We may with justice call such love narcissistic, and can understand why he who has fallen victim to it should relinquish his real, external object of love. The psychological truth of the situation in which the young man, fixated upon his father by his castration-complex, is incapable of loving a woman, is amply proved by numerous analyses of patients whose story, though less fantastic, is hardly less tragic than that of the student Nathaniel.

Hoffmann was the child of an unhappy marriage. When he was three years old, his father left his small family, never to be united to them again. According to Grisebach, in his biographical introduction to Hoffmann's works, the writer's relation to his father was always a most sensitive subject with him.

We shall venture, therefore, to refer the uncanny effect of the Sand-Man to the child's dread in relation to its castration-complex. But having gained the idea that we can take this infantile factor to account for feelings of uncanniness, we are drawn to examine whether we can apply it to other instances of uncanny things. We find in the story of the Sand-Man the other theme upon which Jentsch lays stress, of a doll that appears to be alive. Jentsch believes that a particularly favourable condition for awakening uncanny sensations is created when there is intellectual uncertainty whether an object is alive or not, and when an inanimate object becomes too much like an animate one. Now, dolls happen to be rather closely connected with infantile life. We remember that in their early games children do not distinguish at all sharply between living and lifeless objects, and that they are especially fond of treating their dolls like live people. In fact I have occasionally heard a woman patient declare that even at the age of eight she had still been convinced that her dolls would be certain to come to life if she were to look at them in a particular way, with as concentrated a gaze as possible. So that here, too, it is not difficult to discover a factor from childhood; but curiously enough, while the Sand-Man story deals with the excitation of an early childhood fear, the idea of a "living doll" excites no fear at all; the child had no fear of its doll coming to life, it may even have desired it. The source of the feeling of an uncanny thing would not, therefore, be an infantile fear in this case, but rather an infantile wish or even only an infantile belief. There seems to be a contradiction here; but perhaps it is only a complication, which may be helpful to us later on.

The theme of the "double" has been very thoroughly treated by Otto Rank.[5] He has gone into the connections the "double" has with reflections in mirrors, with shadows, guardian spirits, with the belief in the soul and the fear of death; but he also lets in a flood of light on the astonishing evolution of this idea. For the "double" was originally an insurance against destruction to the ego, an "energetic denial of the power of death," as Rank says; and probably the "immortal" soul was the first "double" of the body. This invention of doubling as a preservation against extinction has its counterpart in the language of dreams, which is fond of representing castration by a doubling or multiplication of the genital symbol; the same desire spurred on the ancient Egyptians to the art of making images of the dead in some lasting material. Such ideas, however, have sprung from the soil of unbounded self-love, from the primary narcissism which holds sway in the mind of the child as in that of primitive

---

5   "Der Doppelganger."

man; and when this stage has been left behind the double takes on a different aspect. From having been an assurance of immortality, he becomes the ghastly harbinger of death.

The idea of the "double" does not necessarily disappear with the passing of the primary narcissism, for it can receive fresh meaning from the later stages of development of the ego. A special faculty is slowly formed there, able to oppose the rest of the ego, with the function of observing and criticizing the self and exercising a censorship within the mind, and this we become aware of as our "conscience." In the pathological case of delusions of being watched this mental institution becomes isolated, dissociated from the ego, and discernible to a physician's eye. The fact that a faculty of this kind exists, which is able to treat the rest of the ego like an object—the fact, that is, that man is capable of self-observation—renders it possible to invest the old idea of a "double" with a new meaning and to ascribe many things to it, above all, those things which seem to the new faculty of self-criticism to belong to the old surmounted narcissism of the earliest period of all.[6]

But it is not only this narcissism, offensive to the ego-criticizing faculty, which may be incorporated in the idea of a double. There are also all those unfulfilled but possible futures to which we still like to cling in phantasy, all those strivings of the ego which adverse external circumstances have crushed, and all our suppressed acts of volition which nourish in us the illusion of Free Will.[7]

But, after having thus considered the manifest motivation of the figure of a "double," we have to admit that none of it helps us to understand the extraordinarily strong feeling of something uncanny that pervades the conception; and our knowledge of pathological mental processes enables us to add that nothing in the content arrived at could account for that impulse towards self-protection which has caused the ego to project such a content outward as something foreign to itself. The quality of uncanniness can only

---

6 I cannot help thinking that when poets complain that two souls dwell within the human breast, and when popular psychologists talk of the splitting of the ego in an individual, they have some notion of this division (which relates to the sphere of ego-psychology) between the critical faculty and the rest of the ego, and not of the antithesis discovered by psychoanalysis between the ego and what is unconscious and repressed. It is true that the distinction is to some extent effaced by the circumstance that derivatives of what is repressed are foremost among the things reprehended by the ego-criticizing faculty.

7 In Ewers' *Der Student von Prag*, which furnishes the starting-point of Rank's study on the "double," the hero has promised his beloved not to kill his antagonist in a duel. But on his way to the duelling-ground he meets his "double," who has already killed his rival.

come from the circumstance of the "double" being a creation dating back to a very early mental stage, long since left behind, and one, no doubt, in which it wore a more friendly aspect. The "double" has become a vision of terror, just as after the fall of their religion the gods took on daemonic shapes.[8]

It is not difficult to judge, on the same lines as his theme of the "double," the other forms of disturbance in the ego made use of by Hoffmann. They are a harking-back to particular phases in the evolution of the self-regarding feeling, a regression to a time when the ego was not yet sharply differentiated from the external world and from other persons. I believe that these factors are partly responsible for the impression of the uncanny, although it is not easy to isolate and determine exactly their share of it.

That factor which consists in a recurrence of the same situations, things and events, will perhaps not appeal to everyone as a source of uncanny feeling. From what I have observed, this phenomenon does undoubtedly, subject to certain conditions and combined with certain circumstances, awaken an uncanny feeling, which recalls that sense of helplessness sometimes experienced in dreams. Once, as I was walking through the deserted streets of a provincial town in Italy which was strange to me, on a hot summer afternoon, I found myself in a quarter the character of which could not long remain in doubt. Nothing but painted women were to be seen at the windows of the small houses, and I hastened to leave the narrow street at the next turning. But after having wandered about for a while without being directed, I suddenly found myself back in the same street, where my presence was now beginning to excite attention. I hurried away once more, but only to arrive yet a third time by devious paths in the same place. Now, however, a feeling overcame me which I can only describe as uncanny, and I was glad enough to abandon my exploratory walk and get straight back to the piazza I had left a short while before. Other situations having in common with my adventure an involuntary return to the same situation, but which differ radically from it in other respects, also result in the same feeling of helplessness and of something uncanny. As, for instance, when one is lost in a forest in high altitudes, caught, we will suppose, by the mountain mist, and when every endeavor to find the marked or familiar path ends again and again in a return to one and the same spot, recognizable by some particular landmark. Or when one wanders about in a dark, strange room, looking for the door or the electric switch, and collides for the hundredth time with the same piece of furniture.

---

8 HEINE, *DIE GÖTTER IM EXIL.*

Taking another class of things, it is easy to see that here, too, it is only this factor of involuntary repetition which surrounds with an uncanny atmosphere what would otherwise be innocent enough, and forces upon us the idea of something fateful and unescapable where otherwise we should have spoken of "chance" only. For instance, we of course attach no importance to the event when we give up a coat and get a cloakroom ticket with the number, say, 62; or when we find that our cabin on board ship is numbered 62. But the impression is altered if two such events, each in itself indifferent, happen close together, if we come across the number 62 several times in a single day, or if we begin to notice that everything which has a number-addresses, hotel-rooms, compartments in railway-trains—always has the same one, or one which at least contains the same figures. We do feel this to be "uncanny," and unless a man is utterly hardened and proof against the lure of superstition he will be tempted to ascribe a secret meaning to this obstinate recurrence of a number, taking it, perhaps, as an indication of the span of life allotted to him. Or take the case that one is engaged at the time in reading the works of Hering, the famous physiologist, and then receives within the space of a few days two letters from two different countries, each from a person called Hering; whereas one has never before had any dealings with anyone of that name. [...]

[...] This is the place now to put forward two considerations which, I think, contain the gist of this short study. In the first place, if psychoanalytic theory is correct in maintaining that every emotional affect, whatever its quality, is transformed by repression into morbid anxiety, then among such cases of anxiety there must be a class in which the anxiety can be shown to come from something repressed which *recurs*. This class of morbid anxiety would then be no other than what is uncanny, irrespective of whether it originally aroused dread or some other affect. In the second place, if this is indeed the secret nature of the uncanny, we can understand why the usage of speech has extended *das Heimliche* into its opposite *das Unheimliche;* for this uncanny is in reality nothing new or foreign, but something familiar and old—established in the mind that has been estranged only by the process of repression.

It only remains for us to test our new hypothesis on one or two more examples of the uncanny.

Many people experience the feeling in the highest degree in relation to death and dead bodies, to the return of the dead, and to spirits and ghosts. As we have seen, many languages in use today can only render the German expression "an *unheimliches* house" by "a *haunted* house." We might indeed have begun our investigation with this example, perhaps the most striking of all, of something uncanny, but we refrained from doing so because the uncanny in it is too much mingled with and in part covered by what is purely gruesome. There is scarcely any other matter, however, upon which our thoughts and feelings have changed so little since the very earliest times, and in which discarded forms have been so completely preserved under a thin disguise, as that of our relation to death. Two things account for our conservatism: the strength of our original emotional reaction to it, and the insufficiency of our scientific knowledge about it. Biology has not yet been able to decide whether death is the inevitable fate of every living being or whether it is only a regular but yet perhaps avoidable event in life. It is true that the proposition "All men are mortal" is paraded in text-books of logic as an example of a generalization, but no human being really grasps it, and our unconscious has as little use now as ever for the idea of its own mortality. Religions continue to dispute the undeniable fact of the death of each one of us and to postulate a life after death; civil governments still believe that they cannot maintain moral order among the living if they do not uphold this prospect of a better life after death as a recompense for earthly existence. In our great cities, placards announce lectures which will tell us how to get into touch with the souls of the departed; and it cannot be denied that many of the most able and penetrating minds among our scientific men have come to the conclusion, especially towards the close of their lives, that a contact of this kind is not utterly impossible. Since practically all of us still think as savages do on this topic, it is no matter for surprise that the primitive fear of the dead is still so strong within us and always ready to come to the surface at any opportunity. Most likely our fear still contains the old belief that the deceased becomes the enemy of his survivor and wants to carry him off to share his new life with him. Considering our unchanged attitude towards death, we might rather inquire what has become of the repression, that necessary condition for enabling a primitive feeling to recur in the shape of an uncanny effect. But repression is there, too. All so-called educated people have ceased to believe, officially at any rate, that the dead can become visible as spirits, and have hedged round any such appearances with improbable and remote circumstances; their emotional attitude towards their dead, moreover, once a highly dubious and ambivalent one, has been toned down in the higher strata of the mind into a simple feeling of reverence.[9] [...]

---

9 Cf. *Totem und Tabu:* "Das Tabu und die Ambivalenz."

[...] I will relate an instance taken from psychoanalytical experience; if it does not rest upon mere coincidence, it furnishes a beautiful confirmation of our theory of the uncanny. It often happens that male patients declare that they feel there is something uncanny about the female genital organs. This *unheimlich* place, however, is the entrance to the former *heim* [home] of all human beings, to the place where everyone dwelt once upon a time and in the beginning. There is a humorous saying: "Love is home-sickness"; and whenever a man dreams of a place or a country and says to himself, still in the dream, "this place is familiar to me, I have been there before," we may interpret the place as being his mother's genitals or her body. In this case, too, the *unheimlich is* what was once *heimisch,* homelike, familiar; the prefix "un" is the token of repression.

III

It may be true that the uncanny is nothing else than a hidden, familiar thing that has undergone repression and then emerged from it, and that everything that is uncanny fulfils this condition. [...]

[...] Our conclusion could then be stated thus: An uncanny experience occurs either when repressed infantile complexes have been revived by some impression, or when the primitive beliefs we have surmounted seem once more to be confirmed. Finally, we must not let our predilection for smooth solution and lucid exposition blind us to the fact that these two classes of uncanny experience are not always sharply distinguishable. When we consider that primitive beliefs are most intimately connected with infantile complexes, and are, in fact, based upon them, we shall not be greatly astonished to find the distinction often rather a hazy one.

The uncanny as it is depicted in *literature,* in stories and imaginative productions, merits in truth a separate discussion. To begin with, it is a much more fertile province than the uncanny in real life, for it contains the whole of the latter and something more besides, something that cannot be found in real life. The distinction between what has been repressed and what has been surmounted cannot be transposed on to the uncanny in fiction without profound modification; for the realm of phantasy depends for its very existence on the fact that its content is not submitted to the reality-testing faculty. The somewhat paradoxical result is that *in the first place a great deal that is not uncanny in fiction would be so if it happened in real life; and in the second place that there are many more means of creating uncanny effects in fiction than there are in real life.*

The story-teller has this license among many others, that he can select his world of representation so that it either coincides with the realities we are familiar with or departs from them in what particulars he pleases. [...]

[...] The story-teller can also choose a setting which, though less imaginary than the world of fairy tales, does yet differ from the real world by admitting superior spiritual entities such as daemonic influences or departed spirits. So long as they remain within their setting of poetic reality their usual attribute of uncanniness fails to attach to such beings. The souls in Dante's *Inferno,* or the ghostly apparitions in *Hamlet, Macbeth* or *Julius Caesar,* may be gloomy and terrible enough, but they are no more really uncanny than is Homer's jovial world of gods. We order our judgement to the imaginary reality imposed on us by the writer, and regard souls, spirits and spectres as though their existence had the same validity in their world as our own has in the external world. And then in this case too we are spared all trace of the uncanny.

The situation is altered as soon as the writer pretends to move in the world of common reality. In this case he accepts all the conditions operating to produce uncanny feelings in real life; and everything that would have an uncanny effect in reality has it in his story. But in this case, too, he can increase his effect and multiply it far beyond what could happen in reality, by bringing about events which never or very rarely happen in fact. He takes advantage, as it were, of our supposedly surmounted superstitiousness; he deceives us into thinking that he is giving us the sober truth, and then after all oversteps the bounds of possibility. We react to his inventions as we should have reacted to real experiences; by the time we have seen through his trick it is already too late and the author has achieved his object; but it must be added that his success is not unalloyed. We retain a feeling of dissatisfaction, a kind of grudge against the attempted deceit; I have noticed this particularly after reading Schnitzler's *Die Weissagung* and similar stories which flirt with the supernatural. The writer has then one more means he can use to escape our rising vexation and at the same time to improve his chances of success. It is this, that he should keep us in the dark for a long time about the precise nature of the conditions he has selected for the world he writes about, or that he should cunningly and ingeniously avoid any definite information on the point at all throughout the book. Speaking generally, however, we find a confirmation of the second part of our proposition—that fiction presents more opportunities for creating uncanny sensations than are possible in real life. [...]

If you haven't read or heard about Freud's ideas before, the portions of "The Uncanny" that discuss the Oedipus complex and castration might have been difficult (and perhaps bizarrely amusing). With a small group of students, use library sources and the Internet to explore these theories in greater depth. Locate and discuss definitions for "Oedipus complex" (or oedipalization), "castration anxiety," and other terms that seem relevant. How does this background information change your understanding of "The Uncanny"? How would you explain these concepts in your own words? What aspects of these theories, if any, seem like reasonable accounts of human psychology?

In a small group of classmates, debate the merits of Freud's theory of oedipalization, especially as he applies it to E.T.A. Hoffmann's "The Sand-Man," which you can read on the Internet. Freud claims, "Elements in the story... seem arbitrary and meaningless so long as we deny all connection between fears about the eye and castration; but they become intelligible as soon as we replace the Sand-Man by the dreaded father at whose hands castration is expected." Is Freud right? Your group should develop arguments both for and against Freud's reading of Hoffmann's story, demonstrating ways Freud's ideas help Hoffmann's story to make sense as well as alternatives to Freud's reading that might make the story equally, or perhaps more, sensible.

Freud discusses the idea of "the double" as a particular source of uncanny feeling. According to Freud, a double involves "the repetition of the same features or character-traits or vicissitudes, of the same crimes, or even the same names." Using some of the ideas Freud associates with doubling (be sure to note which ones you choose), create a fictional character who doubles you. You might think of this person as your evil twin, but then again, a double isn't necessarily evil. What does your double look like? What does your double have in common with you? How are the two of you different? What does the double reveal about you? Create a profile for your double that represents her, him, or it visually as well as through words. Present the profile to your classmates, either in a brief presentation or on a class website.

Freud's "The Uncanny" provides a way to understand Hoffmann's "The Sand-Man," but the ideas in the essay could have much broader applications. Choose one of the other monsters represented in this book, and write an essay that uses Freud's ideas to help explain the monster's significance. How is the monster both familiar and unfamiliar? If the monster represents the return of repressed feelings, what are those feelings? How else might the monster relate to oedipalization—that is, to the psychological formation of people's identities and desires?

MONSTERS

EVIL DOLLS: THE *CHILD'S PLAY* AND *PUPPET MASTER* SERIES

BY L. ANDREW COOPER AND BRANDY BALL BLAKE

Many monsters originate in fairy tales and children's stories, fashioned to reflect the fears of young audiences and to teach about the real-life dangers that the monsters represent. Other monsters take children's dreams—such as the fantasy that toys could come to life and become real playmates—and turn them into nightmares. Tales in which toys come to life, like Carlo Collodi's early nineteenth-century novel *Pinocchio* and the more recent film series *Toy Story* (three films, made in 1995, 1999, and 2010, with a fourth film in the planning stages), have perverse counterparts in the mainstream horror film series that began with *Child's Play* (1988) and the direct-to-video cult horror phenomenon that began with *Puppet Master* (1989). In these films, dolls come to life to commit murder, either turning on the children who play with them or hunting adults who would never expect such danger lurking within figures of innocence.

Child's Play has four sequels: *Child's Play 2* (1990), *Child's Play 3* (1991), *Bride of Chucky* (1998), and *Seed of Chucky* (2004). A remake of the original is slated for release in 2013. The first film in the series begins with serial killer Charles Lee Ray fleeing from police and taking refuge in a toy store. Mortally wounded, he uses a voodoo chant to transfer his soul into a nearby doll, one of the "Good Guy" dolls that are the season's most sought-after children's toy. After an explosion, the possessed doll ends up for sale by a street peddler in a back alley. A Good Guy doll is all Karen Barclay's young son Andy wants for his birthday, and since the dolls are too expensive for a single mother like Karen to afford at full price, Karen overlooks the suspicious circumstances and buys the possessed doll from the street peddler.

The doll's name is Chucky, and he promises to be Andy's "friend to the end," a promise that becomes increasingly grim after Chucky comes to life and murders Andy's babysitter, among others. At first no one believes Andy when he says his doll has come to life; Chucky looks and acts like any other Good Guy when other people are near, only showing his crueler face and using the voice of Charles Lee Ray (provided by horror staple Brad Dourif) around Andy and his victims. Andy's mother and other adults end up thinking the boy has lost his mind, and they blame him for the killings. Meanwhile, Chucky visits the voodoo priest who trained him in the dark arts and learns that in order to escape the confines of the doll's body, which is becoming flesh and blood, he must transfer his soul into the body of the first person to discover that the doll is actually alive—Andy. Ultimately, Karen and a police detective see enough to believe the boy's story, leading to a battle with Chucky in which the doll is burnt and dismembered. However, like movie psychos Michael Myers and Jason Voorhees (see "Movie Psychos and Slashers" in this volume), massive physical damage hardly slows Chucky down.

The next two films in the *Child's Play* series have similar storylines, with Chucky continuing his efforts to transfer his soul into a real human body. However, in *Bride of Chucky*, the tone of the series changes dramatically, veering toward the all-out horror-comedy only hinted at by Chucky's one-liners in the previous films. In *Bride*, Charles Lee Ray's former lover Tiffany (Jennifer Tilly) uses her copy of *Voodoo for Dummies* to reanimate Chucky. The two start fighting almost immediately, and just after Tiffany finishes watching *Bride of Frankenstein* (1935) on TV, Chucky kills her and transfers her soul into a female version of the Good Guy doll that just happens to be wearing a wedding dress. The two set off on a road trip, with a goal of reaching Charles Lee Ray's grave, where they will perform a ceremony to make themselves human again. Of course the two turn on each other in a combination of slapstick and gore that culminates with Tiffany quoting *Bride of Frankenstein*'s climactic line, "We belong dead." They don't die, at least not permanently, as the duo returns in *Seed of Chucky* to deal with Chucky's spawn.

The *Puppet Master* movies feature dolls that differ significantly from Chucky and Tiffany. The film franchise that begins with *Puppet Master* continues in

Puppet Master 2 (1991), *Puppet Master 3: Toulon's Revenge* (1991), *Puppet Master 4* (1993), *Puppet Master 5: The Final Chapter* (1994), *Curse of the Puppet Master* (1998), *Retro Puppet Master* (1999), *Puppet Master: The Legacy* (2004), *Puppet Master vs. Demonic Toys* (2004; as the title suggests, it brings in more living toys from another franchise), and *Puppet Master: Axis of Evil* (2010). The series centers on puppets at least initially created by a man named Andre Toulon, who has an Egyptian spell that allows him to bring the puppets he creates to life. The first film involves a group of psychics called together by a colleague who plans to have Toulon's living puppets kill them all so that he can get away with using Toulon's secret to gain immortality. Other films in the series carry this story both backward and forward, gradually filling in details about how Toulon learned and used the reanimation technique before he was hunted by Nazis (who want the technique for their own evil purposes) during the World War II era and about how the puppets introduced in the first film continue to wreak havoc on the world.

The focus of the films isn't the storytelling but the puppets themselves. Each puppet has a different design and a different, usually extravagant, way of killing people. Their names often hint at how they kill: Blade, Pinhead, Jester, Tunneler, and Leech Woman are the originals that appear in most of the films. The puppets end up being sympathetic to varying degrees as they defend Toulon and fight against people who mistreat them. Seeing who and how the puppets will kill next, while perhaps cheering them on, becomes the primary motivation for the films' narratives and audiences. Quantities of humor and intentional campiness also vary by title, but as a whole, the direct-to-video series thrives on the appeal of the puppets' quirky charm to a loyal cult following.

Figure 24. In *Child's Play*, Andy is ecstatic to receive the Chucky Good Guy doll as a birthday present. This image shows Chucky as if he were just like other Good Guy dolls, with a friendly and harmless expression. A living toy menacing a child is a nightmare version of a common childhood fantasy involving toys that become real-life playmates. Chucky and the Good Guy dolls implicitly exploit children's fantasies, and thus they suggest an undercurrent of social criticism in the early *Child's Play* films: the mass production and marketing of toys like the Good Guys create overwhelming demand among children and challenge parents to spend huge sums on fads that could be harmful or even, as with Chucky, deadly.

Figure 25. In contrast to the doll's friendly and harmful appearance, this image from *Child's Play 2* shows Chucky as he appears to his victims. Chucky often kills people in ironically gruesome ways; he prepares to kill a teacher with a yard stick. Psychologist Joanne Cantor identifies transformations of familiar things into unexpected forms as one of the phenomena children find most frightening.

Figure 26. *Bride of Chucky* veers toward comedy as stitched-together Chucky and his doll "bride" Tiffany become a monstrous couple that recalls the film *Bride of Frankenstein*. The sexual tension and aggressive dialogue between the dolls combine with absurd violence to create humorous (although possibly quite disturbing) situations.

Figure 27. In the original *Puppet Master*, the signature puppet Blade, which is in all the films, brandishes a hook and knife, showing that being life-sized isn't necessary for being a killer.

Figure 28. Two more killer puppets from the original *Puppet Master* prepare to kill people according to their unique designs. The drill on the top of his head allows Tunneler, shown on the top, to do as his name implies. On the bottom, Leech Woman opens her mouth and unleashes leeches on a prone man's body, ready to drain him dry. Both of these puppets, as well as others in the *Puppet Master* series, are vaguely erotic in the ways that they kill, suggesting a link between dolls and sexual fetishism.

EVIL DOLLS: THE CHILD'S PLAY AND PUPPET MASTER SERIES

The *Child's Play* and *Puppet Master* film series are not the only stories that involve evil dolls. Search the Internet for more, finding at least one additional film, one written story, and one story in another medium. What do the different stories about evil dolls have in common? How do they differ? How do representations of the dolls change over time and across media? What fears do the dolls reflect, and how do those fears vary with context?

The caption for Figure 25 refers to transformations, which are also crucial in werewolf stories, as particularly frightening for children. Review information about werewolves included in this book. Then write an essay that connects evil dolls to other monsters.

- What is significant about this connection?

- How do evil dolls carry on traditions found in other monster stories?

- What distinguishes the evil doll as a monster—what does the evil doll *do* and *mean* that adds to a broader understanding of monsters' cultural significance?

Using popsicle sticks, paper cutouts, socks, or any other materials you have handy, create your own evil toy. Bring your evil toy to class, and with a group of other students who have their own evil toys, create a horrific narrative or puppet show that reflects on the imaginative worlds—and perception-distorting fears—of children.

- How does your toy reflect interests or fears you had as a child?

- What do your classmates' toys suggest about their own childhood interests or fears?

- How might you tell a story that reflects on these childhood experiences while also revealing something about your culture at large?

- Would your story focus on horror, or would it involve humor in ways similar to the turn toward humor in *Bride of Chucky*?

- What difference does humor make for your evil toys' meanings?

MONSTERS

SERIAL KILLERS: FROM JACK THE RIPPER TO AILEEN WUORNOS

BY L. ANDREW COOPER AND BRANDY BALL BLAKE

Serial killers receive huge amounts of media attention and inspire countless novels, films, and television shows, including some of the fictional works discussed in this book. In *Creating Cultural Monsters: Serial Murder in America*, Julie B. Wiest claims that "the most common word used in the news and popular media to describe a serial murderer is *monster*," and she remarks that "many serial murderers use that description for themselves" (92). Wiest puts serial killers in traditional monster company, mentioning demons, werewolves, witches, zombies, and others, and she observes, "Their association with traditional monster imagery is especially clear when considering the nicknames given to many serial murderers by the media, which frequently include the words 'ripper,' 'stalker,' 'slasher,' 'butcher,' 'vampire,' and even 'monster.'"

Despite or perhaps because of their ubiquity in popular culture, serial killers are often misrepresented and misunderstood. The United States' Federal Bureau of Investigation (FBI) includes detailed information about serial killers on its website, www.fbi.gov, in an article entitled "Serial Murder: Multi-Disciplinary Perspectives for Investigators." Before officially defining what a serial killer is, the FBI carefully establishes what the serial is *not* by dispelling certain "myths." The first myth is that "serial killers are all dysfunctional loners." Instead, "the majority of serial killers are not reclusive, social misfits who live alone," and "because many serial killers can blend in so effortlessly, they are often overlooked by law enforcement and the public." As examples, the FBI lists Robert Yates, who killed seventeen women while being "married with five children;" the Green River Killer, Gary Ridgeway, who "attended church regularly, read the Bible at home and at work, and talked about religion with co-workers;" and the BTK killer, Dennis Rader, who was "married with two children, was a Boy Scout leader, served honorably in the U.S. Air Force, was employed as a local government official, and was president of his church."

The second myth is that "serial killers are all white males." In fact, "the racial diversification of serial killers generally mirrors that of the overall U.S. population." The third myth is that "serial killers are only motivated by sex," but motivations actually include "anger, thrill, financial gain, and attention seeking," perhaps others. The fourth myth is that "all serial murderers travel and operate interstate," the fifth, "serial killers cannot stop killing," the sixth, "all serial killers are insane or evil geniuses," and the seventh, "serial killers want to get caught." Only after dispelling these myths and discussing other obstacles to defining serial killing does the FBI advance this working definition: "the unlawful killing of two or more victims by the same offender(s), in separate events." The separation of events is particularly important, as many definitions of serial killing require a "cooling off" period between murders that distinguishes them from mass murders (multiple victims killed at once) and spree killings (multiple victims killed over a short period of time).

Myths about serial killers proliferate through fiction, creating what scholar Philip Jenkins describes as a mutually determining relationship between fact and fiction:

> There exists a complex feedback relationship between fact-based and fictitious accounts of the serial murder phenomenon. Fictional accounts often derive heavily from real-life cases, though with significant alteration; while in turn, the fiction has done at least as much to shape popular stereotypes of the serial killer as any avowedly factual book or news program. This is most apparent in the work of Thomas Harris [author of the novel *Silence of the Lambs*], but Robert Bloch [author of the novel *Psycho*] played a comparably influential role in earlier decades. There is also some evidence that actual serial killers may pattern themselves on fictional accounts. (15)

Jenkins also notes the exaggerated fear that many people have of serial killers, commenting, "99.99 percent of Americans will die from causes other than irrational multiple homicide" (47). Jenkins explains the media's overwhelming emphasis on the threat of serial murder by exploring "the wide range of symbolic meanings that have been attached to the phenomenon, and how these meanings have been manipulated for the purposes of a number of interest groups and bureaucratic structures," but he remains uncertain about "whether the specific image of the 'monster' developed in the media before it was popularized by police agencies" (47, 81). He also credits slasher films in the tradition of *Halloween* (1978) for increasing the portrayal of serial killers as monsters and promoting "increasingly inhuman interpretations of the killer's origin and powers" (81).

The history and cultural contexts of serial murder are also fraught with uncertainties either created or perpetuated by popular as well as scholarly representations. The film *From Hell* (2001) and the graphic novel it was adapted from reflect and strengthen a belief that the serial killer is a new phenomenon born with the crimes of Jack the Ripper in England at the dawn of the twentieth century. An opposing viewpoint might look to the crimes of 15th-century Frenchman Gilles de Rais, who raped and murdered children, or 16th-century Hungarian Elizabeth Bathory, who allegedly participated in the murders of dozens of girls, supposedly to bathe in their blood. Turning her attention away from these European precedents, Wiest devotes a considerable portion of her study of serial killers to explaining why contemporary American culture presents "an ideal environment for serial murder" (4). Jenkins, on the other hand, scoffs at the notion that serial killing is a recent or nationally-specific phenomenon, and he attributes such misunderstandings to the cultural uses of serial killer stories: "If serial murder is acknowledged to have a lengthy pedigree in a particular society, then it is implausible to attempt to blame it on recent developments," so in order to make serial killing politically useful, "a certain amount of historical amnesia is necessary, if only as a rhetorical stance" (122).

Although the definition, history, and motivations for serial killing are all debatable, a few murderers show up frequently on people's lists of real-life monsters. The following brief descriptions of some of history's most famous serial killers derive mostly from *Monstropedia: The Monstrous Encyclopedia* and were cross-referenced with studies by Wiest, Jenkins, and others included in this book's bibliography. Note that although the vast majority of serial killers are heterosexual, several of the killers listed here are known to have had homosexual relationships. Jenkins and other scholars have commented on the media's tendency to devote more attention to killers' homosexuality, part of a larger anti-gay tendency to distort information in order to justify prejudices.

Jack the Ripper. Creating the mold by which twentieth-century serial killers are measured, a murderer known as "Jack the Ripper" killed at least five people in the Whitechapel area of London, England. The five commonly agreed-upon victims were all prostitutes killed in 1888; more than six other murders that occurred between 1888 and 1891 have been attributed to the Ripper. Jack the Ripper's name derives from the gruesome ways in which he mutilated his victims' bodies as well as from letters sent to news agencies by someone claiming responsibility for the crimes. These letters fanned a media frenzy, making "Jack the Ripper" famous and creating paranoia about threats that might be hiding in London's lower-class and minority-based communities. Although several "definitive" accounts of the crimes have been published, Jack the Ripper has never been positively identified.

Ed Gein

The exact number of murders committed by Ed Gein in the 1950s is also uncertain; Wiest's and other accounts not overcome by the sensationalism of Gein's case limit the number to two women, which might disqualify Gein from some definitions of "serial killer." However, police found the remains of more than a dozen people when they raided Gein's home in Plainfield, Wisconsin. Local graveyards supplied many of the bodies, which Gein used to adorn furniture, lamps, and windows. He even made articles of clothing out of women's skin so that he could dress up as his mother. As this last detail might suggest, Gein provided inspiration for Norman Bates in various versions and sequels to *Psycho*, Leatherface in various versions and sequels to *The Texas Chain Saw Massacre*, and Buffalo Bill in both novel and film versions of *The Silence of the Lambs*. (Additional information from TruTV.com.)

John Wayne Gacy

Also known as "The Killer Clown" because he dressed as a clown at children's parties, Gacy raped and murdered 33 boys and young men between 1972 and his arrest in December 1978. He strangled his victims and stored most of their bodies in the crawlspace beneath his home. As recently as November 2011, police were using new DNA evidence in attempts to identify some of Gacy's victims.

Ted Bundy

Courtesy of Florida Memory Project

Bundy is known to have strangled or bludgeoned at least three women; he confessed to killing more than thirty and is believed to have killed approximately 35. He was captured in 1977 but escaped twice, taking more victims while he was at large. He fueled debates about the roles of media in real-world violence by claiming that pornography inspired his killings, but given Bundy's proclivity for showmanship, his claims are unreliable.

Jeffrey Dahmer

Dahmer sexually abused, murdered, and partially consumed the bodies of 17 men and boys, drugging and strangling them to death. He was found guilty of murder in 1992 and was killed in prison in 1994.

Aileen Wuornos

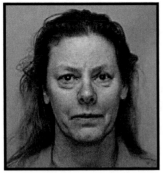

Receiving a great deal of attention because of the relative rarity of female serial killers, Wuornos was found guilty of murdering six men by shooting between 1989 and 1990. She worked as a prostitute; her victims were clients. That she traveled with a female companion and was identified as a lesbian received a great deal of media attention and formed the basis for many scenes in the critically acclaimed film *Monster* (2003).

Explore

Thousands of websites and other sources describe the backgrounds and crimes of serial killers. Investigate some of these sources, paying attention to the rhetoric they use. How do some sources seem to sensationalize serial killers? Which sources would you say are *not* sensational, and what makes them different? Does all the attention that serial killers receive contribute to what some have called an "epidemic" of serial killing in the United States? Why do you think serial killers have captured so many imaginations?

Invent

Fictional and real-life investigators who track serial killers often create profiles based on what they learn from crime scenes and other sources of information about the perpetrators. Based on what you've read, heard, and seen about serial killers, create your own profile of a "typical" serial killer as well as two or three examples that fit your profile. Consider factors such as sex, race, age, and religion as well as the killers' backgrounds and psychological makeup. Compare your profile with classmates' profiles. On what do you agree? On what do you disagree? How might these profiles be useful for catching and/or understanding future serial killers?

Choose one of the serial killers listed above and study one nonfictional account of his or her crimes alongside a fictional account either based on or inspired by the actual events. How and why do the fictions change, elaborate, or manipulate the facts? What is the significance of your comparison? Write an essay in which you answer these questions by closely analyzing details from both accounts.

The "Movie Psychos and Slashers" section of this book (page 211) discusses *Psycho* (1960) and *The Texas Chain Saw Massacre* (1974), two films at least partially inspired by the crimes of Ed Gein, but the killers in these films, Norman Bates and Leatherface, are radically different from one another. In groups, debate the following questions:

- How could one person inspire such radically different characters?

- Do you find these characters more believable now that you know about Ed Gein?

- Does knowing about Ed Gein change your perception of these characters' monstrosity? If so, how?

MOVIE PSYCHOS AND SLASHERS: FROM NORMAN BATES TO FREDDY KRUEGER

BY L. ANDREW COOPER AND BRANDY BALL BLAKE

Some of the most popular monsters of twentieth- and twenty-first-century cinema lack virtually all of earlier monsters' beastly trappings. They don't have claws or fangs: their monstrosity begins on the inside, where the workings of their distorted minds prompt them to do terrible deeds. These monsters kill people for many reasons—chief among them revenge, sustenance, and perverse sexuality—but explanations of their motivations usually fail to account fully for the gruesome ways in which they dispatch innocent victim after innocent victim. That they are completely insane and/or purely evil usually provides the final, irreducible reason for the horrors that unfold onscreen.

Many films contributed to the emergence of the subgenre of the horror film that these monsters inhabit. Most commonly known as "slasher" and "body count" films, the subgenre owes a great deal to drive-in and B-movie horror films of the 1950s and several noteworthy films of the early 1960s, especially Michael Powell's *Peeping Tom* (1960) and Mario Bava's early Italian *giallo* film *Blood and Black Lace* (1964). Among these earlier influences, the film that deserves the most credit for putting the slasher (a word that describes both the subgenre and the type of monster it features) on the map is Alfred Hitchcock's *Psycho* (1960). Althogh *Psycho* isn't always classified as a slasher film per se, *Psycho*'s most famous scene, usually referred to as "the shower scene," sets the standard for the slasher's signature crime (you can find the scene on YouTube or another Internet video site). In this scene, beautiful young Marion Crane, portrayed by Janet Leigh, enjoys the shower in her room at the Bates Motel until the shadow of a womanly form approaches, yanks back the shower curtain, and stabs her repeatedly with a kitchen knife. The scene actually shows little blood and nudity, but Hitchcock's quick cuts between shots of the plunging knife and shots of the screaming victim create such a violent effect that the film is still blood-curdling today. Thanks at least in part to this scene's success, slashers almost always bear common household weapons, such as kitchen knives or garden tools, and they typically hunt their beautiful, young prey—usually women—at moments of vulnerability and undress.

The killer in *Psycho* turns out to be Norman Bates (Figure 29), who has a split personality that prompts him to dress up as his mother (whom he has murdered) and kill any woman to whom he is sexually attracted. Today, most viewers come to the film having already heard something about it—people expect Marion Crane to die as soon as she steps into the famous shower, and few are surprised by the murdering-mother-is-actually-the-son twist. These elements are familiar because they're both legendary in their own right and often imitated, but in 1960, their shock value was supreme. Particularly since the film spends a great deal of time building up Marion as the lead character (and Janet Leigh was an A-list leading lady), her murder defied the original audience's expectations for monstrous spectacle, and Norman's sexual twistedness gave them a type of monster they had rarely seen before.

A sliver of Norman's sexual aberration finds its way into the next psycho spotlighted here. Briefly in the original *Texas Chain Saw Massacre* (1974) and at great length in some of the sequels, chainsaw-wielding Leatherface (Figure 30) wears women's clothing, and he plays a mix of masculine and feminine roles in his entirely male family of psychotic former slaughterhouse workers. More shockingly, in the manner of real-life serial killer Ed Gein (who supposedly inspired *Psycho* as well), he wears his victims' skins: Leatherface's leather-looking masks are actually the faces of victims past. However, interpretations of Leatherface and the family on whose behalf he slaughters young people with a chainsaw tend to focus less on sexuality than on economic class, as the family's backstory frames them as workers dispossessed of their slaughterhouse livings by the mechanization of their jobs (technology, epitomized by the chainsaw itself, also deserves interpretive attention in this film). The family's members, three brothers and a barely-living grandfather, support themselves by killing travelers who stop near their Texas home. The family uses victims' body parts as tools and furniture as well as food.

Although Leatherface certainly played a role, the monster who deserves the most credit for popularizing the slasher as a subgenre is Michael Myers (Figure 31), the lunatic from *Halloween* (1978). As a child, Michael murders his older sister on Halloween night. Fifteen years later, he escapes a mental institution, returns to his home town, steals a supposedly common mask from a local shop (the mask is actually based on the visage of William Shatner, of *Star Trek* fame), and starts stalking young women who remind him of his long-ago deed. Because it's Halloween, he can begin his hunt in broad daylight: when everyone is wearing a mask and trying to scare each other, real threats like Michael's can go unnoticed until it's too late. In addition to exchanging Leatherface's grotesque mask for a plain one and ushering in a fad for horror films based on significant dates, *Halloween* restored an element of the supernatural to slasher monstrosity. When the film's heroine, Laurie Strode (Jamie Lee Curtis), stabs him with needles and knives, *he just keeps coming*. Being an almost invincible monster who stalks beautiful women gives Michael Myers more in common with vampires than slasher fans usually acknowledge, but Michael's brand of slow-moving stalk-and-slash antics nevertheless has a memorable flair.

The psycho in the hockey mask, Jason Voorhees (Figure 32), is perhaps the most recognizable of all these famed fictional killers because of the sheer volume of films associated with the *Friday the 13th* series that spawned him (twelve, from the original in 1980 to the remake in 2009, which really seems to beg for at least one more). Jason's story has him supposedly drowning at a summer camp while the counselors who should have been minding him were too busy having sex to do their jobs; consequently, the series has first his mother and then him getting revenge on libidinous woodsy teens. Jason upped the ante for gore in the slasher subgenre, and he also took Michael Myers's hint of the supernatural to its inevitable, (il)logical conclusion. Starting with *Friday the 13th Part 3*, the 3-D installment in which Jason first dons a hockey mask, the spectacles of young women and men being hacked to pieces lead up to final sequences in which the killer faces similar mutilation. Stabbed, chopped, hanged, and more, Jason removes all subtlety from his immediate predecessor's creepy, monstrous immortality, and sharing in the monster's lack of poise, audiences at *Friday the 13th* films are known for cheering both as the monster kills people and as he is killed. Giving or receiving pain, Jason provides spectacles that are a hoot, and the heavy doses of comedy in some of the films—especially *Friday the 13th Part 6: Jason Lives* (1986), *Jason Goes to Hell: The Final Friday* (1993, part 9, the second film of the series to include

"Final" in its misleading title), and *Jason X* (2001, part 10)—acknowledge the variety of fun that a monster can afford.

Also given to sick humor as well as horror, the final slasher under consideration here is Freddy Krueger (Figure 33), the child-murdering maniac from *A Nightmare on Elm Street* (1984) and its many sequels. Freddy initially haunts the dreams of teens whose parents lynched him after he escaped conviction for murder on a technicality. As someone who returns from death to haunt the living, Freddy is arguably one of the most traditional forms of monster in the catalogue, a ghost. However, he wears straight razors like giant fingernails on one gloved hand and stalks his victims in ways that recall other slashers. Furthermore, since Michael Myers and Jason Voorhees tend to return from fatal encounters, whether such slashers are actually ghosts is already a classification stumper. The question of *what* Freddy is, therefore, opens up a chasm of ontological mystery too deep to fathom here. The question of *how* Freddy operates is far more germane to the narratives of the *Nightmare* series: manipulating dreamscapes by the force of his evil will, he toys with victims until they stop entertaining him, and then he ends both the dreams and the dreamers. Because he is a dream, Freddy can change his size and shape, tricking victims and viewers by taking other forms and overwhelming them by becoming a carnivorous worm, a supersized puppetmaster, and other creatures that give him new abilities as well as new appearances. Later films in the series suggest he ultimately gets his power by devouring the souls of the children he murders; in any case, his limits are only the filmmakers' imaginations (and maybe the size of their special effects budgets).

As you look at the following images (and perhaps see one or more of the films), consider what the psychos' and slashers' appearances, as well as their behaviors, contribute to their monstrosity.

Figure 29. This image shows Norman Bates (Anthony Perkins) near the end of Alfred Hitchcock's *Psycho*. Having just wrapped up an interior monologue in the voice of his mother, Norman uses his sinister expression to show viewers just how psycho he really is. Up to this point, Norman has looked completely sane—at least when not wearing his mother's clothes. Although Norman's monstrosity is entirely explicable according to the laws of known science, the deception of his appearances and the duality of his character recall other monsters who are more than they appear to be.

Figure 30. Leatherface (Gunnar Hansen) shows off his favorite weapon on a sunny Texas day. While wearing the skins of his victims makes Leatherface the stand-out monster in *The Texas Chain Saw Massacre*, the technological weapon and even the bright setting—too vast for anyone to hear victims' screams—are also candidates for monster-hood.

Figure 31. *Halloween's* Michael Myers (Tony Moran) menaces his prey with a kitchen knife in a typical suburban home. The familiar, familial setting suggests that a monster might find you anywhere; as Michael's sister learns at the beginning of the film, the monster might even be kin.

Figure 32. After donning his hockey mask for the first time, Jason Voorhees (Richard Brooker) carries around an intended victim in *Friday the 13th Part 3*. Although she looks helpless here, this young woman eventually engages Jason in a ferocious battle, finally hitting him with a hatchet to the head. The blow slows him down but doesn't stop him: as many teens learn the hard way, the monstrosity of a movie psycho isn't just that he kills but also that he might refuse to die.

Figure 33. Freddy Krueger (Robert Englund) holds up his homemade glove-with-razor-fingers. In *A Nightmare on Elm Street*, he says of his glove, "This is God!" This blasphemous taunt directed at one of his victims highlights a demonic dimension of the killer's ability to invade his victims' dreams, and it also emphasizes a nihilistic undercurrent throughout the slasher subgenre, in which the spectacle of gruesome death is the most salient force available to drive a narrative. This image also provides a glimpse at Freddy's horribly burned skin, a remnant of his lynching at the hands of his victims' parents.

Explore

A tendency to spawn sequels seemingly without end is a defining feature of slasher films, and the tendency to return for one film after another is a defining feature of the monsters the films portray. Find information about the sequels in the *Psycho, Texas Chain Saw Massacre, Halloween, Friday the 13th,* and *Nightmare on Elm Street* series. How would you characterize the changes that take place as movie psychos appear in sequel after sequel? How do their characters and abilities evolve? Why do you think these changes occur? Although slashers are sometimes stigmatized for being sequel machines, earlier monsters, especially Frankenstein's monster and Dracula, have also appeared in large numbers of films. How do these earlier monsters' film follow-ups differ from slashers'? What do these differences suggest about the monsters themselves?

In small groups, plan your own slasher movie, either a sequel involving one of the slashers described here or a film based on a slasher of your own devising. Discuss your monster's appearance, weapon(s), and favorite prey as well as what your film will reveal about the monster's backstory and how developments within the film might contribute to a longer series. How might a slasher from *this* year differ from the classic slashers described above—how should the moment shape the monster? (To turn this conversation into a major assignment, use a camcorder to create a scene from the movie you've imagined.)

Like other monsters, the psycho or slasher provides an index to a culture's anxieties, particularly anxieties related to identity (factors such as race, sex, gender, sexuality, and economic class). Choose one of the movie psychos described here and develop a thesis about the anxieties it reflects. What makes this monster meaningful, and how do its meanings relate to the ways it pursues and dispatches its victims?

Although the psychos and slashers described here are in some ways distinctly contemporary phenomena, in other ways they recall monsters from the nineteenth century and earlier. Brainstorm about connections between one of the psychos and a specific predecessor from before the twentieth century. Do the similarities suggest that particular anxieties or prejudices have spread from one historical moment to another? If so, what are they? If not, how do you account for the connection between the psycho/slasher and his predecessor? Finally, how do differences between the psycho/slasher and his predecessor relate to broader historical changes in representations of monstrosity?

Gerard Jones, an academic and popular success, has written nonfiction, humor, and comic books. While he has created his own comic series, including The Trouble with Girls and Oktane, he has also worked on such classic series as Justice League, Batman, and Green Lantern. His nonfiction books examine topics related to the popular work he pursues. For example, Men of Tomorrow: Geeks, Gangsters, and the Birth of the Comic Book and The Comic Book Heroes: The First History of Modern Comic Books examine the comic industry from a historical perspective, while Killing Monsters: Why Children Need Fantasy, Super Heroes, and Make-Believe Violence tackles more theoretical issues.

Jones's Killing Monsters confounds common views of media violence as a monstrous influence on impressionable minds. His book examines how children use violence—anything from pretending to slay monsters to playing first-person shooter video games to listening to brutal rap lyrics—in order to cope with overbearing problems and emotions that they cannot otherwise face. "Being Strong," the first chapter of this book, discusses Jones's growing realization that violence can help children "to feel stronger, to access their emotions, to take control of their anxieties, to calm themselves down in the face of real violence, to fight their way through emotional challenges and lift themselves to new developmental levels." As you read this chapter, consider your own feelings about media violence as well as your experiences with "pretend" violence.

excerpts from

KILLING MONSTERS

BY GERARD JONES

My first memory is of tearing the monster's arm off.

I had crossed the sea to the hall of these warriors who were being terrorized by a nocturnal beast, boasted over mead that only I could slay it, pretended to sleep until the monster crept in to devour a warrior—and when it came to seize me I leapt up, seized its massive arm in my grip of steel, and held on as we battled through the hall, smashing the wooden walls with our fury, until at last in desperation it tore itself loose of its own limb and fled, bleeding and screaming, mortally wounded to its lair in the fens.

Quite a feat for a five-year-old.

When I was old enough to go to kindergarten, my mother went back to college to get her teaching credential. She hadn't had a lot of high culture in her own upbringing and she made sure that I was more fortunate: she tacked prints from the Metropolitan Museum to all the walls in the house and read classic literature to me at bedtime. She tried Stevenson's poems, *Gulliver's Travels*, Chaucer's *Reynard*. It all rolled off me. If I hadn't asked her about all this decades later, I'd never have known. The only one I remembered was *Beowulf*, with its pagan, barbarian monster-slayer of a hero.

He was a terrible role model. He didn't do any of the things we want our children's heroes to teach: didn't discuss solutions with the group, didn't think first of the safety of others, didn't try to catch the monster without harming it. He bragged, he bullied, he killed, and he even let his allies be devoured to further his plan. Yet, it was Beowulf I wanted to be, and Beowulf I became. I made my mom read it to me over and over, and I caught her when she tried to glide past the most gruesome parts ("The demon clutched a sleeping thane in his swift assault, tore him in pieces, bit through the bones, gulped the blood, and gobbled the flesh . . ."). I carved scenes from his battles into my Playskool blocks with a ballpoint pen and rearranged them in every possible narrative order. Running naked from the bath across the polyester carpet I thumped my skinny chest and roared, "Foe against foe, I'll fight the death!"

I was no warrior in real life. I was a mama's boy. I liked to play in the house and the backyard, liked kids who were my age but not when they got too wild. The prospect of kindergarten terrified me, and so did knowing that my mom was going to be away from home much of every day. But at home, in my own world, I could tear a pillow off the bed with a *"rrrrrrarrr!"* and see the monster Grendel fleeing in terror.

"You were an adorable barbarian," my mom said, helping me dig through a box of my childhood artwork. I found a yellowing pad covered with stick-figure warriors grimacing and flexing their muscles—loaf-like bubbles protruding from line-thin arms—at toothy monsters. I remembered striking that pose—and how strong I felt. Then, with a mock sigh, my mother added, "But I did so want you to be cultured."

As it turned out, I did grow up fairly cultured—or civilized, at least. I was as cooperative, bookish, and conscientious as my parents could have wanted. But I carried that monster-slaying hero inside me the whole time. First as fantasy: Beowulf gave way to King Kong, then Batman, then James Bond. As I outgrew fantasies, he became a scholarly interest. [...]

[...] For all the decades of psychological research attempting to prove that entertainment violence makes children more aggressive, or desensitizes them, or distorts their views of reality, very few studies have asked why they love it or what good it might do them. Hardly any, in fact, have even asked when or why it has a negative effect or how potential negative effects might be ameliorated. Bruno Bettelheim had summed up a great deal of psychiatric research on the benefits of violent fairy tales in his *Uses of Enchantment*, but even he had dismissed mass entertainment out of hand—even though the fantasies, the themes, and the violence of that entertainment often echoed fairy tales and even though it obviously resonated powerfully with millions of modern children.

So I interviewed psychiatrists, pediatricians, family therapists, teachers, screenwriters, game designers, and parents. I read the research. I asked children and teenagers what stories, movies, songs, and games they loved and what they meant to them. I dug back through my own growing up. I watched my son as he tackled the challenges of toddlerhood, preschool, and elementary school, choosing fantasies and entertainment to help him along the way. I gathered hundreds of stories of young people who had benefited from superhero comics, action movies, cartoons, shoot-'em-up video games, and angry rap and rock songs. I found stories of kids who'd used them badly, too, and others who'd needed adult help to use them well. But mostly I found young people using fantasies of combat in order to feel stronger, to access their emotions, to take control of their anxieties, to calm themselves down in the face of real violence, to fight their way through emotional challenges and lift themselves to new developmental levels.

During those same years, however, criticisms of entertainment violence became steadily more intense. The news was replete with stories of teenage violence (even though juvenile crime rates were dropping rapidly), and many of those stories drew connections between the crimes and movies, songs, or video games. The boys who killed their classmates and themselves at Columbine High School were discovered to have loved the video game *Doom*, and its influence soon dominated speculation on what might have influenced them. Congressional committees excoriated the entertainment industry. Prominent psychologists testified that video violence had been proven harmful to children. In March

2000, the American Academy of Pediatrics urged doctors to monitor their young patients' exposure to media violence and warn parents of its dangers. […]

[…] I had been leading workshops in comic-strip creation in which I encouraged kids to put down their own stories and fantasies through words and pictures. As simple as they were, those workshops were sources of an astonishing wealth of juvenile imaginings and experiences. So, drawing upon the wisdom of educators, psychologists, and media literacy experts, I used those as the foundation for what I've come to call the Art and Story Workshops: programs adaptable to every level from preschool to high school that help kids pull together the images, thoughts, and emotions in their minds through individual storytelling in a comic strip-like form. I'd take over a classroom for a day or a week, get the kids talking about their ideas and passions, and challenge them to put them down on paper—in both words and pictures.

Children are usually taught to compartmentalize their communication into either linear narrative or static portraits, but storytelling that is both visual and verbal leads them to transcend the compartments, to experience their thoughts and feelings more completely. Comics also have an inherent funkiness that frees kids to express fantasies that the more adult-approved media inhibit. Visual storytelling unlocks the images they've stored up from cartoons, movies, and video games and helps them make more sense of the media-transmitted stories that fill their environments. The process gives young people a sense of authorship, of authority over their own emotions and the world's influences. It also reveals the way that children use fantasies, stories, and media images in building their sense of self.

What I've learned in the Art and Story Workshops has consistently reinforced my belief that the vast array of fantasies and stories that we tend to dismiss with such labels as "media violence" are used well by children. I've seen young people turn every form of imaginary aggression into sources of emotional nourishment and developmental support. But I'm startled, sometimes, too. I bring in my own biases about what's beneficial and what's not. And sometimes a boy like Philip will smash them.

The theme that day was "power." When I'm working with eighth and ninth graders, I find it useful to have the class agree on an overall theme as a starting point (usually after a very boisterous discussion). After that, every kid is responsible for telling the story that excites him or her most, however silly or sentimental or horrific or tasteless others might find it. I move around the room to help unstick ideas and bolster confidence, but I make it clear that because they are doing it for *themselves*, not for the school, the teacher, or a grade, there are no grown-up restraints or expectations to observe. Philip needed no help; he dove instantly into a humorous comic strip about a wily prostitute who tricks a corrupt police officer.

"Why that?" I asked. "Because I hate hypocrisy," he said, "especially when it acts like it's supposed to be morality." "Like what else?" I asked. That's when one of the girls sitting next to him asked Philip, "Can I tell him?" He nodded, and she told me that Philip had come out as gay a month before. The boys in the class had mostly avoided him since, and his friends now all came from one clique of sensitive, politically minded girls.

As she talked, I noticed Philip and a second girl writing lines of poetry on each other's pages. I asked if they were song lyrics. "Rap lyrics," said Philip proudly, and he and the girls told me about the hip-hop tastes they shared: Dr. Dre, DMX, Snoop Dogg. But, said Philip with obvious passion, his favorite was Eminem. That was what startled me. Eminem was then at the peak of his notoriety for his rageful, homophobic epithets: *"My words are like a dagger with a jagged edge that'll stab you in the head whether you're a fag or a lez."* Philip noticed my reaction and forced a grin. "Don't say what my mom always says."

I asked him what that was. He nursed his thoughts for a moment, and then he poured it out: "She's being really cool about all this. Not like my dad. My dad's really making it hard, telling me it's just a phase, not letting me go to any support groups, blah blah blah. My mom's being really supportive, being there for me no matter what. But she just won't get Eminem. She calls his lyrics 'hate-mongering.' She keeps saying, 'How can you listen to that if you're gay?' 'Why don't you listen to something that makes you feel good about yourself?' And I try to tell her why it *does*."

"Why does it?" I asked.

"Because Eminem has the courage to say who he *is*."

It's easy to fall into the trap of thinking that young people emulate literally what they see in entertainment. That if they like a rapper who insults gays, then they must be learning hostility to gays, and if they love a movie hero who defeats villainy with a gun, then they must be learning to solve problems with violence. There is some truth in that. One of the functions of stories and games is to help children rehearse for what they'll be in later life. Anthropologists and psychologists who study play, however, have shown that there are many other functions as well—one of which is to enable children to pretend to be just what they know they'll *never* be. Exploring, in a safe and controlled context, what is impossible or too dangerous or forbidden to them is a crucial tool in accepting the limits of reality. Playing with rage is a valuable way to reduce its power. Being evil and destructive in imagination is a vital compensation for the wildness we all have to surrender on our way to being good people.

In focusing so intently on the literal, we overlook the *emotional* meaning of stories and images. The most peaceful, empathetic, conscientious children are often excited by the most aggressive entertainment. Young people who reject violence, guns, and bigotry in every form can still embrace the emotional power at its heart. Children need to feel strong. They need to feel powerful in the face of a scary, uncontrollable world. Superheroes, video-game warriors, rappers, and movie gunmen are symbols of strength. By pretending to be them, young people are being strong.

Adults, however, often react to violent images very differently—and in the gap between juvenile and adult reactions, some of our greatest misunderstandings and most damaging disputes are born. Soon after the terrorist attacks of September 11, 2001, many toy retailers reported sharp increases in sales of G. I. Joe and other militaristic toys. But some of those same retailers also began pulling such toys from the shelves, largely in response to parents' requests. Newspaper stories reported that many parents were forbidding violent toys and entertainment in their homes as a reaction to the tragedy. One mother said she'd hidden her son's toy soldiers because "It's bad enough that they see the Army in the airport."

Many of us worried about how we would help children deal with the terror of September 11, but when I went into the classrooms, I found that the children were far less shaken than their parents and teachers. Most of them talked about the horrific images they'd seen with a mixture of anger and excitement—and a lot of them wanted to draw pictures, tell stories, or play games involving planes destroying buildings or soldiers fighting terrorists. This isn't a failure to react appropriately to tragedy: this is how children deal with it. When something troubles them, they have to play with it until it feels safer.

Adults are generally more empathetic, more attuned to the greater world, and are more literalistic than children. We are more likely to feel the pain and anxiety caused by real violence when we see it in make-believe. It troubles us to see our kids having fun with something that we deplore. We fear that they are celebrating or affirming a horror that we desperately want to banish from reality. We want them to mirror our adult restraint, seriousness, compassion, and pacifism. But they can't—and shouldn't—mimic adult reactions. Play, fantasy, and emotional imagination are essential tools of the work of childhood and adolescence.

Anxiety about how our kids will turn out is an inescapable aspect of adulthood. That anxiety is always heightened in times of sudden change or general insecurity about the future. It can be a useful emotion when it helps us notice the ways in which children are using their aggressive fantasies, and when it energizes us to teach them nonviolent solutions to life's problems. It can be destructive, however, if it only heightens our children's own anxieties, or drives them away from us and deeper into a media-based reality, or keeps them from finding the fantasies they need.

In working with children, I've come up against my adult anxieties again and again. But I've also been brought back in memory to their kid's place in life, a place in which they may need precisely the images that their daily life doesn't provide, precisely the stories from which their parents have tried to protect them. For a long time, I resisted looking closely at my own adolescence. I dismissed it as simply too sheltered and assumed that superhero comics had been just a source of excitement for me. It was only when I began seriously exploring the function of aggressive fantasy in children's development that I let myself look fully at what I'd gone through in those years and began to understand why the figure of the hero kept fighting his way to such a central place in my psyche.

When I was thirteen I started cutting school. I didn't have the words to say why. We didn't talk about scary feelings in my house. My parents desperately wanted a polite and civilized home, unlike the ones they'd grown up in. My mother always seemed to be suppressing anger, my father always dodging a confrontation. They let me know in a thousand ways that they wanted a sweet little boy who didn't get angry or greedy or rebellious, and I badly wanted to be that.

They were going through a hard time; I can see that now, but then I didn't know what was happening. My mother would sit in front of the evening news drinking glass after glass of wine ("my anesthetic," she called it, although she wouldn't name the pain), telling me bitterly of a world that had mutilated her liberal ideals with assassinations, riots, war rising crime, and racial violence, telling me as she drank how disillusioned she was as a high school teacher, how appalled she was at the new youth culture. My father would retreat into the back room with the newspaper. They barely spoke to each other and never told me why, and I could never make out their muted arguments behind closed doors.

I didn't know what to do. I hated junior high, felt threatened by what my peers were turning into. I didn't want adolescence, didn't want to have to go into that world my mother talked about. I hung out less and less with my friends, and I wouldn't tell them why. Pretty soon they stopped asking. I started faking headaches so I could stay home from school, even though home was cold and empty. My mother blamed the public school system and put me in a tiny experimental school full of misfits. I didn't protest; somehow it felt like the survival of my fragile world depended on being the nice boy who would fulfill all of his parents' expectations. But by eighth grade I was cutting school to stay home all day and watch TV with the shades drawn. There was nothing on that wasteland of game shows and soap operas that spoke to me, but I kept watching, hoping for something to excite me. Sometimes late at night I would slip out of the house and take long walks alone, looking for I didn't know what. [...]

[...] The character who entranced me, and freed me, was the Incredible Hulk: overgendered and undersocialized, half-naked and half-witted, raging against a frightened world that misunderstood and persecuted him. In normal life he was a government scientist who had to struggle desperately to maintain his altruistic self-restraint—because his own anger set off a reaction in his body that transformed him, uncontrollably, into a brute of raw, destructive power. "Mustn't . . . let . . . myself . . . feel it!" he'd roar, and suddenly his body would explode with muscles that ripped through his clothes, and he'd hurl himself bare-chested and free through the walls around him and thoom into the sky with a mighty leap. The Hulk smashed through the walls of fear I'd been carrying inside me and freed me to feel everything I had been repressing: rage and pride and the hunger for power over my own life.

Suddenly I had a fantasy self who could show me what it felt like to be unafraid of my own desires and the world's disapproval, to be bold enough to destroy what had to be destroyed. I had my Beowulf back. And when he and I came down from the heights with an earth-shattering boom, I saw that we were on open desert beyond the narrow streets I'd been walking. "Puny boy follow Hulk!" roared my fantasy self, and I followed. [...]

[...] After a few years I was done with comics, or so I thought. I moved on to more grown-up heroes and more sophisticated stories, established a career in writing, and resisted looking back at the painful cradle of it all. But once I began talking to kids, I could no longer ignore the Hulk standing there in the middle of my growing up. He hadn't smashed all my problems, but he'd led me to a new sense of myself. He'd helped me play through some of my deepest fears. He'd led me to the arrogant, self-exposing, self-assertive, superheroic decision to become a writer, to start writing the script of my own life.

He also gave me a new way of talking to my parents. Gerry the superhero fan wasn't the same kid as Gerry the nice boy of my mother's imagination. I began to develop fantasies and tastes that she didn't understand and didn't wholly approve of. But she trusted that anything that excited me so much must be doing me some good, and she wanted me to share it with her. My father compared my superheroes with mock disdain to the Shadow and the other violent heroes of the pulp magazines he'd grown up with. They would both listen to me prattle about my favorite characters, writers, and artists. We still didn't talk openly about my angers and frustrations, but at least we talked about my fantasies of being powerful and destructive. I felt that the darker side of myself was being seen and accepted for the first time.

My mother told me years later that her anxieties had eased when she saw my love of superheroes as coming from within me, not as something that had been imposed upon me by the entertainment industry. The comic books were made by others and sold to me as a commodity, but the desire to read them was *mine*. A lot of us stumble over that as parents, blaming what our children see for making them want things, forgetting that it's our children themselves who are doing the wanting. Each child's fantasies and emotional needs are very much his own, even if he shares them with millions of other kids. When we burden those needs with our own anxieties, we can confuse and frighten children about their own feelings. Adult anxieties about the effects of entertainment are sometimes the real causes of the very effects that we fear most. [...]

[...] When we consider children in relation to mass media and pop culture, we tend to define them as consumers, watchers, recipients, victims. But they are also *users* of that media and culture: they are choosers, interpreters, shapers, fellow players, participants, and storytellers. Viewing children as passive recipients of the media's power puts us at odds with the fantasies they've chosen, and thus with children themselves. Viewing them as active users enables us to work with their entertainment—*any* entertainment—to help them grow. Shooter games, gangsta rap, *Pokémon* all become tools for parents and teachers to help young people feel stronger, clam their fears, and learn more about themselves.

In our anxiety to understand and control real-life violence, we've tried to reduce our children's relationships with their fantasies of combat and destruction to vast generalizations that we would never dream of applying to their fantasies about love and family and discovery and adventure. We don't usually ask whether game shows predispose our children to greed, or whether love songs increase the likelihood of getting stuck in bad relationships. But when aggression is the topic, we try to purée a million games and dreams and life stories into statistical studies. We ask absurdly sweeping questions like, What is the effect of media violence on children? as if violence were a single, simple phenomenon of which sandbox play-fights and mass murder were mere variations, as if the evening news and *Reservoir Dogs* and Daffy Duck were indistinguishable, as if children were like trees in an orchard who could all be raised to identical form by the same externalities. Many forces have been shown to contribute to aggression: religious fervor, patriotic fervor, sports rivalry, romantic rivalry, hot summer nights. Entertainment has inspired some people to violence, but so have the Bible, the Constitution, the Beatles, books about Hitler, and obsessions with TV actresses. We don't usually condemn those influences as harmful, because we understand them better, we understand why people like them and the benefits most of us draw from them. What's lacking is an understanding of aggressive fantasies and the entertainment that speaks to them.

"Narrative deals with the vicissitudes of human intentions," writes the great psychologist Jerome Bruner in *Actual Minds, Possible Worlds*. "And since there are myriad intentions and endless ways for them to run into trouble—or so it would seem—there should be endless kinds of stories." My work with kids and entertainment has been a discovery of stories. Every story of a superhero or a monster or an angry rapper—even the video game that looks so simplistic at first glance—resonates with the personal stories of its audience. And every one becomes a different story depending on the listener, the viewer, the player. A child chooses a particular movie or game because his unique story has led him there, and he weaves a new, personal narrative out of the fantasy and play it inspires. [...]

[...] Children want to be strong, secure, and happy. Their fantasies will tell us what they feel they need to attain that, if we pay attention. But we need to look beyond our adult expectations and interpretations and see them through our children's eyes. First, we need to begin disentangling the fears and preconceptions that have prevented us from doing so.

In small groups, discuss what "violence" is. Begin by looking up definitions and synonyms of the word. Then discuss the different types of violence you've encountered—in reality, in books, on the Internet, on television, in video games, in song lyrics, etc. Are there differences in these types of violence? Why? What types of violence do you find "monstrous"?

As Jones emphasizes, critics have argued for years that media violence can have a negative impact on children. Find examples of these arguments online or in your library. Then examine the rhetoric used. How much of the language is based on pathos? Logos? Ethos?

- What kind of evidence are the authors using to support their arguments, and how does their evidence compare to Jones's?

- What information or examples are missing from their arguments?

- What information or examples are missing from Jones's?

All of the stories selected for this book are violent in some manner. Choose one of the fictional selections, and list the types of violence it involves. Then consider whether that violence might help readers or viewers to release aggressive or violent feelings of their own—to achieve what is known as "catharsis." Brainstorm ways in which the story might encourage a cathartic experience. What role does the monster of the story play in that catharsis? Does violence against the monster relate to the emotional release? If so, do you find this violence to be more beneficial or harmful to the reader/viewer? To society as a whole? Why?

Did you, like many of the young people Jones encountered, use aggressive fantasies to overcome adversity as a child? Did you pretend to be a monster or hero? If so, which ones? If not, what type of make-believe violence did you participate in? Create a comic in which you use words and images to analyze how make-believe violence affected you as a child.

MAJOR ASSIGNMENTS

MAJOR ASSIGNMENT #1
DEFINITIONS

BACKGROUND

Jeffrey Jerome Cohen, Judith Halberstam, and other writers included in this volume have attempted to define "monster" in various ways. Instead of offering a singular, dictionary-style definition, Cohen offers seven "theses" about monsters as reflections on cultures, beginning with the idea that a monster is "an embodiment of a certain cultural moment—of a time, a feeling, and a place" (4). Halberstam remarks that "monsters are meaning machines," and ultimately she suggests, "The monster always represents the disruption of categories, the destruction of boundaries, and the presence of impurities and so we need monsters and need to recognize and celebrate our own monstrosities" (21, 27). While these and other definitions of the term share a tendency to view monsters as cultural metaphors, they differ in many respects. These differences stem in part from the authors' different backgrounds, audiences, and purposes and in part from the difficulty of fitting a single definition (or even multiple definitions) to a phenomenon as diverse as monstrosity.

ASSIGNMENT

At the end of the semester, reread the definition of "monster" that you wrote previously. Consider what you have learned about monsters since forming these ideas. Now, write an essay discussing how your definition of the word "monster" has changed. Your essay should include your beginning-of-semester definition and an *extended* definition that represents your current thinking. Compare your two definitions, and use evidence from this book and/or your independent research to reflect on and explain the similarities and differences between them.

MODE AND GENRE

This assignment requires two types of writing. First, the *extended definition* should elaborate your ideas beyond a typical dictionary definition. Not only must you put your definition into your own words, but you must also expand it with discussion of physical details, psychological characteristics, behavioral tendencies, and historical associations. Second, the comparison requires you to analyze and draw conclusions about *what* has remained the same, *what* has changed, and *why* those similarities and differences make sense in light of evidence.

RESEARCH AND INVENTION QUESTIONS

These questions can inspire and guide your thinking. You do not need to answer all of them in your final definition.

- What sorts of creatures (categories, archetypes, etc.) do you want to make sure your definition includes?

- What sorts of creatures (categories, archetypes, etc.) might your definition exclude?

- How does your definition relate to or change definitions of the "human"?

- How does your definition relate to boundary-dwelling, Othering, and similar concepts explained in this book?

- How does your definition take into account the changes that have occurred to monsters (or categories/archetypes of monsters) over time?

- How does your definition differ from other definitions, such as Cohen's or Halberstam's, that appear in this book?

- What elements from others' definitions do you want to include?

- Looking at your beginning- and end-of-semester definitions, which elements differ? Which are the same? How might you explain these differences and similarities?

MAJOR ASSIGNMENT #2
IDENTITIES

BACKGROUND

Throughout this book, we have stressed that monsters have historically been used for identity construction, particularly through Othering—in which the dominant society (Self) condemns those who are different and represents them as monstrous. However, most monsters are closer to the Self than they initially seem. For example, in both *An American Werewolf in London* and *The Strange Case of Dr. Jekyll and Mr. Hyde*, the protagonist transforms into a monstrous creature and must consequently come to a new understanding of his own identity. Is he a person or a monster? Where does one being end and the other being begin? Although transforming into a monster highlights questions such as these, literal transformations like Dr. Jekyll's aren't necessary to raise questions about our perceptions of identity. In fact, monstrous transformations can reflect on how identities in general are formed.

ASSIGNMENT

Create a photo essay that examines how monsters reflect upon and construct identity (your identity or identity in general). Resist simple categorization; try to avoid falling into dichotomies such as good/evil, black/white, and us/them. Include a short reflection piece that explains the meaning behind your essay. The reflection should explain what you intend the photo essay to convey and what idea(s) in the photo essay might not come across, or might not come across in the same way, in a print essay.

MODE AND GENRE

A photo essay could take the form of a series of images (printed or in a slide format), a collage/montage, a Prezi (with images embedded within images), or a similar combination of images. However, you need to remember that the way the images are presented, combined, and sequenced has a large impact on the statement you make. The reflection piece allows you to interpret and explain your images, but you should make sure the essay itself presents your statement without depending on the reflection to make an impression.

RESEARCH AND INVENTION QUESTIONS

- Identity can be defined in a number of different ways. How can you define identity in order to make your argument focused and specific?

- What is the connection between photographs and identity? How might that connection help you develop your essay?

- What can you communicate with images that you might not be able communicate with words? What strategies can you use to represent ideas you would normally express through words by using images instead?

MAJOR ASSIGNMENT #3
MEDIA

BACKGROUND

As this book's introduction, bibliographies, filmography, and game-ography suggest, monsters have a long and diverse history. They have appeared in the art and literature of virtually every culture in every part of the world, and they have also appeared in every medium for communication, from the oldest forms of oral storytelling to the newest developments in digital gaming. Just as a monster's historical, cultural, and geographic contexts shape its forms and meanings, so does its medium. The medium through which people represent their monsters fundamentally affects what those monsters are, how they appear, and why they're significant.

ASSIGNMENT

Choose a type or category of monster and research representations of it in at least three different media, finding stories, images, or other takes on the monster not discussed at length in this book (if the monster is merely mentioned, it's fair game). You might, for example, look at the Chupacabra or the Wendigo as it has appeared in a short story, a television show, and a feature-length movie. As you identify representations of your monster, also examine people's responses to those representations. To find responses, you might look up newspaper reviews, journal articles, or blogs; you might also conduct your own primary research through surveys or interviews. When you have finished gathering your data, analyze it and develop a thesis about the differences the media make in both the representations and the responses. Explain, illustrate, and defend your thesis through a website that you design or through another type of non-linear argument that involves both text and images. [*Note*: This assignment might be individual or collaborative, depending on your instructor's requirements.]

MODE AND GENRE

Non-linear arguments involve opportunities and challenges that differ from the linear arguments that appear in typical academic essays. A "linear" argument follows a pre-determined sequence: it presents first one idea, then another, then another, usually through a series of paragraphs or other chunks of information that the audience encounters in a fixed order, following a straight line. By contrast, a "non-linear" argument arranges information in a manner that usually allows audiences to create their own sequences, making choices about what to encounter next based on cues provided by features of the argument's design. Interacting with design cues allows audiences to *navigate* the argument's non-linear text. One of the most familiar non-linear texts is a hypertext, which is common on websites. Most websites are non-linear because their designs include menus, links, tags, rollovers, and other features that provide access to information based on things the audience does (such as clicking on a link). When you visit a website's homepage, you choose where to go next based on the information that interests you. Similarly, a successful non-linear argument will present audiences with enough information to make informed choices about the ways to navigate through ideas in order to reach conclusions about interrelated topics. Your design should help audiences find what they want when they want it, allowing them to make sense of your claims about the representations and responses uncovered during your research while persuading them that your claims are valid.

You and your instructor should decide on the most appropriate way to complete this assignment based on the technology and time available. You don't have to know computer code to design a website: you can use special software to build a site from scratch, or with your instructor's permission, you can use templates or other resources that simplify the design process. Many templates are available for free online. Alternately, instead of designing an actual website, you might create a diagram on paper that represents a non-linear argument. This diagram might look like a flow chart or family tree: it arranges chunks of information (usually in boxes, comparable to a single page on a website) in a pattern that uses lines or other connections to show the paths audiences might take from one chunk to others. Instead of a diagram on paper, you might also create a "card sort," using a note card for each chunk of information (again comparable to a single page on a website) and using string or something else to show the paths audiences can take from one card to others. Just like pages on a website, the chunks of information on your diagram or card sort can include both text and images.

RESEARCH AND INVENTION QUESTIONS

- What category or type of monster do you want to know more about?

- What cultural, historical, and/or geographic context would you like to learn more about by studying its monsters?

- What media are you most interested in studying: print, film, painting, performance, Web media, video games, something else?

- What do the media you choose have in common? What makes them different?

- Where are you most likely to find responses to the representations you've identified? Why are the responses you find there likely to help you understand the differences that the media make in the representations?

- What differences are *inherent to* the representations of the monsters? What differences arise from people *responding to* the representations?

- How might you use a non-linear design to arrange information and claims about your representations and responses *more efficiently*? (For example, instead of repeating information every time it's relevant, a website might just provide a link to a single page that contains that information every time it's relevant.)

- How can using non-linear design both reflect and convey the purpose of your argument?

- How might non-linear design help to meet audiences' varying needs for background information, examples, and additional information that is helpful but not essential for your argument?

- How can you combine images and words in ways that make information more comprehensible and persuasive?

- How can you use elements such as type size, fonts, and colors to make sure information is easy to see, read, and access?

- How might your design incorporate help or additional resources for people with disabilities?

- How can you incorporate citations and other cues that acknowledge the sources of your information and help to build your authority?

MAJOR ASSIGNMENT #4
FICTION AND NONFICTION

BACKGROUND

While many of the selections in this book focus on fictional monsters that have infused the imagination over the years, the term "monster" arises throughout works of nonfiction as well. Often, it appears in critical examinations of fictional monsters, as can be seen in the excerpts within this book from Jeffrey Jerome Cohen and Judith Halberstam as well as the analyses of various films, such as *American Werewolf in London* and *Candyman*. However, other works of nonfiction also incorporate or discuss monsters—for example, those that examine serial killers (as in Lionel Dahmer's reflections on his son's crimes), terrorists, child abusers, and similar human horrors or that examine accounts of supposedly "real" monsters, such as Bigfoot or the Abominable Snowman. While both types of writing explore monstrosity, they may do so for different purposes, use different language, even focus on different details. In addition, tone and meaning may differ—for example, fiction and nonfiction differ in the ways they use symbolism, sensationalism, and sympathy. Finally, the fictional and nonfictional forms change our perceptions of monsters and monstrosity.

ASSIGNMENT

In groups, create a thirty-minute radio show that examines the concept of monstrosity. You must choose whether your show is fictional or nonfictional and then narrow that choice down into a type of radio show; these choices will help shape your content. Write a script that focuses on (1) a particular monster or (2) an aspect of monstrosity, and analyze examples as you discuss your topic. If you can access such software, record your performance using free podcast applications (such as Garage Band or Audacity), and be aware of production issues particular to sound recordings, such as sound quality and ambient noise.

After creating your narrative, write a short reflection essay that explains the choices your group made in developing your radio show, focusing on why your group chose fiction or nonfiction and how that choice affected your presentation of monstrosity.

MODE AND GENRE

Radio shows highlight orality and speech over other aspects of communication. Nonfictional radio shows have many forms, from the informational or opinion-based radio shows of NPR to the upbeat (and sometimes intentionally obnoxious) morning shows of local music stations. Fictional radio shows, a highly popular method of entertainment between the 1920s and the 1950s, often tell stories, using sound effects and music to build suspense as they narrate events. While these categories of radio programming would seem to be distinct from each other, sometimes the line between fiction and nonfiction on the radio becomes blurry, as in Orson Welles' production of *The War of the Worlds*, which caused widespread panic when audiences for its original broadcast in 1938 heard it and believed real monsters were invading Earth. Listeners could not tell the difference between fiction and nonfiction and believed that an actual alien invasion was occurring.

Once you choose the genre for your radio show, you should research that genre in order to learn and be able to recreate its conventions. For example, a morning radio show may include discussion among the radio hosts, interviews with guests, call-in segments, sound effects (such as applause), contests, and music. Also, you should plan your show's structure. For example, a thirty-minute show might be interrupted by commercials, news updates, traffic and weather updates, information identifying the show and the radio station, etc., and these interruptions might create distinct segments and/or significant pauses. Fictional shows, on the other hand, more likely base their structures on the story being told, with commercials and other information before and after the narrative or at moments of particular dramatic interest.

Strictly aural forms present a number of challenges. For example, radio producers must decide about using host(s) and/or narrator(s), how many characters and/or voices to incorporate, and how to integrate sound effects. In addition, they must determine how (and whether) to frame their material in a way that suggests fictional or nonfictional status.

RESEARCH AND INVENTION QUESTIONS

- In general, what are the differences between fiction and nonfiction? How do they present information? What types of information do they cover?

- How do representations of monsters differ between fiction and nonfiction? What characteristics of monstrosity are generally emphasized in works of fiction? Of nonfiction?

- What are the differences between fictional and nonfictional radio shows? How can you tell which category you're listening to if you start listening to the show in the middle of a broadcast?

- What types of radio shows do you like to listen to? How can your likes and dislikes help you better formulate a model for your show?

- How might the needs of the listening audiences affect the development of your radio show? Toward what audience(s) should you direct your show? (Keep in mind that developing programming towards specific audiences often helps to focus content.)

- How does using an oral medium change the structure of your ideas? The incorporation of your analysis?

- How is the "monster" characterized? Defined? Described?

- How could your representation of monstrosity have differed if you had chosen the other category—fiction versus nonfiction (or vice versa)? How might the tone of your program change? How would the difference change the meanings associated with the monster you discuss?

MAJOR ASSIGNMENT #5
VIOLENCE

BACKGROUND

Some monsters are friendly or at least non-violent, but most of the monsters in this book—and arguably most monsters—threaten people with violence. As a result, representations of monstrosity are often violent, and that violence is sometimes controversial. At least since the time of Ancient Greece, philosophers and politicians have been arguing about the potentially harmful effects of violent spectacles, whether those spectacles be gladiatorial contests, movies in the *Texas Chain Saw Massacre* series, or first-person-shooter video games. Anthropologists, sociologists, psychologists, cultural critics, and other professional researchers have studied the effects of exposure to violent media from many different angles. While some say that laboratory and field studies have conclusively shown a correlation between exposure to violent media and violent behavior, others disagree. In any case, *correlation* between exposure and behavior does not prove *causality*, which is almost always difficult to prove scientifically.

Scientists may not have reached total consensus about whether exposure to violent spectacles through media causes violent behavior, but representations of violence are still routinely condemned for corrupting their readers, viewers, and players. These condemnations often raise questions about whether—and to what degree—violent media should be controlled or censored. In the United States, the ratings systems for movies and video games, which help to determine who gets access to certain representations, are examples of media industries controlling exposure to the violent content they produce. Because of these ratings systems, recent film sequels about the murders committed by movie psychos and the latest evolution of zombies in the *Resident Evil* game franchise are less accessible than they would be otherwise. Violent monsters, then, both represent cultural taboos against violent behaviors and *are*, to an extent, culturally taboo, forbidden to some people in some circumstances. These creatures are already boundary dwellers: fear that they could inspire violent behavior encourages some people to put up boundaries against them—and even against depictions of them—making monsters off-limits for representation.

ASSIGNMENT

Take a position on whether representations of monsters that behave violently, or against whom violence is perpetrated, risk creating or encouraging violent behavior in the people who encounter those representations. Express your position in an opinion essay that uses appropriate appeals (logos, pathos, ethos) to convince your audience that your position is correct. The essay should take the form of a newspaper editorial or a blog. Be sure to consider the political, social, and cultural implications of your position.

MODE AND GENRE

Editorials and blogs usually focus on their authors' opinions, but the strongest works in these genres usually rely on detailed research and other evidence to help convince audiences that the authors' opinions are correct (or at least worth considering seriously). While use of evidence requires a certain level of rigorous argumentation, editorials and blogs often distinguish themselves from formal essays through humor and other appeals to emotion. Anecdotes and testimonials are more common forms of evidence in these genres than they are in formal essays. While the media for editorials vary, they're mostly associated with print (in newspapers and magazines), while the blog (a shortened form of "web log") typically involves interactive computing. Writing is arguably the primary mode in both genres, but the medium could allow you to rely on visual and digital rhetoric as well.

RESEARCH AND INVENTION QUESTIONS

- Do you think violent media cause violent behavior? Why or why not? If your answer isn't a simple "yes" or "no," what keeps you from making a yes-or-no claim?

- Who do you see as the audience for your argument? What concerns might your audience have about the effects of violence? How will you address these concerns?

- What background information do you need to find (research) and cite in order to support your position for this audience? What sorts of studies have been done on the effects of violent media? Who did the studies? In what types of publication do the results appear, and what do the types of publication tell you about the studies?

- What representations of violent monsters have been most controversial? Why?

- What are common legal and cultural attitudes toward censorship where you live? How do you feel about censorship? Other than censorship, how might people who believe violent media cause violent behavior limit the threat?

- If you were to publish this editorial or blog, what type of publication might be most appropriate? Examples of possibilities include newspapers (you might consider different regional papers), a magazine (you might consider different types of magazines, such as news magazines or science magazines), and established web communities (blogs are often associated with particular organizations that have common social, political, or professional purposes).

Monsters

FILMOGRAPHY

FILMS

28 Days Later (2002)
Alien (1979)
The Blob (1958)
Bride of Frankenstein (1935)
Creature from the Black Lagoon (1954)
Curse of Frankenstein (1957)
Dead Alive (a.k.a. *Brain Dead*) (1992)
Dracula's Daughter (1936)
The Evil Dead (1981)
The Exorcist (1973)
The Fly (1986)
Freaks (1932)
Fright Night (1985)
Godzilla (1954)
The Golem (1920)
The Hills Have Eyes (1977)
House of Wax (1953)
Invasion of the Body Snatchers (1956)

King Kong (1933)
Love at First Bite (1979)
Monsters, Inc. (2001)
Monster Squad (1987)
The Mummy (1932)
Nosferatu (1922, 1979)
Plan 9 from Outer Space (1959)
Rosemary's Baby (1968)
Scars of Dracula (1970)
Shaun of the Dead (2004)
Suspiria (1977)
Terminator (1984)
The Thing (1982)
The Tingler (1959)
Underworld (2003)
Wolf (1994)
The Wolf Man (1941)

TELEVISION SHOWS

The Addams Family
Being Human
Bewitched
Buffy the Vampire Slayer
Charmed
Dark Shadows
Doctor Who
The Munsters

Supernatural
Tales from the Crypt
True Blood
The Twilight Zone
V
The Walking Dead
The X-Files

GRAPHIC NOVELS AND COMICS

Gaiman, Neil. *The Sandman*
Mignola, Mike. *Hellboy*
Moench, Doug, et al. *Batman & Dracula: Red Rain, Bloodstorm, Crimson Mist.*
Moore, Alan. *From Hell, League of Extraordinary Gentlemen, V for Vendetta.*
Niles, Steve. *30 Days of Night*

VIDEO GAMES

American McGee's Alice
Bioshock
Castlevania
Doom
God of War
Half-Life
House of the Dead
Resident Evil
Shadow of the Colossus
Silent Hill

OTHER GAMES

Call of Cthulhu
Dungeons & Dragons (esp. *Ravenloft*)
Magic: The Gathering
Pokemon
Vampire: The Masquerade

WORKS CITED

Bell, Rachael, and Marilyn Bardsley. "Ed Gein: The Inspiration for Buffalo Bill and Psycho." *TruTV Crime Laboratory: Crimnal Minds and Methods*. Turner, A Time-Warner Company, 2011. Print. 12 Dec. 2011.

Brooks, Max. *World War Z: An Oral History of the Zombie War*. New York: Three Rivers Press, 2006.

Cantor, Joanne. *Mommy I'm Scared: How TV and Movies Frighten Children and What We Can Do to Protect Them*. New York: Harcourt Brace, 1998. Print.

Carter, Angela. "The Company of Wolves." *The Bloody Chamber*. New York: Penguin, 1979. 110–118. Print.

Cohen, Jeffrey Jerome. "Monster Culture (Seven Theses)." *Monster Theory*. Minneapolis, MN: U of Minnesota Press, 1996. 3–25. Print.

Cooper, L. Andrew. *Gothic Realities: The Impact of Horror Fiction on Modern Culture*. Jefferson, NC: McFarland, 2010. Print.

Finucane, Ronald C. *Miracles and Pilgrims: Popular Beliefs in Medieval England*. Totowa, NJ: Rowman and Littlefield, 1977. Print.

Freud, Sigmund. "The Uncanny." *Laurel Amtower, Professor of English and Comparative Literature*. San Diego State University, n.d. Web. 15 Dec. 2011.

Gilmore, David. *Monsters: Evil Beings, Mythical Beasts, and All Manner of Imaginary Terrors*. Philadelphia: U of Pennsylvania Press, 2003. Print.

Halberstam, Judith. *Skin Shows: Gothic Horror and the Technology of Monsters*. Durham, NC: Duke University Press, 1995. Print.

Jenkins, Philip. *Using Murder: The Social Construction of Serial Homicide*. New York: A. de Gruyter, 1994. Print.

Jones, Gerard. *Killing Monsters: Why Children NEED Fantasy, Super Heroes, and Make-Believe Violence*. New York: Basic Books, 2002. Print.

Mellor, Anne K. "Frankenstein: A Feminist Critique of Science." *One Culture: Essays in Science and Literature*. Ed. George Levine and Alan Rauch. Madison: University of Wisconsin Press, 1987. 287–312. *Frankenstein; or, the Modern Prometheus*. Ed. Stuart Curran. Pennsylvania Electronic Edition. University of Pennsylvania, Web. 10 Dec. 2011.

Monstropedia: The Monstrous Encyclopedia. Monstropedia.com, 14 Sept. 2011. Web. 12 Dec. 2011.

Shelley, Mary. *Frankenstein*. Ed. J. Paul Hunter. New York: W.W. Norton & Co., 1996. Print.

Stevenson, Robert Louis. *The Strange Case of Dr. Jekyll and Mr. Hyde*. Ed. Katherine Linehan. New York: W.W. Norton & Co., 2002. Print.

Stoker, Bram. *Dracula*. Ed. Nina Auerbach. New York: W.W. Norton & Co., 1996. Print.

Wilson, Natalie. "Civilized Vampires Versus Savage Werewolves: Race and Ethnicity in the Twilight Series." *Bitten by Twilight: Youth Culture, Media, & the Vampire Franchise*. Ed. Melissa A. Click, Jennifer Stevens Aubrey, and Elizabeth Behm-Morawitz. New York: Peter Lang, 2010. 55–70. Print.

Wiest, Julie B. *Creating Cultural Monsters: Serial Murder in America*. Boca Raton, FL: CRC Press, 2011. Print.

LIST OF ILLUSTRATIONS AND FILMS CITED

Figure 1: "Health Care Monster." *About.com: Political Humor*. Creators Syndicate. Sept. 2009. Web. 12 Dec. 2011.

WORKS CITED

Figure 2: Von Holst, Theodore. *Frontispiece to Frankenstein 1831*. 1831. Tate Britain, London. *Wikimedia Commons*. Web. 10 Dec. 2011.

Figure 3: *Frankenstein*. Dir. James Whale. *Frankenstein: The Legacy Collection*. Universal Studios, 2004. DVD.

Figure 4: *Mary Shelley's Frankenstein*. Dir. Kenneth Branagh. Sony Pictures Home Entertainment, 1998. DVD.

Figure 5: *Night of the Living Dead*. Millennium Edition. Dir. George A. Romero. Elite Entertainment, 2002. DVD.

Figure 6: *Night of the Living Dead*. Millennium Edition. Dir. George A. Romero. Elite Entertainment, 2002. DVD.

Figure 7: *Night of the Living Dead*. Millennium Edition. Dir. George A. Romero. Elite Entertainment, 2002. DVD.

Figure 8: *Night of the Living Dead*. Millennium Edition. Dir. George A. Romero. Elite Entertainment, 2002. DVD.

Figure 9: *Dawn of the Dead*. Divimax Edition. Dir. George A. Romero. Starz / Anchor Bay, 2004. DVD.

Figure 10: *Dawn of the Dead*. Divimax Edition. Dir. George A. Romero. Starz / Anchor Bay, 2004. DVD.

Figure 11: *Day of the Dead*. Divimax Special Edition. Dir. George A Romero. Starz / Anchor Bay, 2003. DVD.

Figure 12: *An American Werewolf in London*. Dir. John Landis. Universal Pictures, 2005. DVD.

Figure 13: *An American Werewolf in London*. Dir. John Landis. Universal Pictures, 2005. DVD.

Figure 14: *Dracula*. Dir. Tod Browning. *Dracula: The Legacy Collection*. Universal Studios, 2004. DVD.

Figure 15: *Horror of Dracula*. Dir. Terence Fisher. Warner Home Video, 2002. DVD.

Figure 16: *Bram Stoker's Dracula*. Dir. Francis Ford Coppola. Sony Pictures Home Entertainment, 1992. DVD.

Figure 17: *Bram Stoker's Dracula*. Dir. Francis Ford Coppola. Sony Pictures Home Entertainment, 1992. DVD.

Figure 18: "Edward; crest: *Twilight* Saga *Eclipse* Poster." JPEG. *Movie Poster Warehouse*. Movieposter.com, 2011. Web. 9 Dec. 2011.

Figure 19: "Wolf Pack: *Twilight* Saga *New Moon* Poster." JPEG. *Movie Poster Warehouse*. Movieposter.com, 2011. Web. 9 Dec. 2011.

Figure 20: *Candyman*. Special Edition. Dir. Bernard Rose. Sony Pictures Home Entertainment, 2004. DVD.

Figure 21: *Candyman*. Special Edition. Dir. Bernard Rose. Sony Pictures Home Entertainment, 2004. DVD.

Figure 22: *Candyman*. Special Edition. Dir. Bernard Rose. Sony Pictures Home Entertainment, 2004. DVD.

Figure 23: *Candyman*. Special Edition. Dir. Bernard Rose. Sony Pictures Home Entertainment, 2004. DVD.

Figure 24: *Child's Play 2*. Dir. John Lafia. *Chucky: The Killer DVD Collection*. Universal Studios, 2011. DVD.

Figure 25: *Child's Play 2*. Dir. John Lafia. *Chucky: The Killer DVD Collection*. Universal Studios, 2011. DVD.

Figure 26: *Bride of Chucky*. Dir. Ronny Yu. *Chucky: The Killer DVD Collection*. Universal Studios, 2011. DVD.

Figure 27: *Puppet Master*. Dir. David Schmoeller. *The Midnight Horror Collection: Puppet Master*. Echo Bridge Home Entertainment, 2010. DVD.

Figure 28: *Puppet Master*. Dir. David Schmoeller. *The Midnight Horror Collection: Puppet Master*. Echo Bridge Home Entertainment, 2010. DVD.

Figure 29: *Psycho*. Dir. Alfred Hitchcock. *Alfred Hitchcock: The Masterpiece Collection*. Universal Studios, 2005. DVD.

Figure 30: *The Texas Chain Saw Massacre*. Dir. Tobe Hooper. Geneon [Pioneer], 2003. DVD.

Figure 31: *Halloween*. Dir. John Carpenter. Starz / Anchor Bay, 1999. DVD.

Figure 32: *Friday the 13th, Part 3*. Dir. Steve Miner. *Friday the 13th: From Crystal Lake to Manhattan*. Paramount, 2004. DVD.

Figure 33: *A Nightmare on Elm Street*. Dir. Wes Craven. *The Nightmare on Elm Street Collection*. New Line Home Video, 1999. DVD.